19×5/69
9/91

VISUALIZING PROJECT MANAGEMENT

KEVIN FORSBERG

HAL MOOZ

AND

HOWARD COTTERMAN

FOREWORD BY NORMAN R. AUGUSTINE
PRESIDENT AND CHIEF EXECUTIVE OFFICER
LOCKHEED MARTIN CORPORATION

JOHN WILEY & SONS, INC.
NEW YORK · CHICHESTER · BRISBANE · TORONTO · SINGAPORE

To Cindy, Connie, and Maureen
who provided more support
than they should have had to.

This text is printed on acid-free paper.

Copyright © 1996 by John Wiley & Sons, Inc.
Published by John Wiley & Sons, Inc.

All rights reserved. Published simultaneously in Canada.

Reproduction or translation of any part of this work beyond that
permitted by Section 107 or 108 of the 1976 United States Copyright
Act without the permission of the copyright owner is unlawful.
Requests for permission or further information should be addressed
to the Permissions Department, John Wiley & Sons, Inc.

This publication is designed to provide accurate and authoritative
information in regard to the subject matter. It is sold with the
understanding that the publisher is not engaged in rendering legal,
accounting, or other professional services. If legal advice or other expert
assistance is required, the services of a competent professional person
should be sought.

Library of Congress Cataloging-in-Publication Data:

Forsberg, Kevin.
    Visualizing project management / Kevin Forsberg, Hal Mooz : written by
Howard Cotterman.
       p.   cm.
    Includes bibliographical references.
    ISBN 0-471-57779-0 (alk. paper)
    1. Project management.   I. Mooz, Hal.   II. Cotterman, Howard.
III. Title.
HD69.P75F67   1996
658.4′04—dc20   95-52250

Printed in the United States of America

10 9 8 7 6 5 4 3 2 1

FOREWORD

There are a thousand reasons for failure but not a single excuse.

Mike Reid

It is every manager's unending nightmare: In today's world of increasing complexity, there is less and less tolerance for error. We see this daily in the realms of health care, product safety and reliability, transportation, energy, communications, space exploration, military operations, and—as the above quote from the great Penn State football player Mike Reid demonstrates—sports. Whether the venue is the stock market, a company's customer base, consumers, government regulators, auditors, the battlefield, the ball field, or the media, "No one cares"—as the venerated quotation puts it—"about the storms you survived along the way, but whether you brought the ship safely into the harbor."

Over the course of my own career in aerospace, I have seen an unfortunate number of failures of very advanced, complex—and expensive—pieces of equipment, often due to the most mundane of causes. One satellite went off course into space on a useless trajectory because there was a hyphen missing in one of the millions of lines of software code. A seemingly minor flaw in the electrical design of the Apollo spacecraft was not detected until Apollo 13 was 200,000 miles from Earth, when a spark in a cryogenic oxygen tank led to an explosion and the near-loss of the crew. A major satellite proved to be badly nearsighted because of a tiny error in grinding the primary mirror in its optical train. And, as became apparent in the inquiry into the Challenger disaster, the performance of an exceedingly capable space vehicle—a miracle of modern technology—was undermined by the effects of cold temperature on a seal during a sudden winter storm. Murphy's Law, it would seem, has moved in lock-step with the advances of the modern age.

THEORETICALLY, SUCCESS IS MANAGEABLE

In the grand old days of American management, when it was presumed that all problems and mistakes could be controlled by more rigorous managerial oversight, the canonical solution to organizational error was to add more oversight and bureaucracy. Surely, it was thought, with more managers having narrower spans of control, the organization could prevent any problem from ever happening again. Of course, this theory was never confirmed in the real world—or, as Kansas City Royals hitting instructor Charlie Lau once noted regarding a similar challenge, "There are two theories on hitting the knuckleball. Unfortunately, neither one works."

The problem with the strategy of giving more managers fewer responsibilities is that no one is really in charge of the biggest responsibility: Will the overall enterprise succeed? I recall the comment a few years ago of the chief executive of one of the world's largest companies, who was stepping down after nearly a decade of increasingly poor performance in the marketplace by his company. He was asked by a journalist why the company had fared so poorly under his tutelage, to which he replied, "I don't know. It's a mysterious thing."

My observation is that there is no mystery here at all. After decades of trying to centrally "manage" every last variable and contingency encountered in the course of business, Fortune 500 companies found themselves with 12 to 15 layers of management—but essentially ill-prepared to compete in an increasingly competitive global marketplace. Or, as I once pointed out in one of my Laws, "If a sufficient number of management layers are superimposed on top of each other, it can be assured that disaster is not left to chance."

A NEW LOOK AT PROJECT MANAGEMENT

Today's leaders in both the private and public sectors are rediscovering the simple truth that every good manager has known in his or her heart since the first day on the job: *Accountability* is the one managerial task that cannot be delegated. There must be *one* person whose responsibility it is to make a project work— even as we acknowledge the importance of teamwork and "worker empowerment" in the modern workplace. In other words, we are rediscovering the critical role of the *project manager*.

The importance of the project manager has long been noted in our nation's military procurement establishment, which has traditionally considered the job to be among the most important and most difficult assignments in peacetime. Performed properly, the project management role, whether in the military, in civilian government, or in business, can make enormous contributions and can even affect the course of history.

Challenges of this technology-focused project management role are particularly noteworthy for the insights they provide into the broader definition of project management. Perhaps the greatest of these is inherent in technology itself. In the effort to obtain the maximum possible advantage over a military adversary or a commercial competitor, products are often designed at the very edge of the state of the art. But as one high-level defense official noted in a moment of frustration over the repeated inability of advanced electronic systems to meet specified goals, "Airborne radars are not responsive to enthusiasm." In short, managerial adrenaline is not a substitute for managerial judgment when it comes to transporting technology from the laboratory to the field.

Despite considerable tribulations—or, perhaps *because* of them—the job of the technology-focused project manager is among the most rewarding career choices. It presents challenging work with important consequences. It involves the latest in technology. It offers the opportunity to work with a quality group of associates. And over the years, its practitioners have generated a large number of truly enormous successes.

THE LURE OF PROJECT MANAGEMENT

This brings me to the broader observation that the project manager's job, in my opinion, is one of the very best jobs anywhere. Whether one is working at the Department of Defense, NASA, or a private company, the project manager's job offers opportunities and rewards unavailable anywhere else. Being a project manager means integrating a variety of disciplines—science, engineering, development, finance, and human resources—accomplishing an important goal, making a difference, and seeing the result of one's work. In short, project management is "being where the action is" in the development and application of exciting new technologies and processes.

The principles of successful project management—picking the best people, instilling attention to detail, involving the customer, and, most importantly, building adequate reserves—are no secret, but what is often missing in the literature on the subject is a comprehensive, easy-to-understand model. This is one of the many compelling aspects of *Visualizing Project Management*. The authors have taken a new, simplified approach to visualizing project management as a combination of sequential, situational management actions incorporating a four-part model—common vocabulary, teamwork, project cycle, and project management elements. The beauty of their approach is that they portray management complexity as process and discipline simplicity.

Kevin Forsberg, Harold Mooz, and Howard Cotterman are eminently qualified to compose such a comprehensive model for successful project management. They bring a collective experience unmatched in the commercial sphere. One author has spent his entire career in the high-tech commercial world; the two others have more than 20 years each at a company (Lockheed Corporation, which is part of the new Lockheed Martin Corporation) that established a reputation strongly supporting the role of the project manager. Collectively, the authors have had many years successfully applying their "visualizing project management" approach to companies in both the commercial and the government markets. Their technical skill and work-environment experience are abundantly apparent in the real-world methodology they bring to the study and understanding of the importance of project management to the success of any organization.

SUMMARY

As corporate executives and their counterparts in the public sector expect project managers to assume many of the responsibilities of functional management—indeed, as we look to project managers to become "miracle workers" pulling together great teams of specialists to create products of enormous complexity—we need to make sure that the principles and applications of the project management process are thoroughly understood at all levels of the organizational hierarchy. This book will help executives, government officials, project managers, and project team members *visualize*, then successfully *apply* the process. I recommend this book to all those who aspire to project management, those who must supervise it in their organizations, or even those who are simply fascinated with how leading-edge technologies make it out of the laboratory and into the market.

—Norman R. Augustine
President and Chief Executive Officer
Lockheed Martin Corporation

ABOUT THE AUTHORS

Kevin Forsberg, Ph.D., is co-principal and co-founder of the Center for Systems Management which serves international clients in project management. Dr. Forsberg draws on 27 years of experience in applied research, system engineering, and project management, followed by 13 years of successful consulting to both government and industry. While at the Lockheed Palo Alto, California, Research Facility, Dr. Forsberg served as deputy director of the Materials and Structures Research Laboratory. He earned the NASA Public Service Medal for his contributions to the Space Shuttle program. Dr. Forsberg received his B.S. in Civil Engineering at Massachusetts Institute of Technology and his Ph.D. in Engineering Mechanics at Stanford University.

Hal Mooz is co-principal at the Center for Systems Management, one of two successful training and consulting companies he founded that specialize in the disciplines associated with project management. Mr. Mooz has won and successfully managed highly reliable, sophisticated satellite programs from inception to operations. His 22 years of experience in program management was followed by 15 years of experience installing project management into federal agencies, government contractors, and commercial companies. He is co-founder of the Certificate in Project Management at the University of California at Santa Cruz. Mr. Mooz received his ME degree from Stevens Institute of Technology.

Howard Cotterman is president of Cognitive Corporation, which specializes in computer-based training. Mr. Cotterman has held key posts and managed a broad range of projects from real estate development, to publishing, to the computer and semiconductor industries. His 30 years of project management experience began with the development of IBM's first microprocessor in the mid-1960s and includes development and manufacturing projects at NCR, Intel, and Rockwell International. Mr. Cotterman received his B.S. and M.S. degrees in Electrical Engineering from Purdue University.

ACKNOWLEDGMENTS

Visualizing Project Management draws on project management consulting experience and the training of over 20,000 project management practitioners conducted by the Center for Systems Management, headquartered in Cupertino, California. The authors wish to acknowledge the many contributors to the development of the process and quality of content, especially John Chiorini for sharpening the message and clearing out the extraneous, and Shirley Devan and Jeff Owen for their creativity in developing the many illustrations.

CONTENTS

PART II
THE ESSENTIALS OF
PROJECT MANAGEMENT

INTRODUCTION

A SUCCESSFUL FUTURE DEPENDS ON SUCCESSFUL PROJECTS

Whether you're a middle manager on the endangered list or already up to your armpits in alligators as a project manager, your future may well depend on achieving success in the challenging project environment. In his recent *Fortune* article,[1] Thomas Stewart likened the deepening cuts in middle management to the extinction of the dinosaur, with project managers evolving to rule the corporate jungle. "Like his biological counterpart, the project manager is more agile and adaptable than the beast he's displacing, more likely to live by his wits than by throwing his weight around. Says William Dauphinais, a partner at Price Waterhouse: 'Project management is going to be huge in the next decade. The project manager is the linchpin in the horizontal/vertical organizations we're creating.' Project management is 'the wave of the future,' says an in-house newsletter from General Motors' technology and training group, which exhorts, 'We need to raise the visibility and clout of this job responsibility!'"

The project manager may well be the hero of the American workplace as Tom Peters, author of *In Search of Excellence*, asserts in his more recent book, *Liberation Management*. He observes that, even though he is a self-avowed "middle manager basher,"

> "The project manager is the linchpin in the horizontal/vertical organizations we're creating."

most of the people attending his training seminars are themselves middle managers. Says Peters, "Middle management, as we have known it since the railroads invented it right after the Civil War, is dead. Therefore middle managers as we have known them are cooked geese." His answer to his clients facing a dead end, ". . . create projects."

What's all this fuss about projects? After all, a project can be any temporary undertaking carried out to achieve specified results within well-defined cost, schedule, and technical boundaries. Well, it's those precise boundaries, coupled with that temporary organization, that give project management its unique challenges and rewards. To see the picture, visualize the intensity and hubbub of a theater production, a building construction site, or a new product development.

> Project management techniques have evolved from various niches to be the mainstream and mainstay of management, in general.

Near-maximum productivity improvements have already been wrought from executive and external pressures to work harder and longer, and with capital improvements such as computers. In fact, automation of day-to-day tasks is one trend that's driving the middle manager to extinction. Now project management is being widely recognized as the next productivity frontier. Recent trends have moved this most complicated of management processes to center stage. The concepts described here are the precursors of future management practices.

IT'S ALARMINGLY COMMON FOR PROJECT TEAMS TO FAIL

> Success in the dynamic project world depends on integrating the best techniques available with what's valid among conventional wisdom.

Although the vital role of projects has been widely acknowledged, project teams continue to fail. Some do well, but most do not. Yet, the most basic techniques have been available, as Stewart quips, literally from day one, ". . . the first practitioner having been God, who gave himself six days in which to turn the void into the world, then turned operations management over to Adam, who promptly made a hash of it. (Unlike corporate project managers, however, God got to define what he meant by 'six days' and had unlimited resources.)"

In our experience, failure often results from fundamental confusion over precisely what is involved in successfully managing a project from inception through completion. While excellent managers are usually cognizant of the full scope of management thinking, others limited by one-dimensional thinking often make uninformed decisions from the wrong theory. At best, this locks them into mediocre performance. At worst, it leads to project failure.

Being temporary, projects often bring together people unknown to each other. The newly formed group usually includes specialists motivated by the work itself and their individual contributions. Teams of highly skilled technicians make costly errors —even fatal ones—simply because the members fail to understand or follow a disciplined, systematic approach to project management. This factor remains most critical to project success: the availability of an effective and intuitive project management process—one that the project group will quickly buy into and build their team upon.

> The most critical success factor is the availability of an effective and intuitive project management process.

YOU CAN'T RELY ON PERSONAL EXPERIENCE AND INTUITION ALONE

No matter how much intuition and experience you have, you can't rely on personal experience alone as you navigate through the increasingly complex and dynamic project environment. On the other hand, management excellence cannot be taught any more simply than professional quarterbacking, Olympic gymnastics, or being a great artist. No matter how much innate management talent you start with, you need input from others as well as your own experiences to attain excellence.

Our own management roles range from high-tech CEOs to general contractors, from industry leaders to new ventures. As professional trainers, our clients hail from the ranks of AT&T, Emerson Electric, GTE, government agencies such as NASA, and dozens of other organizations which through over 20,000 trainees are now claiming the benefits of our project management model.

> Our field-tested model helps you to understand every piece of the project puzzle and to visualize how each fits into the overall picture.

Having successfully completed many complex government and commercial projects, we developed this text by combining our own experiences as managers and trainers with those of our clients. Providing hundreds of real case studies, our clients challenged us to perfect techniques and tools that they could propagate upward, downward, and laterally throughout their own organizations. They spurred us to confront tradition, constructively—to challenge conventional wisdom here as we have in our training programs.

It is difficult, even for the most experienced project team, to effectively manage a complex process without a complete understanding of every piece, and an ability to visualize how each part fits into the overall picture. We introduce intuitive models in Part I to enable you to visualize the relationships before getting involved in the supporting application details of Part II.

As in solving any puzzle, it helps to know how many pieces there are. Rather than present the full inventory of management techniques, we decompose them into 10 essential and unambiguous management elements. We separate the planned, sequential project cycle events from those situational management and leadership elements that we portray in an orthogonal, three-dimensional model.

Improvements should be measured both on a personal and an organizational basis.

Those of you considering a commitment to project management can use this foundation to support and enhance your own experiences. If you're already an experienced manager, we're confident our model and visual aids will clarify your management thinking, extend your comfort zone, and make dramatic performance improvements—yours as well as your organization's.

These are just some of the ways this book will make a difference.

ENDING UP WITH THE GOLDEN GOOSE

Regardless of your position or your speciality, you can ensure a successful future through project management.

Not every manager and every organization can benefit from creating projects during this time of transition. If you are unable to cope with things such as matrix ambiguities and responsibility without authority, you may be better off focusing on a support management role or supervising repetitive operations. By becoming a project manager, you'll trade job insecurity for a host of other uncertainties, including the very nature of your next project. On the other hand, if you thrive on adventure or aspire to the ranks of executive or general management, projects are your best training ground. Achieving the payoff depends more on your personal attitude than position—be it an executive, as one interfacing with project teams, or as a project manager or team member.

Fortunately, the efforts you make now to revitalize the project environment, or to create one, can pay high dividends to your entire organization. The project team can be a catalyst for culture changes that may be needed elsewhere. This team catalyst can also become the most significant competitive edge a firm can wield in this technology-driven, time-compressed era. Whereas technology is surprisingly easy to clone, a well-integrated, highly productive project culture, tailored to your needs, is an invaluable proprietary asset.

> Whereas technology is surprisingly easy to clone, an integrated, highly productive project culture, tailored to your needs, can be your proprietary golden goose.

PART ONE

VISUALIZING PROJECT MANAGEMENT: REALIZING SUCCESS

This book has been organized to achieve two goals: (1) your visualization of what project management is all about at the concept level; then (2) defining how to apply those concepts, together with the tools to do the tailoring.

Part One enables you to visualize the major relationships. We progressively assemble a composite view of the project management process much as the video camera does for dynamic sports such as gymnastics and football. The sports fan initially sees the total activity—the gymnastics routine or the collective movements of the football team. Then, zooming in for a close-up or replaying in slow motion, the viewer sees the precise maneuvers and subtle techniques that result in an Olympic or Superbowl performance. In this way, Part Two gets you involved in the supporting application details.

Finally, by zooming out in Chapter 8, you regain the broad perspective, but now with the awareness of details needed to appreciate the complexities of the total performance.

1

WHY IS PROJECT MANAGEMENT A CRITICAL ISSUE?

It is best to do things systematically, since we are only human and disorder is our worst enemy.

Hesoid,
8th century B.C.

THE FUTURE OF MOST ORGANIZATIONS DEPENDS ON SUCCESSFUL PROJECTS

Whether for survival or to sustain market leadership, projects are the key in the new era of world competition. Projects affect the vital aspects of any business:

- Developing new products and services that meet customer needs.
- Shortening time-to-market for new developments.

For some businesses, such as construction and aerospace, projects are the only product.

3

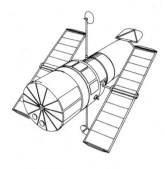

The Hubble Telescope is one of the most highly publicized project failures *and* successes (repair mission).

- Improving efficiency and productivity.
- Strengthening competitive positions in national or world markets.

IT'S ALARMINGLY COMMONPLACE FOR PROJECT TEAMS TO FAIL—SOME DO WELL, BUT MOST DO NOT

Almost daily we are made aware of projects that have failed or not met customer expectations. Past examples include the Denver airport which suffered from both software and construction deficiencies, the Challenger disaster, the AT&T telephone system shutdown, the Hubble Space Telescope, and many others. Concurrent with these troubled projects are those that meet or exceed expectations. The Olympics are perhaps the best examples. They routinely accomplish difficult objectives on time and usually with substantially—sometimes surprisingly—higher profits. (Los Angeles' Olympics profit was $100,000,000—ten times that expected.)

Project performance is very team-dependent.

Widely varying project results would lead one to conclude—quite correctly—that project success is too often dependent on the specific team. Since projects and project teams are temporary, their performance may be incorrectly attributed to the luck of the draw. But any team can succeed when it is committed to the fundamentals of project management and insists on applying them consistently and systematically.

WHY DO PROJECTS HAVE A DISMAL PERFORMANCE RECORD?

Project Management is not well-understood.

Failure often results from fundamental confusion over precisely what is involved in managing a project successfully from inception through completion. Even experienced managers often disagree on important aspects, like the blind men that encounter the elephant and reach different conclusions concerning the nature of the beast. In the parable, the man feeling the tail concludes the elephant is like a rope, while the man holding the trunk decides the elephant is like a snake, and so forth. Project reality is such a complex organism that personal experience alone provides a biased view.

In an atmosphere of confusion—internally and externally—it's no wonder that projects are often poorly implemented. Typically, waste, inefficiency, and costly errors are compounded as hoards of new personnel are added in a futile attempt to recover from the incorrect practices that caused the failures.

Many projects fail by repeating either the technical or business mistakes of others, which we refer to as *Lessons Learned.* For example, the SeaSat Satellite failed in orbit when an arc across the solar array slip rings caused a catastrophic power supply failure. A prior project at the same company had solved this problem, discovered in a thermal vacuum chamber test before the launch. A *Lessons Learned* analysis developed by the project team after a project is complete would be invaluable to other project managers, present and future. But there is usually no mechanism for the lessons to get into the hands (and minds) of those who would benefit most. Furthermore, project teams are dispersed to other projects just at the time they should be documenting those learning experiences. Perhaps Thoreau had this predicament in mind when he queried, "How can we remember our ignorance, which our growth requires, when we are using our knowledge all of the time?" Of all the project management concepts, *Lessons Learned* from prior failures and successes is the most neglected. Project requirements should include such lessons, but even when documented, they're usually not readily accessible.

To succeed, the project team needs training and support from above. Unfortunately, relatively few companies comprehend the full power of project management. The more difficult the times, the greater the need to effectively manage projects. Successful companies of all types have discovered that a transition to project management is essential to improve or sustain high business performance. So why do troubled companies appear reluctant

> In an atmosphere of confusion, adding people usually compounds poor performance.

> *Lessons Learned* from prior failures and successes are too often neglected.

TABLE 1.1   Upper Management Frequently Gives Lip Service to Project Management

	Proactive ☺	Reactive 😐	Slow React ☹	Lip Service ☹ ☹	No Interest ☹ ☹ ☹
Project Training	All levels	Project team	Managers only	None	None
Management Support	Continuously involved	Reference manual	Reluctant	Impossible edicts	Sink or swim
Management Process	Up-to-date	Standard	As customer demands	Counter-productive involvement	None
Funding & Budgets	Planned	Controlled	By variances	No budget authority	Excess spending with cash cow
Project Mgr Authority	Fully empowered	Selective delegation	Reluctant to delegate	Responsibility w/o authority	Unspecified
Project Controls	Comprehensive and effective	Basic	Force fit	Arbitrary	Uncontrolled
Communications	Open to broad scrutiny	Formal	Defensive	Avoided	Closed to any scrutiny

to make necessary cultural changes? As managers rise in the organization, they often suffer a gradual loss of perspective regarding the change process itself. Too many executives are reluctant to leave their comfort zones and depart from tradition. They typically don't embrace or emphasize disciplined project management on any level. Their behavior can range from being reactive to showing no interest as contrasted with the ideal proactive management attitude (Table 1.1).

WHY IS PROJECT MANAGEMENT SO DIFFICULT?

Several major challenges, unique to projects, add to the demanding business environment discussed above. In this section we highlight the difficulties inherent in a project's temporary nature, those inherited from misguided management, and others contributed by the need for nontraditional organizations.

For simple projects or complex, the only certainty is uncertainty in the increasingly demanding project environment. Our training programs continually provide candid, in-depth visibility into dozens of projects each month which reveal trends that threaten government and commercial enterprise alike. Some austerity measures are a one-way road. Here are a few of the more familiar signs of the times:

- Layoffs and early retirement.
- Attrition without replacement.
- Dependence on overtime and subcontractors.

Marketplace shifts often force abrupt changes of direction. Longer projects face particularly elusive targets. Budget and contingency planning rarely account adequately for market shifts and schedule slips—a double-edged sword. A prolonged project can face inflated labor and material costs, and then eroded market prices when it eventually shoulders its way into the marketplace. Competitive danger signs include:

- Greater market-window risks.
- More contenders carving available markets.
- Reduced profit margins

Conditions such as inflation/recession cycles, lack of borrowing power, and stockholder pressures have always existed, but not to the degree they do now, especially when coupled with technology shocks and dealing in unstable international markets, together with worldwide competition. Diversionary pressures include:

- High rate of technology change.
- More attention to legal, ethical, and fair conduct.
- Greater international involvement.

Uncertainty . . . is the only certainty.

Plans don't scale, demanding more and more from less and less.

Tougher competition demands shorter time-to-market and squeezes the break-even point.

Outside influence, often distracting, is becoming relentless.

Inside pressure is being compounded by the other trends.

Reaching new heights of efficiency and productivity, while laudable, may overemphasize means. When carried to extreme, this can be divisive and divert teams from their primary goals leading to:

- Stressful, conflict-ridden atmosphere.
- Higher demands from a shrinking staff.
- More specialization and reorganizations.

Productivity improvements wrought from automation and from pressure to work harder and longer need to be replaced by the elimination of costly errors through disciplined project management.

Inadequate skills
It's rare to find personnel with the requisite set of broad skills

Staffing challenges contribute significantly to the difficulty of project management. Selecting the right project manager is critical to project success. The project manager must fulfill the requirements of the customer or user, must answer to senior management by generating a fair return on investment, and must provide a stimulating, positive work environment for the project team. Project managers must be skilled in technical, business, legal, financial, and personnel matters. Above all, project managers must be selected for their leadership qualities. They must be able to deal with all levels of stakeholders which are often international and multicultural.

The nature of teams.
Teams are formed of a diverse group of talented individuals with little or no experience working together.

Project management is made difficult by the urgent need for a new group to achieve proficiency as a team. The temporary nature of project teams often brings together people who have little or no experience working together. Furthermore, people who are attracted by project assignments are generally motivated by intangible factors such as the work itself or the technical challenge, rather than being part of the team. The newly formed group usually includes specialists who have excelled as individual contributors. Some key team members may even be working part-time. This independence—both managerial and technical—conflicts with the interdependence required for teamwork.

Project managers must often overcome stigma resulting from a lack of training or inherited from previous misapplication of the most vital project management methods. To the uninitiated, a structured process can appear to be overbearing and bureaucratic—even to slow progress and stifle creativity. As in most complex processes, a partial implementation or one crippled by ignorance is worse than none at all. People who use the techniques or tools must be skilled enough to apply them for maximum effectiveness and to achieve support from the team. Misapplied techniques and tools will often lose their effectiveness and poison others against them—possibly forever. This pollution has been happening for years. Unfortunately, the personnel base has been poisoned against good techniques as well as bad. The negative biases are most likely to come from those with:

- Misperceptions based on weak project management.
- Bad experiences resulting from flawed processes.
- Misinterpretations of prior failures.
- Little training or none at all.
- Fears about tight controls.

The fears about tight controls are a major source of negative bias, particularly from the technical community, which often confuses project controls with lack of creative freedom. This bias may have resulted from arbitrary controls that didn't make sense or were never explained. Experienced managers know, however, that appropriate controls enhance rather than inhibit creativity. Such controls free the project team to be creative in finding solutions, rather than being distracted by the day-to-day confusion of misdirected project activity. Our surveys, summarized next and addressed in Chapter 8, were taken over many years and across diverse industries. They reveal that, in the absence of a strong project management culture, the most effective techniques are often not considered important for project success. Even worse, the project team is likely to be biased against the very techniques

Negative bias.
Team members may be biased against good tools by bad prior experience.

The personnel base has been poisoned against good techniques as well as bad.

Project controls are often confused with a lack of creative freedom.

critical to project success, believing they don't really work and should be avoided.

The project manager faces the challenge of converting the negative and neutral attitudes into passionately positive ones.

Opinions about project management, like those about Management by Objectives and Total Quality Management, are seldom neutral. People tend to be either fully committed or extremely negative, depending on their own experiences or perceptions. We designed a survey to be administered to participants entering our training classes. The survey measures the participants' candid attitudes about "how they value" a selected group of important project management techniques prior to receiving training. The results are summarized in Chapter 8. The wide range of responses, with most techniques falling below the 50 percent acceptance level, suggests that the majority of project personnel will not cause these tools to be incorporated into their organization or even support them if they are installed. With so many flawed and incomplete implementations of project management, it's no wonder negative attitudes continue to propagate. The project manager faces the challenges of assessing both individual and team attitudes on each issue and converting the negative and neutral attitudes into passionately positive ones. We address this challenge in Chapter 8.

Projects defy tradition. Traditional management methods simply don't apply.

Projects are quite different from traditional operations. A common form of project is historically exemplified by a construction industry project or by DOD- and NASA-contracted developments that typically create projects among many geographically and nationally dispersed companies. When the project team has completed its objectives, it is disbanded and its members seek new assignments through their skill center home organization. Still other project organizations are formed by one company at the core which then uses other companies and subcontractors as skilled resources. In all cases, project team members typically serve two managers, the project manager performing as their task manager and a permanent functional manager who guarantees the technical performance of the temporary resource.

The evolution of a typical project, such as a new product or new business development, usually follows three steps as shown in Figure 1.1.

FUNCTIONAL ORGANIZATION   PROJECT ORGANIZATION

1. PROPOSAL: A project often starts in a functional organization with a proposal or in response to an external request.

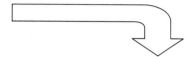

2. DEVELOPMENT: For the development phases, a cross-functional team is formed and empowered.

3. PRODUCTION: For standard production and/or operational support, it is common to return to a functional form of management.

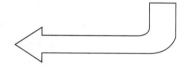

FIGURE 1.1   The evolution of a typical project.

Traditional management approaches deal well with the first and third of these three steps. They do not do well during step two—the heart of project management. Traditional working conditions have meant stability, continuity, and security. Conventional wisdom and traditional management textbooks have emphasized the need for the manager to create a productive work environment and a consistent climate including:

> Conventional wisdom seldom holds true for projects. In many cases, it's dead wrong.

- Stable work environment.
- Minimum of conflict among employees.
- Ambitious employees driven to be their personal best by perks and personal competition.
- Simple, clear reporting structure and organization.
- Responsibility matched with authority.
- Maximum creative freedom.

There's very little that's conventional in the project environment. So conventional wisdom seldom holds true. In many cases, it's dead wrong.

As depicted by Figure 1.2, projects are as important to institutions as leaves are to a tree. Traditional management models focus on the enduring organizations—the roots—such as functional departments. By contrast, project management is more narrowly focused on the specific objectives of the project at hand. Like task forces and other temporary groups, project teams are drawn from various long-term permanent organizations. But unlike other temporary groups, projects are managed to a defined plan including a budget, schedule, and specific output—usually a product or service. Projects are requirements-driven. The customer or user defines the requirements to be met by the project team. This may be done through an intermediary, such as the marketing organization.

Unlike the activities that occur wholly within traditional, functional organizations, project work depends on lateral flow. Therefore, projects lend themselves to some form of matrix organization, such as shown in Figure 1.3. Horizontal dotted line interfaces need to be encouraged and strengthened rather than used reluctantly as exceptions to the linear chain of command.

> Projects should not be forced into traditional structures used for repetitive or long-term work.

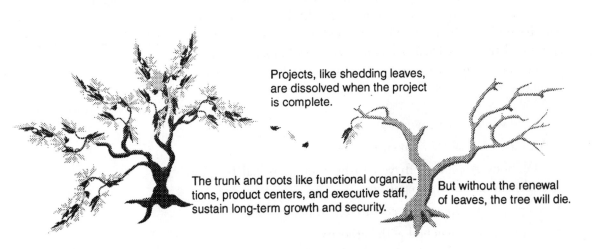

Projects, like shedding leaves, are dissolved when the project is complete.

The trunk and roots like functional organizations, product centers, and executive staff, sustain long-term growth and security.

But without the renewal of leaves, the tree will die.

FIGURE 1.2 Projects are like the leaves on a tree.

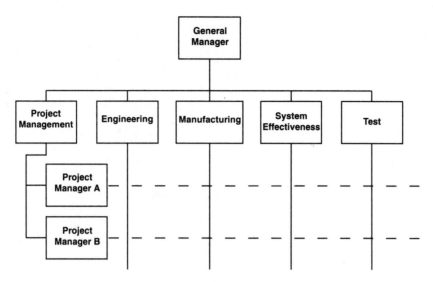

FIGURE 1.3   Typical matrix organization.

The nontraditional aspects and complexity of project management make it difficult to instill in others and install as a culture. This is exacerbated by the mixed heritage discussed earlier and the lack of training. Even when training is available, it is often based on models that are oversimplified and inadequate. For example, many models confuse and intermix sequential activities and ongoing processes. In the next chapter, we address the role of models in concisely describing project management and the specific limitations of current models.

Project Management is difficult to describe succinctly

2

WHY MODEL PROJECT MANAGEMENT?

The power of a science seems quite generally to increase with the number of symbolic generalizations its practitioners have at their disposal.

Thomas Kuhn,
The Structure of Scientific Knowledge

WHY MODEL ANYTHING?

- *Models help to explain how things work.* Abstractions can be personalized and explained by math models or expressions. What young student of science hasn't been enlightened by a physical model of the reciprocating engine or of a molecule?

- *Models can broaden our perspective* as does a desktop globe or a model of the solar system.

- *Models provide a common conceptual frame of reference* just as the common vocabulary does for communications.

- *Models can express rules more simply,* often replacing explicit rules or providing a strong complement.

From road maps to wind tunnels, models help us to avoid costly errors and dead ends.

- *Models clarify relationships, identify key elements, and consciously eliminate confusion factors.* In Thomas Kuhn's words, ". . . all models have similar functions. Among other things they supply the group with preferred and permissible analogies or metaphors."

Models enable us to visualize the big picture. Visualization can be as powerful a technique for achieving high performance and success in business as it is in fields such as sports. Top athletes first perform successfully in their minds before competing. They experience their winning achievement visually—see it— even feel it. NASA researcher, Dr. Charles Garfield, reports that most peak performers are visualizers. Businesspeople who need to persuade others, such as sales personnel or entrepreneurs, benefit from visualizing their situation and the response they expect. Visualization—a right brain activity—is a vital characteristic of leadership, another right brain activity. We employ this technique to gain insight into the logical and systematic project management process—a left brain activity. Visualization can broaden your perspective on all aspects of your job. Lead from your right, manage with your left.

Psychologists agree that most people have insight and creative abilities far beyond those used routinely. Albert Einstein is just one of many people believed to have overcome traditional Western society left-brain learning patterns. He was able to "see" three-dimensional pictures in his mind before he wrote equations. He emphasized the importance of visualization to his own working methods when he said, "The words of the language as they are written or spoken do not seem to play any role in the mechanism of thought. The psychical entities which serve as elements in thought are certain signs and more or less clear images which can be voluntarily reproduced and combined." Experts now believe that visualization, and the subsequent intuition improvements from right-brain thinking, can be developed with time and training.

It's empowering, even for the most experienced project manager, to comprehend the complex project management process with a complete understanding of every piece, and an ability to visualize

Improved visualization and intuition can be developed with time and training.

how each fits into the overall project picture. But many practitioners and even trainers don't see the big picture. Furthermore, all current approaches to project management lack sufficient clarity and detail to be applied routinely and effectively by the project team. This void leads to numerous problems, including the single most common and expensive one: insufficient understanding of user requirements. This often results in deficient initial design, painful redesigns, and expensive time delays (Figure 2.1).

THE FAR SIDE   By GARY LARSON

FIGURE 2.1 Visualization without confirmation through a common language can produce a flawed vision of reality. The results can be equally misleading whether we see the world through the optimist's rose-colored glasses or through a "bugy" lens as this Far Side cartoon depicts. (THE FAR SIDE © 1994 FARWORKS, INC./Dist. by UNIVERSAL PRESS SYNDICATE. Reprinted with permission. All rights reserved.)

With a well-defined project management process in place and the model in mind, it becomes relatively easy to:

- Convey to the team how the project will be managed.
- Communicate with others about the health and progress of the project.
- Assess the risk of alternate paths and take advantage of emerging opportunities.

THE ESSENTIALS OF A PROJECT MANAGEMENT MODEL

> It is impossible to install a process if the model can't be quickly understood and confirmed.

Several experts have identified the general criteria for an effective model, to which we have added specific criteria for project management:

- *Explicitly—and operationally—defined* as to structures, variables, and relationships.
- *Obviously valid and intuitive* to all project stakeholders. If a model has to be studied each time it's applied, it has minimal—perhaps even negative—value.
- *General applicability* throughout the project environment in a way that accounts for the complexity and dynamics of the project process and the special role that project requirements play.
- *Validated empirically* in the real project world.

> The model defined in this book, fully-installed as a culture, can dramatically improve your project success rate.

To implement an effective process, the model must be intuitive because it is impossible to install if it can't be quickly understood and affirmed (it is difficult to install even if it is affirmed). Installing a well-defined "best in class" project management culture, based on the model defined in this book, coupled with training and certifying key team members, can dramatically improve the success rate of projects. To consistently succeed, project-intensive organizations must ultimately come to this realization.

The first step towards defining an explicit model is to provide a vocabulary. In this chapter, we have already used several terms that likely conjure up differing images, depending on each reader's background. Examples are analogies, metaphors, systems, paradigms, and the term "model" itself used many times in this section.

The definitions that follow, from *The American Heritage Dictionary of the English Language, Third Edition,* explain the terms within the context used in this book:

Analogy: Similarity in some respects between things that are otherwise dissimilar. A comparison based on such similarity.

Construct: A concept, model, or schematic idea. A concrete image or idea.

Depict: To represent in a picture or sculpture. To represent in words; describe.

Intuition: The act or faculty of knowing or sensing without the use of rational processes; immediate cognition. Knowledge gained by the use of this faculty; a perceptive insight.

Metaphor: A figure of speech in which a word or phrase that ordinarily designates one thing is used to designate another, thus making an implicit comparison. One thing conceived as representing another; a symbol.

Model: A schematic description of a system, theory, or phenomenon that accounts for its known or inferred properties and may be used for further study of its characteristics.

Paradigm: An example that serves as pattern or model.

Process: A series of actions, changes, or functions bringing about a result: the process of digestion; the process of obtaining a driver's license.

Relationship: A logical or natural association between two or more things; relevance of one to another, connection. The way in which one person or thing is connected with another.

Structure: Something made up of a number of parts that are held or put together in a particular way. The way in which parts are arranged or put together to form a whole. The interrelation or arrangement of parts in a complex entity.

System: A group of interacting, interrelated, or interdependent elements forming a complex whole. An organized set of interrelated ideas or principles. A set of objects or phenomena grouped together for classification or analysis. An organized and coordinated method; a procedure.

THE LIMITATIONS OF CURRENT MODELS

This section focuses on the need to avoid adoption of any model based on a superficial relationship. We often hear strong preferences voiced for one model to the exclusion of all others. This is dangerous. It is important to take advantage of the wide array of management models by understanding their limitations and then applying them appropriately. For example, some models are useful primarily for visualization and comprehension, while others are better suited for day-to-day management.

In this section, we critique several popular models. This has two purposes:

- To use the strengths and contributions of each model to enhance the visualization process.
- To be aware of the important omissions in popular portrayals of the project flow.

We will begin by revisiting a classic: Henri Fayol's[1] widely accepted management principles, originally published in 1916, outline what is necessary for effective general management. His 5 elements:

Planning,
Organizing,
Coordinating,
Commanding,
Controlling

Most management models are based on Henri Fayol's 5 elements and 14 principles.

continue to be popularized by today's project management practitioners as they struggle to accurately describe and model the nature of project management. Combined with Fayol's 5 elements, his 14 principles provide a structure for management direction:

1. Division of work.
2. Responsibility matched to authority.
3. Discipline.
4. Unity of command.
5. Unity of direction.
6. Subordination of the individual's interests to the general interest.
7. Remuneration of personnel.
8. Centralization.
9. Scalar chain (line of authority).
10. Order.
11. Equity.
12. Stability of tenure of personnel.
13. Initiative.
14. Esprit de corps.

Project managers perform the traditional management functions of planning, organizing, coordinating, directing, and controlling. The fact that most of the management texts written since 1916 are based on the Fayol structure, with only minor variations and embellishments, is a tribute to the timelessness of this conventional wisdom. We will often refer to this classical model, confirming the general principles that apply to project management and identifying those that do not. Four principles among Fayol's 14 principles, namely responsibility matched to authority, unity of command, scalar chain of command, and stability are often omitted because they are not desirable in the project environment. This is but one reason a new structure is needed for project

Four principles among Fayol's 14 are often missing and not desirable in the project environment.

management. We will return to this subject in Chapter 3 when we define the project management elements.

Next, we will summarize four current models or structures representing the technical aspect of projects. While these models are popular portrayals of the technical project cycle and enhance the visualization process, they all have important omissions. Part of the problem is that there is no widely understood or universally accepted approach to managing the technical aspect of projects. Furthermore, some popular approaches err in the sequencing of project events. More importantly, they fail to differentiate between sequence-driven and situation-driven management aspects. Viewing the project solely as a sequence of events paints a distorted and biased image of the overall project management process.

These last two problems became apparent when we set out to model the technical processes that drive the project cycle. We started with a commonly accepted circular diagram (Figure 2.2), used by a leading government agency to manage complex, highly technical projects. This model, with its visible flaws, proved

> There is no universally accepted approach to managing the technical aspect of projects.

> Most approaches fail to differentiate between sequential and situational events.

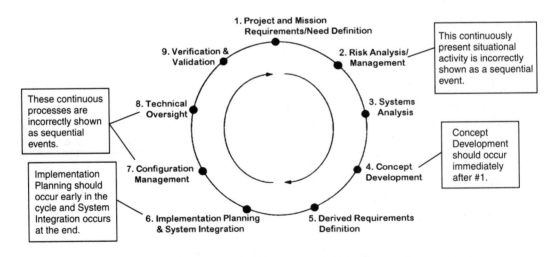

FIGURE 2.2   This circular model has several flaws.

highly instructive. In this and other two-dimensional models, continuously present situational activities, such as risk analysis/management, are incorrectly shown as sequential events.

Some models, such as one Department of Defense representation of the technical aspect of their project cycle (Figure 2.3), depict hardware-related events as independent from software-related events. The false conclusion that these two vital project paths can and should be managed separately until final system integration has resulted in the failure of many projects.

Figure 2.3 and the Waterfall model (Figure 2.4) assume that work downstream should not begin until upstream uncertainties are resolved and major reviews (control gates) have been satisfied. This well-known graphic representation, developed by Dr. Winston W. Royce,[2] presents the software project cycle as a series of diagonal steps vertically paced from upper left to lower right. This process has been designated the waterfall model, since project activity flows from the top to the bottom in discrete, sequential, linear phases. In complex, high-risk projects this is

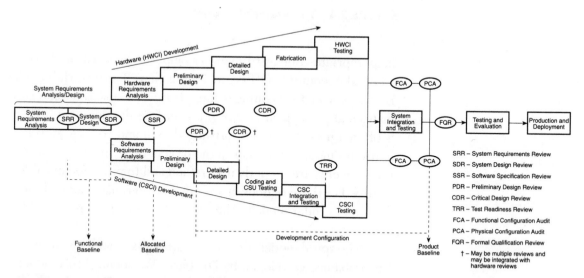

FIGURE 2.3 **Hardware-related events, in the upward path, are erroneously separated from the software events in the downward path.**

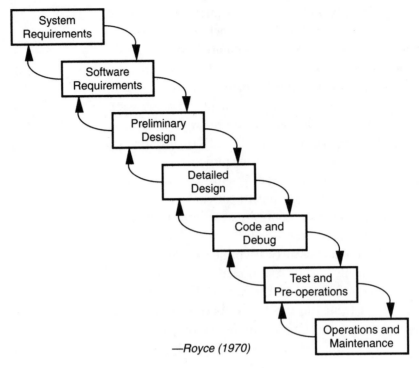

—*Royce (1970)*

FIGURE 2.4 The waterfall model.

inappropriate. Rona Stillman, a computer scientist at the U.S. General Accounting Office, maintains that "The waterfall model is risk-averse. It encourages unrealistic cost and schedule estimates and the appearance of problem-free development." There is often a need to initiate software design and coding, as well as hardware modeling, earlier in the project cycle to ensure that the requirements are properly understood and to prove technical feasibility. For these reasons, many organizations have not embraced these and similar models. They are not adaptable to most real life situations.

The spiral model (Figure 2.5) attempts to address the previous problems. Developed by Dr. Barry W. Boehm,[3] this model is widely used in software development projects. To resolve the deficiencies mentioned above, Dr. Boehm addresses the need for

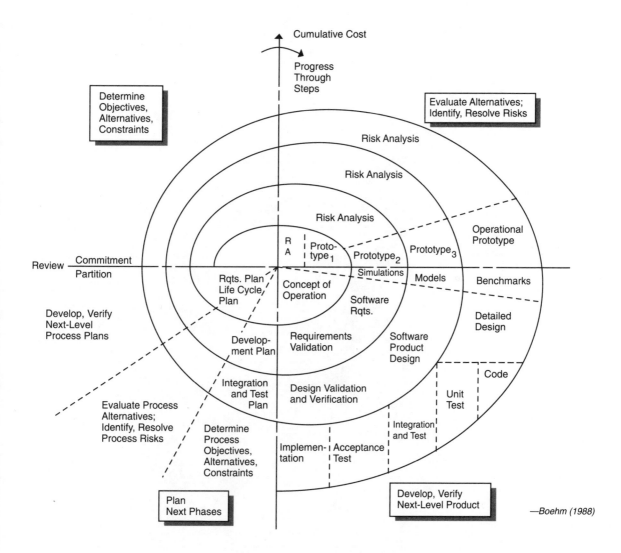

FIGURE 2.5 The spiral model.

early feasibility modeling. While the model does achieve his objective of risk mitigation, the spiral representation can be confusing. The radial time base is inconsistent with standard modeling formats and the model obscures the reviews necessary to control the evolving timebase.

3

VISUALIZING PROJECT MANAGEMENT

Hundreds of people can talk for one who can think, but thousands can think for one who can see. To see clearly is poetry, prophecy, and religion—all in one.

John Ruskin,
Modern Painters

THE FOUR ESSENTIALS FOR EVERY PROJECT

The dictionary defines a team as a group of people working or playing together. But anyone watching a swarm of 6-year-olds playing at soccer, with each child focused on his or her own performance, knows that definition lacks something.

Imagine the challenges faced by a newly formed orchestra, composed of highly trained specialists, each capable of a solo performance (Figure 3.1). When they come together for a short-term engagement, they depend on four essentials:

- Common *vocabulary* of musical symbols.
- Commitment to *teamwork*.

- Musical score (*project cycle* plan).
- Conductor and baton movements (leadership and *management elements*).

We developed the overall model described in this chapter to provide an easily-referenced visual depiction of the project management process. To aid in understanding and communication, the model had to differentiate between practices that are ever present, those that are sequential, and those that are situational. As we visualize the structure of each essential and the relationships among them, vocabulary and teamwork are seen as perpetual properties of a project, while the project cycle and management

FIGURE 3.1   Our image of a great project team is an orchestra, each member capable of solo performances, but committed to teamwork.

elements embody the sequential and situational properties, respectively (Figure 3.2).

We decomposed the project management process into fundamental and unambiguous components. We continued the decomposition process until we identified the most fundamental components: three Project Cycle Aspects and ten Project Management Elements. In the case of the Management Elements, we listed every technique and tool that we and other project management practitioners use successfully. Several hundred were identified. The next step was to categorize the techniques according to how we use them. For instance the work breakdown structure, WBS dictionary, project network diagrams, critical path analysis, scheduling, estimating, and others naturally fit into a planning group. Similarly, the techniques of measuring overrun, under-run, earned value, and others naturally fit within a group we called Project Status. We iterated this step until all techniques and tools fit naturally into homogeneous groups, forming a ten-element structure.

Techniques and tools that provided multiple benefits were located where most significant. For instance, phase transition

> The several hundred successful techniques and tools fit naturally into ten homogeneous groups.

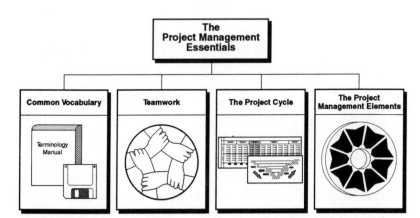

FIGURE 3.2 The project management essentials. *Vocabulary* and *Teamwork* are perpetual properties of projects. The *Project Cycle* and *Management Elements* embody the sequential and situational properties, respectively.

reviews (known as *control gates*) provide the team with visibility as to what is happening, but the most significant benefit of control gates is to provide project control for management. Therefore control gates are categorized as a Project Control technique.

We've validated our model by extensive user experience, having used it to train thousands of project management practitioners. Our graduates confirm this model's unique ability to succinctly convey the necessities for project management success. Clients report that they have significantly improved project performance by basing their culture on this model. We are further gratified with feedback that this concept has helped even the most experienced project managers better understand their role and become even more effective in their career.

After their introduction below, each of the following four chapters focuses on one essential.

Our model has been installed, validated, and refined by the most experienced project managers who report significant performance improvements.

Terminology Manual

The trends toward specialists, each with their own language, coupled with the global and temporary aspects of projects, necessitate the definition of a common vocabulary for each project—even small ones.

A COMMON VOCABULARY—CONSPICUOUS BY ITS ABSENCE

In the previous section, we identified the four essentials through the imagery of an orchestra. When we remove any one of those essentials, a very different picture appears. If you've ever had to recover lost luggage in a foreign country without a common language, you don't have to imagine the disaster that can be bred by misunderstanding.

We are constantly reminded of the consequences of vocabulary breakdown in our training sessions, which vary across a wide range of industries. Some terms we use to teach the practice of project management are confused with similar or identical terms used in the context of a particular business or technical field. For example, the term "proactive" has a prominent role in our project management vocabulary. Our usage reflects the term as defined by *The American Heritage Dictionary of the English Language; Third Edition:*

> Acting in advance to deal with an expected difficulty; anticipatory: not reactive, but proactive steps to combat terrorism.

This usage confuses some people. "Proactive," as used in psychology, refers to a type of memory interference where newly learned facts contribute to forgetting older information, a significant project management problem that we'll return to later.

Another prominent project management word, "status," has nothing to do with stature. The project management context is usually unambiguous, but what troubles some people is our use of "statusing" as a verb. Project Statusing, one of our ten project management elements, is defined in the last section of this chapter.

We will define terms and jargon as we introduce them, a practice that we encourage for every project team. Vocabulary problems lead to conflict and can destroy teamwork. Therefore, a common vocabulary is necessary before you can develop teamwork

PROJECT TEAMWORK

Teamwork is often defined as working together to achieve a common goal. However, this definition falls short of the scope of project teamwork. The work portion of teamwork—that is, the creative effort needed—is usually not well understood. Because of this, real teamwork is only partially achieved.

The fundamentals of teamwork are:

- Common goals.
- Acknowledged interdependency and mutual respect.
- A common code of conduct.
- Shared rewards.
- Team spirit and energy.

Most project teams, including the stakeholders, fail to adequately address these teamwork factors. Of these five factors, the most often overlooked is the common code of conduct. All too often, managers assume that a code of conduct is implied and

Conflict and confusion may drive team members into incorrect practices—even to performing incorrect work.

The visual evidence of teamwork . . .

The coffee pot is never left empty for teammates!

understood even though it hasn't been explicitly defined and agreed to. This can lead to tension and separation among the team members, destroying teamwork.

Without a commitment to teamwork, daily project activity would resemble the floor of the New York Stock Exchange. And it's difficult to imagine a talented group of musicians making good music without a common score and a conductor. Even in "self-directed" teams, the leadership role is filled circumstantially by various team members. And while it is possible for a leaderless group to become a team, it is a time-consuming process at best and likely to fail in today's rapid paced project environments. With company survival riding on project successes, we doubt any CEO would gamble on the odds of creating effective leaderless project teams—any more than preseason ticket buyers would gamble on the emergence of a conductor-less orchestra.

THE SEQUENTIAL PROJECT CYCLE

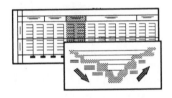

Successful project cycles, the key to achieving consistency from project to project, usually embody a strategy that works and lessons learned that serve as a template.

All projects have a cycle. It may not always be documented and it may not be understood, but there is a sequence of events through which the project passes—the project cycle (Figure 3.3).

Professional project management organizations usually have a standard or template project cycle that includes their preferred sequence of events. This is then tailored to the special characteristics of the project at hand. The resultant project cycle becomes the parent or driver of the logical project network that will be developed during planning.

The cycle has *Periods* (such as Study, Implementation, and Operations), and *Phases* within the periods (such as Concept Definition and Verification). They also include Activities such as Trade-off Candidate Concepts, Products such as System Concept Document, and Control Gates or Phase Transition Reviews such as System Concept Review (Figure 3.4).

Known by a variety of names that help to characterize it, the project cycle has been called: budget cycle, acquisition cycle, implementation cycle, and others. A complete project cycle contains

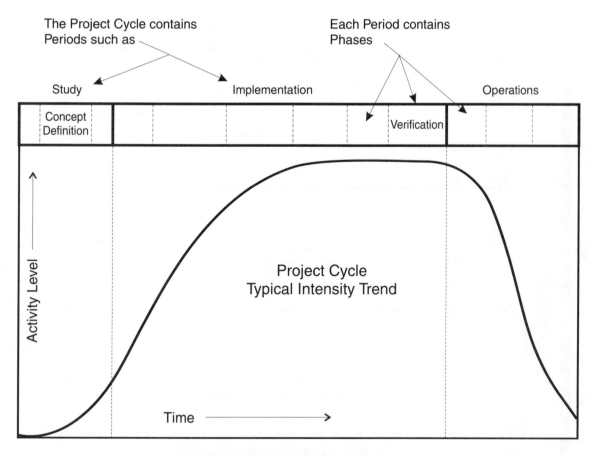

The Project Cycle contains
Periods such as

Each Period contains
Phases

Study   Implementation   Operations

Concept
Definition

Verification

Activity Level

Project Cycle
Typical Intensity Trend

Time

FIGURE 3.3   The sequential project cycle.

all of these—the framework for project-unique tactics as well as strategic plans.

There are three aspects that can be viewed as layers of our project cycle. Each layer—Budget, Business, and Technical—contains its own set of events. The interwoven events for the three aspects constitute the total cycle (Figure 3.5).

The technical cycle identifies the activities and events required to provide the optimum technical solution in the most efficient manner, a system engineering responsibility. The technical process spans from determination of user wants to validation that the project solution satisfies the user. This includes the sequences

The technical aspect of the project cycle is best visualized as a vee.

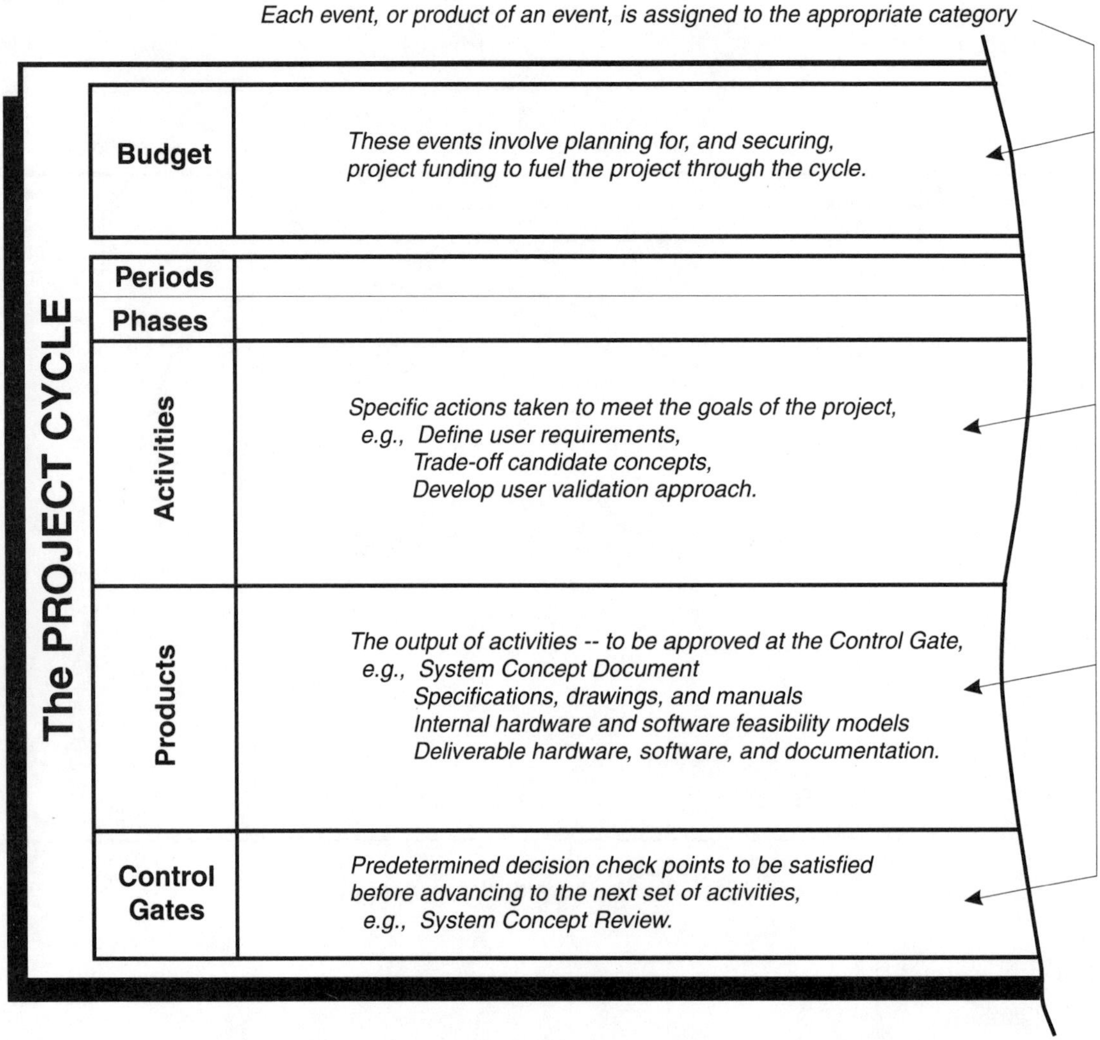

Each event, or product of an event, is assigned to the appropriate category

Budget	*These events involve planning for, and securing, project funding to fuel the project through the cycle.*

Periods

Phases

Activities	*Specific actions taken to meet the goals of the project, e.g., Define user requirements, Trade-off candidate concepts, Develop user validation approach.*
Products	*The output of activities -- to be approved at the Control Gate, e.g., System Concept Document Specifications, drawings, and manuals Internal hardware and software feasibility models Deliverable hardware, software, and documentation.*
Control Gates	*Predetermined decision check points to be satisfied before advancing to the next set of activities, e.g., System Concept Review.*

The PROJECT CYCLE

FIGURE 3.4   Our recommended format for the project cycle.

for decomposition, definition, integration, and verification as shown in a simplified version (Figure 3.6). The process is best visualized when portrayed in a vee format, rather than purely horizontal, to illustrate moving from system requirements and concepts down to detailed part and assembly processes and then

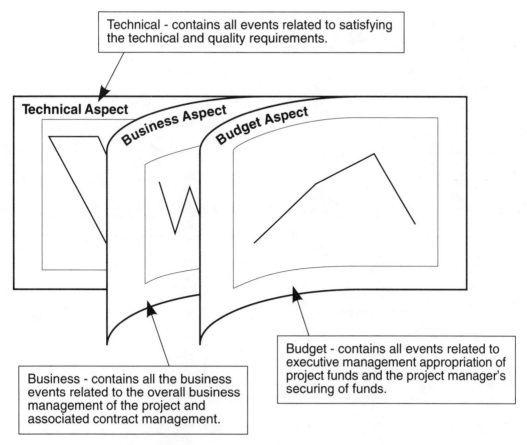

Technical - contains all events related to satisfying the technical and quality requirements.

Technical Aspect

Business Aspect

Budget Aspect

Business - contains all the business events related to the overall business management of the project and associated contract management.

Budget - contains all events related to executive management appropriation of project funds and the project manager's securing of funds.

FIGURE 3.5   The three aspects of all projects.

upward consistent with fabrication and integration of the system elements into the completed system. Also included are the activities associated with risk and opportunity management. The simplified version follows the basic vee chart developed by NASA as part of the Software Management and Assurance Program.

Work should not progress beyond a decision point until the project manager and the buyer are ready to baseline the progress and control the decisions agreed to at that point. Unlike the commonly held view of the Waterfall model, there is no prohibition against doing exploratory design and analysis early in the cycle. In

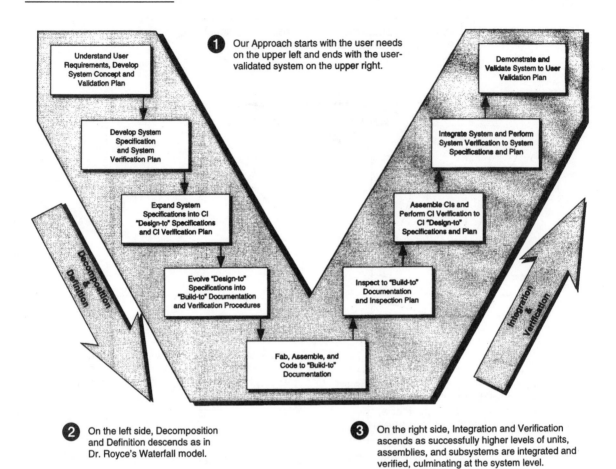

1 Our Approach starts with the user needs on the upper left and ends with the user-validated system on the upper right.

Understand User Requirements, Develop System Concept and Validation Plan

Develop System Specification and System Verification Plan

Expand System Specifications into CI "Design-to" Specifications and CI Verification Plan

Evolve "Design-to" Specifications into "Build-to" Documentation and Verification Procedures

Fab, Assemble, and Code to "Build-to" Documentation

Inspect to "Build-to" Documentation and Inspection Plan

Assemble CIs and Perform CI Verification to CI "Design-to" Specifications and Plan

Integrate System and Perform System Verification to System Specifications and Plan

Demonstrate and Validate System to User Validation Plan

Decomposition & Definition

Integration & Verification

2 On the left side, Decomposition and Definition descends as in Dr. Royce's Waterfall model.

3 On the right side, Integration and Verification ascends as successfully higher levels of units, assemblies, and subsystems are integrated and verified, culminating at the system level.

FIGURE 3.6   The basic Vee model.

fact, hardware and software requirements-understanding models and/or technical feasibility models may be required at the outset.

At each level there is a direct correlation between activities on the left and right sides of the vee. This is deliberate. For example, the method of verification to be used on the right must be determined on the left for each set of requirements developed and documented at each decomposition level. This minimizes the chances that requirements are specified in a way that cannot be measured or verified.

The right side of the vee directly corresponds to the left—the rationale for the shape.

The quasi-independent relationship between the sequence of project events (in the plane of the vee) and the situationally-applied processes, is illustrated by orthogonal planes (Figure 3.7a and b).

We define the System Engineering Process to be the application of the SA&D Subprocess and the SI&V Subprocess to the technical aspect of the project cycle. In Chapter 6, we address the system engineering process in more detail.

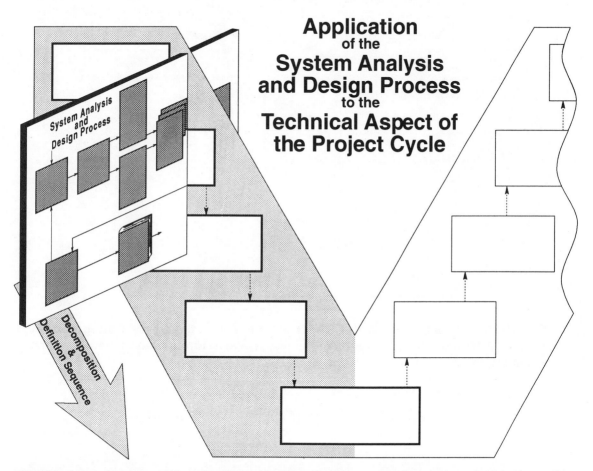

FIGURE 3.7a The System Analysis & Design (SA&D) subprocess plane represents those activities that must be performed situationally as the project proceeds down the left side of the Vee. This SA&D subprocess is repeated at all levels of system decomposition and definition for each design decision that requires trade-off analysis. It will be repeated many times within a phase to satisfy the requirements for the corresponding core control gate.

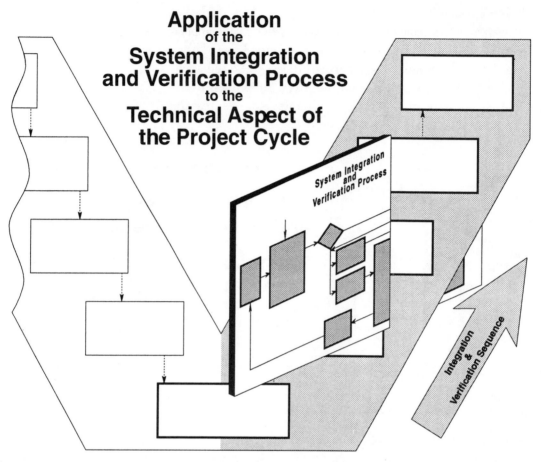

FIGURE 3.7b **The counterpart of the SA&D subprocess is the System Integration and Verification (SI&V) subprocess, an iterative process repeated throughout the integration and verification sequence as illustrated in the diagram.**

THE SITUATIONAL PROJECT MANAGEMENT ELEMENTS

Technical, schedule, and cost performance do not naturally work together. They are opposing forces that require compromise based on knowledge of the project's priorities, continuous forecasting, statusing, and corrective action. The management elements, summarized here, provide the necessary techniques and tools to be situationally applied to manage the project cycle.

Many texts and organizations attempt to apply the Fayol model to projects (reviewed in the last chapter and depicted in the first column of Table 3.1). While the Fayol model and its recent derivatives (second column) have a timeless validity to ongoing general management, they have critical deficiencies related to project management and the relatively short duration of projects. They do not address the unique role of Requirements as the project initiator and driver. Even more significantly, they do not provide enough detail to adequately manage the highly complex project processes, particularly those of high-risk, high-technology projects. In order to provide greater comprehension of what is required, we have expanded these models. The resulting 10 elements, applied to every stage of the cycle, identify those indispensable responsibilities of project management that are too often misunderstood, minimized, or ignored in practice. This is not simply another academic reorganization. Lack of attention to these details is precisely the kind of omission that dooms projects.

The added and changed elements are shown in bold. For project control, the distinction between being proactive and reactive, noted in the last column, is particularly significant. Project Control embodies those techniques that help ensure that events happen as planned, and that unplanned events do not happen, whereas the three variance control elements define the means for detecting and correcting unplanned results.

Because they are situational, the techniques must be applied responsively, relative to the active project phase and the specific team or individual circumstances at the time. An example is the Organization Options element that is applied frequently as the

---

Technical, schedule, and cost performance are opposing forces that require compromise.

Our model adds details that are too often misunderstood, minimized, or ignored in practice.

Lack of attention to these details is precisely the kind of omission that dooms projects.

Situational management depends on the appropriate application of each technique . . . skillfully.

Projects sometimes fail by misapplication of excellent techniques.

TABLE 3.1 Relating the Ten Elements to Traditional Models

Fayol (1916)	Recent Derivatives	Our Ten Element Model	Rationale for Expansion	Major Focus
		Requirements	Failure to manage requirements, which initiate and drive projects, is the major cause for failure.	Formulate *Proactive*
Organizing	Organizing	Organizing		
	Staffing	**Project Team**	Teams are newly formed for each project and include subcontractors and outsourcing.	
Planning	Planning	Planning		
		Risk & Opportunity Management	Usually ignored in the project environment and a significant cause of project failures.	
		Project Control	Often improperly implemented as monitoring. Many failures are due to a lack of proper controls.	
Controlling	Controlling	**Visibility**	Visibility systems must be designed and implemented to keep all stakeholders informed.	Variance control
Coordinating		**Status**	Hard measurement of progress and variance, as opposed to the more typical activity reporting.	*Reactive*
Commanding	Directing	**Corrective Action**	Innovative actions required to get back on plan.	
		Leadership	Creation of team energy to succeed to the plan.	Motivate

project moves from phase to phase and changes its organization form to satisfy the objectives of the active phase. Similarly, the element of Project Visibility will contain those techniques to be considered and applied by the team to optimize the visibility of the active project cycle phase.

The 10 project management elements are the team's toolbox (Figure 3.8) and, therefore, should contain the best and most effective methods in each category. This implicitly depends on the team being skilled in the application of all of the techniques and tools—which is often not the case. Projects do fail by misapplication of excellent techniques.

The ten elements are summarized next and detailed in Chapter 7.

Project Requirements covers both the creation and management of requirements. It includes requirement identification, substantiation, documentation, concept selection, specification, decomposition, definition, integration, verification, and validation. Techniques and tools include system analysis and design, requirements traceability, accountability, modeling, and others. This element is situational rather than sequential since new requirements are apt to be introduced at almost any point in the project to be managed concurrently with the maturing requirements.

Organization Options considers the strengths and deficiencies of various project structures, for example, how each resolves accountabilities, responsibilities, and promotes teamwork and communications. Complex projects do not have to lead to complex structures, and there is no single "best" organization. There are

The project risk, size, and management style determine the formality of application, but not whether a particular element will be present or not—all are essential for project success.

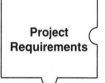

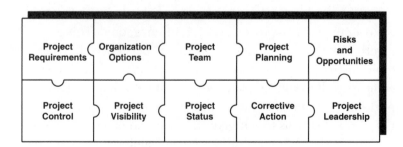

FIGURE 3.8 The team's toolbox.

many options including matrix, integrated product teams, and integrated project teams—even "skunk works." This element is personnel-independent and provides the basis for selecting and changing the structure appropriately as the project progresses from concept to deactivation.

The *Project Team* element addresses the personnel dependencies of the project. It provides the techniques and tools for determining the appropriate mix of personnel and for staffing the project. Selection criteria consider character traits, qualifications, and the specific skills demanded by the challenges of each project phase. Competency models that include necessary attributes and qualifications form the basis of selection for key positions such as the project manager, the business manager, the system engineer, the planner, and the subcontractor manager. The best management approach may require that some key players are changed as the project progresses from development to deployment.

Project Planning starts with the team's conversion of project requirements into team task authorizations including delivery schedules and resource plans. But it doesn't end there. Too often planning is done once and is then forgotten as the project strays from its intended path. To respond to new information and events, updated planning is required to make adjustments in each phase progression. The planning process should include both manual and computer tools which support the best tactical approach for accomplishing project objectives consistent with the project cycle constraints. We teach the use of a powerful technique called "cards on the wall" described in Chapter 7.

Risks and Opportunities management is an important part of the overall planning process, yet it is often ignored. This jeopardy, together with the uniqueness of the associated techniques and tools, justifies treatment as a separate element. This element encompasses the identification and evaluation of both risks and opportunities. It includes techniques for determining and managing the planned actions to mitigate the risks and enhance the opportunities. Risks and opportunities are encountered and can be discovered at any point in the project cycle, so the techniques and tools of this element must be applied perceptively as the project progresses. It is not uncommon for both of these factors to be ignored by the project team and many projects have failed as a result.

Project Control is often misunderstood because many projects have a project controls organization that reports status rather than controlling. Controlling the project is necessary to ensure that planned events happen as planned and that unplanned events don't happen at all. In our method, project control is recognized as process control where every aspect that needs to be controlled must have a standard, a control authority, a control mechanism, and a variance detection system. Using schedule control as an example, the standard is the master schedule, the authority is the business manager, the mechanism is the change board, and the variance detection is the status review. Categories of controlled processes may include security, safety, configuration management, requirements, schedule, cost, and so on. Many projects fail when their control systems are not in place or are circumvented.

Project Visibility encompasses all of the techniques used by the project team and stakeholders to gather data and disseminate information so as to ensure that the project team communicates effectively and is informed as necessary about relevant project activity. It includes manual techniques like MBWA (management by walking around) and project information centers as well as electronic techniques such as voice mail, video conferencing, and fax. The visibility system and associated techniques must be designed to serve the active project phase and its organizational structure.

Project Status is frequently confused with project activity. Project status is not simply activity, but comprehensive measurements of performance against the plan to detect unacceptable variances and determine the need for corrective action. Status should encompass schedule, cost, technical, and business progress. The evaluation and measurement should also include the rate of change of the variance if not corrected. Earned value and other systems are included in this technique and tool set.

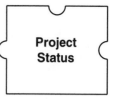

Corrective Action is the culmination of variance management and emphasizes that good reactive management is necessary for effective project management. Corrective Actions are the

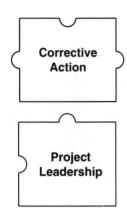

actions taken to return the project to plan and usually take place during Project Statusing, or shortly thereafter. The techniques may include overtime, added work shifts, an alternate technical approach, new leadership, and so on. Projects that ignore variances and fail to implement corrective action are usually out of control.

Project Leadership is the most important of the 10 project management elements. Leadership is the mortar that holds together all other elements of project management and ensures that all the others are properly implemented and effectively used. It represents the ability to inspire—to ensure that project members are motivated on both the individual and team level to deliver as promised within the desired project management culture. Leadership emphasizes doing the right things, while doing things right is a primary management responsibility. Leadership depends on the skillful application of techniques such as handling different personalities and maturity levels, reward systems, and team composition and rewards. History has confirmed that, without strong leadership, the team is likely to stray from cultural fundamentals and implement high-risk, failure-prone short cuts. If the team is fully trained in the worth of the elements and are believers in the process, then the need for strong leadership is reduced.

VISUALIZING THE PROJECT MANAGEMENT PROCESS

Presenting the project management elements in two-dimensional table form and as pieces in a puzzle is useful for discussing the relationships among them. However, to illustrate the more complex relationship between the situationally-applied management elements and the sequential project cycle, we need to employ a third dimension (Figure 3.9).

Once a project cycle is defined, each of the three aspects must be managed situationally by the application of the project management elements. As an example, Project Requirements, one of the 10 management elements, occurs throughout the cycle as

We begin by depicting the first nine project management elements as the spokes of a wheel, held together by its rim, Project Leadership (the tenth element)

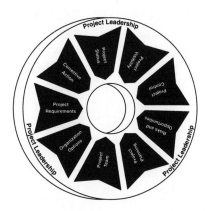

In relationship to the wheel, the sequential project cycle can be visualized as an axle. If the project is to succeed in a financial as well as technical terms, all aspects of the project must be considered and simultaneously managed, as depicted by the three core sections of the axle.

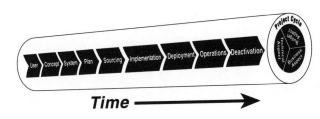

Time ⟶

The axle and wheel assembly represents the overall process. Most crucial to our project management approach is the separation of sequential and situational aspects of the project into separate domains. The axle represents the sequence of events of the project cycle and the wheel represents the situational application of the ten management elements to lead the project through the cycle. The relationship among the project cycle phases (the axle) and the management elements (the wheel) is orthogonal and dynamic, as the wheel moves along the axle with time.

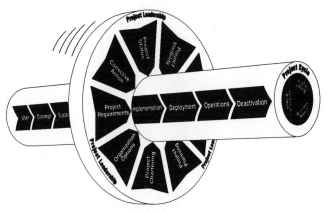

FIGURE 3.9   The orthogonal model.

the original requirements evolve in detail and as new requirements are introduced into the project irrespective of the phase of the cycle currently being managed. Similarly, Project Planning occurs in each and every phase in order to prepare for the subsequent phases. We will return to this model, and to those presented for the technical aspect, as we implement the process in Part Two.

PART TWO

THE ESSENTIALS OF PROJECT MANAGEMENT

In Part One we presented a birdseye view of the management playing field—environment, concepts, roles, and goals. Part Two zooms in on application details in depth. In Chapter 8 we assess the future implications.

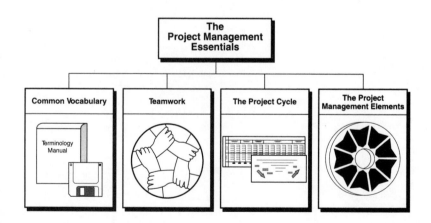

4

PROJECT
VOCABULARY

**Precision of communication is important, more important
than ever, in our era of hair-trigger balances, when a false,
or misunderstood word may create as much disaster as a
sudden thoughtless act.**

James Thurber,
Lanterns and Lances

A disaster such as that described by Thurber occurred when
the term *qualified* was not understood and not responded to
during the prelaunch readiness review of the space shuttle Challenger, leading to the O-ring failure and causing the tragic deaths
of seven astronauts.

TO SUCCEED AT PROJECT MANAGEMENT,
YOU FIRST HAVE TO COMMUNICATE CLEARLY

We can't discuss the other three project management essentials—
Teamwork, the Project Cycle, and the 10 Elements—without a
common vocabulary. The successful practice of project management involves areas of conflict that can only be resolved with

clearly defined terms. For example, communications problems lead to conflict and destroy teamwork, therefore a common vocabulary is necessary before you can develop teamwork.

TO COMMUNICATE CLEARLY, YOU FIRST HAVE TO THINK CLEARLY

John Beckley[1] articulates the essence of clarity, "It isn't hard to write something which, if a person takes the time to study it, is absolutely clear. But writing that has to be studied is not good communication. The meaning of good writing is so immediately clear and obvious, it doesn't have to be studied."

Beckley tells the following story about a man who wrote to a government bureau asking if hydrochloric acid could be used to clean the tubes in his steam boiler. This was the bureau's reply:

> "Uncertainties of reactive processes make the use of hydrochloric acid undesirable where alkalinity is involved."
>
> In appreciation, the man wired back: "Thanks for the advice. I'll start using it next week."
>
> Washington wired back urgently, but still in the bureaucratic jargon: "Regrettable decision involves uncertainties. Hydrochloric acid will produce sublimate invalidating reactions."
>
> This extra courtesy prompted this acknowledgment: "Thanks again. Glad to know it's O.K."
>
> Finally, another urgent, but unmistakable, message: "DON'T USE HYDROCHLORIC ACID! IT WILL EAT HELL OUT OF YOUR TUBES!"

We've historically criticized lawyers and politicians for their confusing, often incomprehensible, prose. It seems intended to obscure rather than to clarify events. But in a similar fashion, managers and technical people often try to sound managerial or technical.

Unfortunately, Orwellian "doublespeak" has proliferated to all segments of politics and business, often in the form of jargon that finds us blaming everything on "paradigms" or a lack of

To communicate precisely, you have to think clearly and use a common vocabulary.

"Snow jobs"—intended or not—can backfire. Your words may mean something quite different to your listener.

Jargon needs to be used as a means, rather than becoming an end, for communicating.

"infrastructure." On the other hand, capitalizing on new technologies and practices can be facilitated by carefully defined jargon.

Acronyms can simplify communication if they are uniformly understood by the team. Remember to leave the jargon behind and to spell out the acronyms when making presentations or writing for audiences outside the project environment. If acronyms are used, define them as they are introduced and provide a glossary. We've included a Glossary for the acronyms used in this book.

> All too frequently, when an engineer sounds as if he's speaking a foreign language—one composed mostly of acronyms—it's because he wants to.

The truly impressive communicator doesn't set out to impress anybody—just tries to get ideas across in the simplest, clearest fashion. Such a person is likely viewed as an outstanding communicator and project contributor.

WE ALL SPEAK ENGLISH, DON'T WE?

Many words, which are viewed as synonyms in common usage, have unique and distinct meanings in a technical sense. Stress and strain, commonly used interchangeably to refer to personal anxiety, refer to quite different technical phenomena, as do the project management terms, validation and verification. Few people confuse "bread" with its chief ingredient, "flour," but the ingredient, "cement," is often used incorrectly to refer to "concrete."

The assumption that we have a common language, when we don't, can have far worse consequences than trying to communicate nonverbally. After all, as jargon and jabberwocky proliferate, the language of choice will often revert to that more trustworthy standby: body language.

A leading corporation recently asked us to participate in a team session convened to identify risks, opportunities, and appropriate actions for a major new project. It was the first time the complete team had been brought together so the project manager opened the meeting with a 40-minute overview of the project. We jotted down some 20 terms we didn't understand and later asked the team members which of the terms they understood. Over half

> The listener's ego may discourage seeking clarification.

the group didn't understand any of the 20 terms. Without a clarifying reference, the team didn't get the important message the
project manager was trying to convey. But each remained silent
assuming the others knew. The most dangerous assumption was
on the part of the project manager who assumed everyone understood.

A major U.S. corporation recently signed a contract with a
foreign government to rebuild that country's entire communication structure without understanding the meaning or implications
of many of the contract provisions.

To prevent misunderstandings, one U.S. government agency
includes electronic and printed versions of their terminology
manual with their Request For Proposal so that all proposals are
based on the same definitions. Such techniques are now proliferating to other project environments.

It can be very costly to assume people understand when they don't.

EACH PROJECT NEEDS ITS OWN TERMINOLOGY MANUAL

In order to make this point in our training sessions, we ask the
class to define several commonly used terms. We frequently select
the following five from a substantial list of misunderstood terms:

Prototype, Baseline, Qualification, Verification, Validation
The class usually erupts into a great debate as they argue among
themselves as to the correct meanings. The debate continues in-
conclusively until our project management terminology manual is
used to clarify the meanings. There is a need for a common vocabulary, which should exist at the project level, since:

- Schools don't have, and consequently don't teach one.
- Most companies don't have a common vocabulary.
- Words are used differently across projects, companies, and
  industries.
- Terminology manuals, when they exist, are often imprecise.
- There is little effort to fix the problem.

A terminology manual, tailored to the project at hand, can go a long way toward fixing the problem. It needs to consider the terminology appropriate to the industry, company, and the specific project. The cardinal rule in constructing a project vocabulary is to make sure every item added is fully justified and carries its own weight. It must contribute more to understanding than it detracts as potential excess verbiage. Try first to use ordinary language to represent a needed concept, using short words where possible. Only if the resulting expression is unduly burdensome, should a new term or acronym be coined or borrowed from a related field or industry. In the latter case, the use of the existing nomenclature should clarify, rather than mislead, through its similarities.

We surveyed several widely used terminology manuals (including NASA, DoD, and IEEE) and found them all to be unclear and imprecise, often "relating" terms to other terms rather than explicitly defining them. This led us to develop a terminology manual for our training courses. The result is about the size of this book with over 1000 definitions for acronyms, terms, control gates, and documents. The definitions below for the five terms used to introduce this section are excerpts from our terminology manual.

Prototype and *Model* are commonly used terms in product development projects. The term prototype infers a model built by Manufacturing under Engineering surveillance. It is built to released drawings with production-worthy parts and processes. This is the definition intended by the customer for a recent development project. But the prime contractor interpreted "prototype" to mean an engineering model that could be based on commercial or even consumer parts bought at the local Radio Shack—a costly mistake. To avoid this surprise, their project terminology manual should have included (at least) the following definitions:

> *Model—Engineering.* A technical demonstration model constructed to be tested in a simulated or actual field environment. The model meets electrical and mechanical performance specifications, and either meets or closely

> A secondary benefit of a project terminology manual is the rise in everyone's sensitivity to the need for precise communications.

> Desktop computers now make it easy to provide access to the project's terminology manual as a shared database.

approaches the size, shape, and weight specifications. It may lack the high-reliability parts required to meet the reliability and environmental specifications, but is designed to readily incorporate such changes into the prototype and final production units. Its function is to test and evaluate operational performance and utility before making a final commitment to produce the operational units. Also called an Engineering Development Model.

Model—Mock-up. A physical demonstration model, built to scale, used early in the development of a project to verify proposed design fit, critical clearances and operator interfaces.

Model—Production. A production demonstration model, including all hardware, software, and firmware, manufactured using production drawings, production tools, fixtures and methods. Generally, the first article of the production unit run initiated after the Production Readiness Review (PRR). A Prototype model, also built from production drawings may precede the PRR, to provide confidence to authorize fabrication of the production model.

Prototype—Hardware. A specification-compliant production readiness demonstration model developed under engineering supervision that represents what manufacturing should replicate. All design engineering and production engineering must be complete and the assembly must be under configuration control. Prototype acceptance test data are presented at the Production Readiness Review (PRR).

The term "rapid prototyping" has lost all meaning—it is neither rapid nor prototyping.

In software, models such as screen designs or algorithms are often referred to as prototypes, hence the ambiguity of the term needs to be explicitly noted in the definition:

Prototype—Software. An imprecise term, currently with multiple meanings. A "rapid prototype" is usually a software requirements demonstration model, which provides a simulated representation of the software system functionality and operator interface. The model facilitates early Customer-

Supplier agreement of the system design approach. A software prototype may also be a technical demonstration model. Except with "Evolving Prototypes," the code is usually discarded once the model has served its purpose.

Baselines are the progressively documented set of functional, performance, and physical characteristics, mutually agreed upon by Customer and Provider, that define the evolving definition of the "to be delivered" item, as well as the project management plan for the project. (Note: Items that have not been mutually agreed upon between Customer and Provider are not part of the Baseline.) Three baselines established during the System Development Phase are the System Specification Baseline, "Design-to" Baseline, and "Build-to" Baseline.

Qualification is the process of testing and analyzing hardware and software configuration items to prove that the design will survive the anticipated accumulation of acceptance test environments plus its expected handling, storage, and operational environments plus a specified qualification margin. Qualification usually includes temperature, vibration, shock, salt spray, software stress testing, and other testing.

Verification is proof of compliance with specification performance requirements. Verification may be determined by test, analysis, inspection, or demonstration.

Validation is the process of providing evidence that a system meets the needs of the User.

SOME CRITICAL CONTROL GATES HAVE CRITICALLY CONFUSED TITLES

While the definition of control gates involves more than terminology, some titles themselves have been a source of confusion. We will use this section to clarify particularly egregious nomenclature. Control gates will be discussed in more depth in the next chapter.

The government has defined control gates that are common to many projects. Since these definitions are being broadly adopted by commercial industry in international environments, it is important to alert new users to misleading nomenclature. Some control gate titles are incorrectly based on their position relative to design approval (e.g., being "critical" to or "preliminary" to design approval).

The *Preliminary* Design Review (PDR) is actually the *final* "Design-to" specification and verification plan review. But in most PDRs you can count on only three things: coffee, donuts, and artist sketches of the project. Specifications (major evidence to be evaluated) are often conspicuous by their absence, as are verification plans, having not been developed. Because it's "prelim," everyone in the room is easily contented, but should not be. This confusing terminology may well cause the team to miss their milestone requirements. Countless hours are wasted in PDRs that don't satisfy the criteria for the review.

All control gates are the *final* point for important project decisions. Even though one of the better known control gates is called CDR—Critical Design Review, all control gates are critical events in the project cycle. The most critical of all design reviews is the System Concept Review where the system concept is approved, thereby locking in the life-cycle costs and risks.

> The preliminary design review may be the most *critical* review of the project.

A FEW FOR THE BOOK (THIS BOOK, THAT IS)

In general, we will define the jargon and terms used in the book as they are introduced. Here are a few exceptions. The meaning of terms such as customer and provider, as used in the Software Prototype definition above, seem obvious. But when users, buyers, and sellers enter the picture, roles can be confused. For example, a major airline may be the customer for an airplane that has many users, such as crew and passengers. The major airline, as the customer, may define the user requirements. Small charter services are both final buyers and users, but they would probably buy a "standard" airplane defined by the manufacturer. In this case, we designate the customer (as seen by the development project team) to be the aircraft manufacturer's marketing department. Since we use these terms liberally in the remaining chapters, we include their definitions here.

> *User* The final party for whom the service or product is being provided. There are many types of users; here are some examples: product user, operational user, service user, future user. All four types drive the user requirements and provide constraints on the product.
>
> *Customer* The buyer of the project team's product or service. The customer is responsible for defining the user requirements through interaction with the intended user (for contracts) or knowledge of the user community (for proprietary products or services).
>
> *Provider* The final seller in the project chain, usually the project team itself.
>
> *Buyers* All the intermediate parties in the project chain which must be satisfied by the corresponding Sellers. For example, the project manager can be viewed as the buyer of services provided by a support organization or other contractor/seller.
>
> *Sellers* All the intermediate parties in the project chain which respond to the buyers.
>
> *Stakeholder* Any individual, group, or organization that can affect, or be affected by, the project.

YOU CAN LEAD A HORSE TO WATER . . .

Project managers should hold their teams accountable to the project vocabulary. It is reasonable to have team members certify that they have read the project terminology manual and that they are committed to using it.

"Accountability" is an important part of every project's vocabulary.

5

TEAMWORK

One man may hit the mark, another blunder; but heed not these distinctions. Only from the alliance of the one working with and through the other, are great things born.
Saint-Exupery,
The Wisdom of the Sands

Team effectiveness relies on many things: chemistry, attitudes, and motivational sources. Achieving real teamwork depends on:

1. Forming a group capable of becoming a team,
2. Creating and sustaining a teamwork environment, and
3. Inspiring teamwork growth through leadership.

In this chapter, we focus on the second of these, a perpetual property of projects, which is also the second essential to successful project management. In Chapter 7, we address the project management elements for team formation and leadership. Team formation emphasizes the techniques for selecting the right people and defining their roles—an ongoing process throughout the project cycle. The motivational techniques needed to sustain the project team are an integral part of Leadership.

Of all the challenges facing project teams, the greatest involves the people themselves.

WHY DO SO MANY TEAMS FAIL?

Few terms are as evocative of today's desired work setting as "team" and "teamwork."

Teamwork, so essential to effective project performance, receives considerable attention today. We want our project staffs to become empowered teams—perhaps even self-directed teams. We organize our work groups into Integrated Project or Product Teams. We use Tiger Teams to solve problems. To manage quality achievement, we team with our customers. We have Continuous Improvement Teams. We agonize over the impact of telecommuting on teamwork. And then with all this emphasis on team and teamwork, we still collect groups of workers, tell them they're empowered, leave them alone, and hope that a functioning team somehow emerges from that forced proximity of a small conference room.

When teamwork fails, it's seldom due to lack of good intentions.

If that wished-for team fails to emerge from that self-discovery process, maybe we'll organize an event called a "team build," at an off-site location. The staff discusses goals and generates mission statements. The event is full of good social activities—perhaps the traditional "build a tower out of soda straws"—

The special recognition usually given to the "team" portion of teamwork makes members aware of the need for cooperation.

Yet many teams fail.

Most team efforts fail because of insufficient attention to the WORK involved.

FIGURE 5.1 The "work" in teamwork.

even some outward-bound type of outdoor experience like a "trust fall." Then, full of sociable camaraderie, we go back to work and watch the team that started to jell so nicely in the woods or at the conference site fall quickly and quietly apart, back into the group of individuals with whom we started. (See Figure 5.1.)

Failure usually results from a lack of knowledge about the work that goes into creating and sustaining teamwork. Inadequate leadership fails to create the environment in which teams can be effective. Furthermore, potential team members are seldom trained to share their efforts to accomplish team goals. The team may assume they know more about teamwork than they do. So we need to be able to differentiate between superficial teamwork and the real thing.

Once a group is formed, the people tend to believe they are a team, even when they're not.

THE FUNDAMENTALS OF AN EFFECTIVE TEAMWORK ENVIRONMENT

Effective teams share several common characteristics. They can articulate their common goal which they are committed to achieve. They acknowledge their interdependency coupled with mutual respect. They have accepted a common set of boundaries on their actions—a common code of conduct for the performance of the task. They have accepted the fact that there is one reward they will all share. Add team spirit and a sense of enjoyment when working together, and the result is a smoothly functioning team.

Our metaphor for a team, depicted in Chapter 3, is a good orchestra, with a common score and a conductor. Both need direction from a commonly defined script (project plan or score) and need direction from a single point of accountability for setting the tempo of the project. However, having a conductor just wave the baton (or a project manager authorize tasks, its functional equivalent in today's project environment) is insufficient to build and sustain a team.

Our dilemma today is that we can't take the time or risk for self-directed group discovery. And merely having a project manager and a kick-off event is insufficient to sustain real teamwork.

The image of an orchestra reflects today's real project environment and the real nature of operating project teams.

So, where do the shared goals, the sense of interdependency, the common code of conduct, and the shared rewards come from? That's the work of creating teamwork.

COMMON GOALS

Significant involvement leads to a sense of responsibility for—and therefore commitment to— project goals.

From a classical management definition, project team members usually represent a heterogeneous group of people from various line responsibilities. For this reason as well as the nature of project people and the teamwork culture, each team member wants involvement and proactive participation in management activities. These include planning, measuring, evaluating, anticipating, and alerting others to potential problems.

Building teamwork begins with clearly defining the group objectives and outlining the various roles and responsibilities required to accomplish the objectives. Gaining consensus on the top level goal is often easy. You must probe to the second or third tier to reveal and resolve conflicts. With the visibility of that team activity, ask each member of the group, "do you really want to be a member of this team?" "Yes" identifies a potential team member.

ACKNOWLEDGED INTERDEPENDENCY AND MUTUAL RESPECT

We concur with Stephen Covey's assertion: "The cause of almost all relationship difficulties is rooted in conflicting or ambiguous expectations around roles and goals."[1] In the team environment, mutual respect, relationships, roles, and interdependencies are inextricable and develop in concert.

At the beginning, one very revealing team effort is defining roles. After team orientation and goal setting, the task of preparing personal job descriptions provides a maturity calibration point and offers an important way of getting feedback and confirmation regarding team role perceptions. These steps are the vehicle for the team to acknowledge interdependency and to establish expectations:

- Define the specific functions, tasks, and individual responsibilities.
- Develop an organizational structure and define team interdependencies.
- Define the scope of authority of each member.

Some roles are informal, including personal activities such as tutor, interpreter, cheerleader, or troubleshooter. While there are usually formal, written responsibilities for project managers and leaders, team members' roles are too frequently informal. As each member is added to the team, it is a wise, proactive practice for that new member to define his/her roles and to have those roles acknowledged by the rest of the team and the project manager, and then adjusted as appropriate, to create team synergy and minimize discord.

> All roles and mutual dependencies need to be acknowledged by all project members.

Later, in the planning process, the Cards-on-the Wall technique (discussed in Chapter 7) provides a unique team building opportunity. As the schedule network evolves, interdependencies are easily recognized.

You can have very well defined responsibilities, but if the interdependencies are not acknowledged, there is no basis for teamwork—only well structured individual effort. For interdependencies to be recognized, there must be an acceptance of, and respect for, the roles that must be filled by each team member.

Like teamwork itself, mutual respect is easier said than done. You need to be aware of, acknowledge, and accommodate both strengths and weaknesses—yours and others'.

Role biases can be a major roadblock to respect. And that can even lead to potholes, as one of the authors learned long ago when mixing asphalt for a road resurfacing project. The contractor personnel took great pleasure in fooling the state inspector. A faulty scale allowed too much sand in the mix, causing the inspector to approve every bad batch. The workers thought it was a great joke until they depended on those roads. Many years later, the potholes are still a grim reminder of our deficient mix, and especially, of our deficiency in appreciating the inspector's vital role.

> Mutual Respect means accepting the need for the role performed by each team member and respecting their competency, especially if it is outside your field of expertise.

In a production environment, manufacturing often sees quality assurance (QA) as an enemy to be circumvented, rather than a vital member of the team necessary to project success. Conversely, QA has been known to stop production lines just to exercise their independence.

The space shuttle tile program demonstrates how teamwork, based on mutual respect, can mean the difference between success and failure. In the transition from research to production, problems occurred that no one knew how to solve. Manufacturing and QA personnel worked together very effectively, helping each other resolve the many technical challenges. Responsibilities for traditional QA tasks were even shifted between organizations when people on the production line found a better way to do things. A true cooperative and lasting team spirit, based on mutual respect, was developed between manufacturing and QA.

Though respect is earned, it begins by putting one's critical attitude aside and giving others the benefit of the doubt, without being condescending or patronizing. By keeping an open mind, you can acquire respect for your lack of specific skills, for another's competency, and for traditionally adversarial roles.

A COMMON CODE OF CONDUCT

The right time to address legal and ethical issues is while they are only potential problems—before they become a career-limiting lesson learned. When it comes to conduct, just as in planning, an ounce of prevention is worth a pound of cure.

While legal and ethical issues have been receiving widespread attention in the news media, most of that has focused on government contracts where many watchdog organizations are hard at work. These more formalized government guidelines demonstrate the scope of the issue. We are now seeing this investigative process moving swiftly into the commercial arena, software piracy being just one recent example. The most obvious conduct issues are usually well-documented by company or government policies. But they may not be well known to all team members. And the gray areas, especially those involving contractor and customer interfaces, may not be understood or interpreted consistently. The project manager is responsible for reviewing these issues, together with the relevant company policies, to ensure that all team

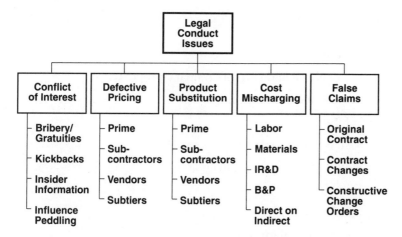

FIGURE 5.2 Legal conduct issues.

members are sensitized to potential problems. Figure 5.2 provides an overview of the legal conduct issues to review with the team.

Ethical conduct issues are more difficult to enumerate. Ultimately, one has to depend on personal values to navigate through the possible conflicts that can occur between company practices, laws/regulations, and management direction. When dichotomies persist, these guidelines may help:

- Seek higher management guidance to confirm difficult choices for conflicts among the various codes of conduct.
- If asked to operate in a potentially improper manner, make sure that the request is written and verify it with the cognizant authority.
- Report any improper conduct, anonymously if necessary.

Ask yourself: "Would I be embarrassed if my behavior appeared on the front page of the newspaper?"

To be effective, a common code of conduct needs to:

- Establish rules of behavior.
- Reach consensus on the definition of an ethical code of conduct.
- Document the most significant factors.

Categories to consider include:

Customer relations.

Personal use and care of company property.

Attendance and work hours.

Safety.

Sexual harassment.

Smoking, alcohol, and drug abuse.

Gambling.

Falsification of records.

Acceptance of gifts.

Standards of quality.

Ask each potential member of the team: "Will you really abide by these rules of conduct?" "No" removes the potential member from the team.

SHARED REWARDS

Effective team rewards begin with fair and equitable compensation for each position on the team. You can devise awards which can be earned by the entire team or individual members. The concept of shared rewards suggests dividing a bonus by the number of contributors. Shared cash awards should be given in small amounts so more can share, or spent on team recognition.

Money spent on pizza for all may even be more effective than a bonus given to the most outstanding contributor.

TEAM SPIRIT AND ENERGY

This quality depends on personal attitudes as well as company culture and begins with:

- An agreement to pool resources.
- Interdependence rather than independence.
- Desire to do whatever is necessary to succeed.
- Placing team needs above one's own needs.

Instilling teamwork cooperation often begins with uninstalling the "me-first" competition culture deeply scripted in most people by their education and business experience.

Independent thinking alone is not suited to the interdependent project reality. Putting the team ahead of oneself, however, does not mean the elimination of strong "pacesetters." The driver-type personalities need to exercise their assertiveness and energy without dominating their teammates. This sometimes involves subtle leadership techniques.

TECHNIQUES FOR BUILDING AND SUSTAINING TEAMWORK: THE WORK OF TEAMWORK

Creating and sustaining effective teamwork requires on-going work on the part of all team members. Many team building efforts fail either because essential techniques are unknown or applied inappropriately by participants unaware of the situational nature of project management and leadership.

> Teams don't always need managers to do things right, but leaders always need teams doing the right things.

While team building is a total team responsibility, we will focus first on what the project manager can do to foster and nurture a fledgling team. First, we need to refine our image of the team as an orchestra led by the project manager. In the project reality, the project manager is both the composer and the conductor. To quote Peter Drucker,[2] "This task requires the manager to bring out and make effective whatever strength there is in his or her resources—and above all in the human resources—and neutralize whatever there is as weakness. This is the only way in which a genuine whole can ever be created."

> The project manager is the most responsible for sustaining a whole that is larger than the sum of its parts.

Like any other development process, there is a gestation period involved. The project manager must avoid over-directing and smothering the team. On the other hand, too much freedom can cause a new team to founder. The project manager must:

- Clearly define unambiguous responsibilities.
- Define and communicate a project process and style.
- Delegate wherever possible.
- Empower the team to be accountable.
- Balance support with direction as required.
- Train the team, by example, to operate as a team.

- Deal with under-performers who drag the team down.
- Establish team-effort rewards.
- Design the tasks and work packages in a way to encourage teamwork.

The leadership techniques discussed next pertain especially to building teamwork.

TEAM KICKOFF MEETINGS

The kick-off meeting may be the best opportunity the project manager has to communicate the project vision to the team in relationship to their work.

The kick-off meeting should be a working session. When properly led by the project manager, it can provide each team member with a sense of organization, stability, and personal as well as team accomplishment. Proper leadership includes a detailed agenda. In *Dynamic Project Management,*[3] the authors offer a detailed agenda for the team kick-off meeting. Emphasizing this opportunity to commit the team members to a common goal, they list eight meeting goals, including:

As in football, a successful kick-off has the team lined up and heading for the common goal(post).

1. Introduce project team members.
2. Review the team mission and develop supporting goals interactively.
3. Determine reporting relationships.
4. Define lines of communication.
5. Review preliminary project plans.
6. Pinpoint high-risk or problem areas.
7. Delineate responsibilities.
8. Generate and obtain commitment.

TEAM PLANNING AND PROBLEM SOLVING

In a team context, these are excellent team building tools, offering opportunities for training, environment setting, and reinforcement. For planning and network development, we use a technique called "Cards on the Wall," described in Chapter 7, to involve the project team in the planning process. It facilitates team buy-in on the planned actions. Once created, the plan will need to be revisited by the team at each phase transition point to ensure that it remains valid and that current plans incorporate previous lessons learned.

> Planning, like problem solving, is a continuing activity, not a one-time event.

DEFINING AND COMMUNICATING A DECISION PROCESS AND STYLE

Even though leadership style and the decision process will vary with the project situation, most managers have a preferred or default style which needs to be communicated to the team. This is detailed in the section on leadership in Chapter 7. In many project environments, a consensus decision process fosters teamwork and is more effective than the extremes of unilateral or unanimous decision-making, depicted in Figure 5.3.

A consensus decision process consists of a thorough discussion until all team members have had a fair hearing and all members are committed to accept and support the group decision. Reaching a consensus may require compromises, but it does *not* involve:

- Voting or averaging.
- Bargaining or trading-off.
- Steam-rolling or flipping a coin.

Consensus decision-making is most effective when:

- You don't know who has the expertise.
- Your facts are insufficient to decide and you need the judgment of a group of involved personnel.
- You need the commitment of the group for the implementation.

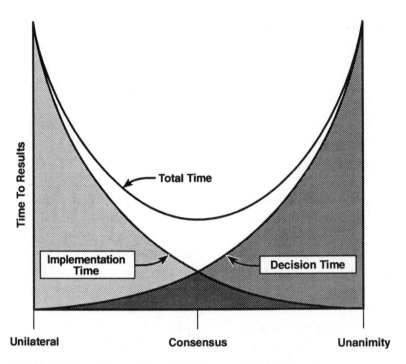

FIGURE 5.3   Alternative decision processes.

Setting the decision environment is not a one-time activity. Let's say you've decided to operate throughout the project on a consensus basis. You find that it works well for team planning of the project, but not as you get into the actual work. Individual contributors with differing work habits and desire for flexible work schedules make consensus building at each decision point cumbersome. Finally, as you hit a real crisis in the program, you can't wait for the team. You make a decision unilaterally and that irritates everyone on the project. The urgency of the situation called for a change in style—an important right for the leader. But teamwork suffered when you changed your style without letting the team know when or why the change was necessary. An effective leader would reveal the reasons when announcing the planned change.

PROJECT INFORMATION CENTERS

Centers where staff can review current information on the project in near-real-time offer an efficient means to share information. Sharing information with the team is a way of reinforcing the vision and setting a good communications example. Current information also enhances the team's ability to reach a shared reward. But what information do you share and how often do you share it? Typical project dynamics suggest that selecting relevant information throughout the project is essential because as the project changes, so does the type of information needed, as well as its timeliness. Out-of-date status charts and schedules vividly reveal a lack of attention to the details of project management and the unimportance of team communication.

> The Project Information Center should portray timely, accurate, and relevant information.

DEALING WITH UNDER-PERFORMERS WHO DRAG THE TEAM DOWN

All too often project managers are reluctant to lose a warm body because of scarce human resources. This can be shortsighted. The under-performer may represent more of a drag than his or her contribution represents. It also sends the wrong message to the remainder of the team. They need to know exactly what kind of performance it takes to earn security.

> When removing a team member, the manager needs to let the others know why—in direct, simple terms.

TEAM EVENTS AND CELEBRATIONS

These are opportunities for creative team building. Events that simulate the project environment through outdoor activities, for example, are extremely useful at start-up time. There is also a continuing need for team rebuilding throughout the project as new challenges are faced and especially as new project members join. The techniques, useful in the later stages of the project, should focus more closely on the actual project where lessons learned can be incorporated into the event.

> Be careful not to leave someone out!

Look for positive events and report them publicly at staff meetings and project reviews. Enlist the customer when appropriate. Go off-site . . . even pizza and beer (no money is no excuse).

TRAINING

Training is leadership.

As formal courses or as an integral part of any team activity, training can contribute significantly to teamwork. Project management courses, such as the those we conduct for our clients, are only the starting point for training—an on-going management responsibility. Senior team members should take any opportunities to reinforce the team principles presented in formal training sessions.

REWARD ACHIEVEMENT

Good performance needs to be rewarded—what gets rewarded gets done.

Remember that rewards come in many forms and, wherever possible, recognize group contributions as did the shared rewards discussed earlier.

Rewarding achievement is the one technique that most consider easy to apply. There is a talent, however, in rewarding performance effectively. For example, if you like to start meetings by recognizing good performance, you're obliged to make sure you're aware of the supporting details. Many a compliment backfires by irritating someone else who contributed to the work while the recipient was just the most visible (or worse, the highest ranking). Paying for accomplishments is another traditional reward that has to be done judiciously.

REINFORCEMENT

Techniques used to remind team members of the continuing requirements of working as a team includes: focusing on the common goal once established and accepted by the team; maintaining respect for the functions, roles, and positions within the team; acceptance of interdependencies; continued acceptance of the evolving common code of conduct; and adjusting the shared rewards as the project matures. The leader must emphasize the essentials of teamwork throughout the project. Posters and slogans around a team room (reminding people of important things) can be helpful.

WHEN IS YOUR GROUP REALLY A TEAM?

Teamwork, like motherhood and apple pie, is something everyone claims to believe in. People tend to believe they're a team, even when they are not. The surest way to get off on a false start is to convene the troops for a kick-off session that is little more than a pep talk. It may feel good to you, but it won't last. Likewise, the surest way to a dead stop is to use teamwork techniques sparingly or only as reactions to problems.

> You need to confirm that your leadership is working on an on-going basis as measured by observable behavior.

Positive Indicators:	*Negative Indicators:*
A positive cooperative climate prevails.	A climate of suspicion and distrust exists.
Information flows freely between team members.	Information is hoarded or withheld.
No work is considered beyond an individual's job description. If it needs to be done and you can do it, then do it!	Finger-pointing and defensiveness prevails.
Interpersonal interactions are spontaneous and positive.	Counterproductive subgroups and cliques begin to form.
The collective energy of the team is high.	"Fear of failure" causes individuals to avoid or postpone making important decisions.
Real teamwork focuses the energy of a diverse group of individuals, having different personality traits and skills, to optimally accomplish a common goal.	The absence of teamwork doesn't lead just to low productivity, it creates a counterproductive environment which saps the energy of the group and demotivates the individuals.

6

THE PROJECT CYCLE

Every step of progress the world has made has been from scaffold to scaffold, and from stake to stake.
Wendell Phillips,
Speech Oct. 15, 1851

This chapter is about project management scaffolding, the Project Cycle. It's about progressing from stake to stake—the Control Gates we introduced in Chapter 3. The foundation is our recommended format for the project cycle with its budget, business, and technical aspects (Figure 6.1).

DEFINE A PROJECT CYCLE OR WANDER THROUGH THE INSTITUTIONAL FOREST

In our training and project management experience, we often encounter two types of project travelers,

1. Those who follow a project cycle and accept it because it's dictated by their customers or management.
2. Those who don't define a project cycle, having not previously heard of the concept.

Even though all projects travel through a sequence of events, the road may not be mapped or the route may not be clearly understood.

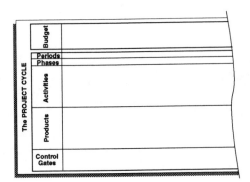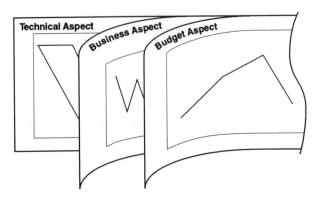

FIGURE 6.1 The project cycle format and the three aspects.

The former tolerate the concept because compliance is directed, and the latter reject it because it appears too formal and bureaucratic. Both are victims of a failure to appreciate the power of the project cycle as a road map for an enterprise and as a flexible and effective risk management tool.

In the absence of a clear and desirable sequence of actions to be taken on a project, and without the major milestones (control gates) for reviewing progress, project teams are left to create their own sequence models or wander in the corporate forest hoping they are navigating correctly. In this competitive era requiring short time-to-market, the institutionalized project cycle becomes the time-proven road from which you can take shortcuts—but only if you know the regular route first.

The impact of not establishing a project cycle can be devastating, as the case of a national HMO that had to rebuild a new hospital. Historically, in the absence of a defined project cycle, the HMO's management had not been involved in decisions such as where to build, or even whether to build new or expand an existing structure. On one recent occasion when the facilities department undertook a project to build a new hospital, general opinions were gathered informally and no sign-off was required.

> An appropriate project cycle, adhered to by all stakeholders, ensures doing the project once and doing it right.

There were no control gates to involve the appropriate stakeholders—such as doctors—and to get formal approvals at the right time and by the right stakeholders. For example, the doctors (the major users) were not required to approve the dimensionally correct floorplan. As a result, after the hospital was built, the doctors didn't like it and directed facilities to do it over!

In this chapter, we will present a template that can be applied to a wide range of projects, in both government and commercial environments. This framework can be used to proactively manage projects through a sequence of defined events that are:

- Disciplined,
- Orderly, and
- Methodical.

Since not all events and features in our template pertain to a specific organization or project, you need your own version. To define a project-specific cycle, each feature and event in your template must be carefully considered, resulting in a conscious decision to include it or not. This avoids errors of omission while taking advantage of a comprehensive field-tested format. We will return to the tailoring process after reviewing the project cycle content.

Our project cycle template is divided into three periods: the Study Period, the Implementation Period, and the Operations Period. These periods correspond to the three major stages of the project as it progresses from an identified user need, through concept determination, implementation, and ultimately to production and/or user operation.

Figure 6.2 depicts representative government and commercial periods and phases along with our project cycle template discussed below.

The customer determines the need and user requirements and then contracts with the provider (ultimately, the project team) to develop the product or service. The customer could be a government agency, a commercial enterprise, or a company's internal marketing department.

> We define the project cycle as an orderly sequence of integrated activities, performed in phases, leading to success.

> Any feature eliminated from a proven template should be justified.

> Most disciplined companies follow some version of a project cycle that is divided into periods and further divided into phases.

> Even though projects can be initiated very differently, they are subject to the same project management process once the requirements are established.

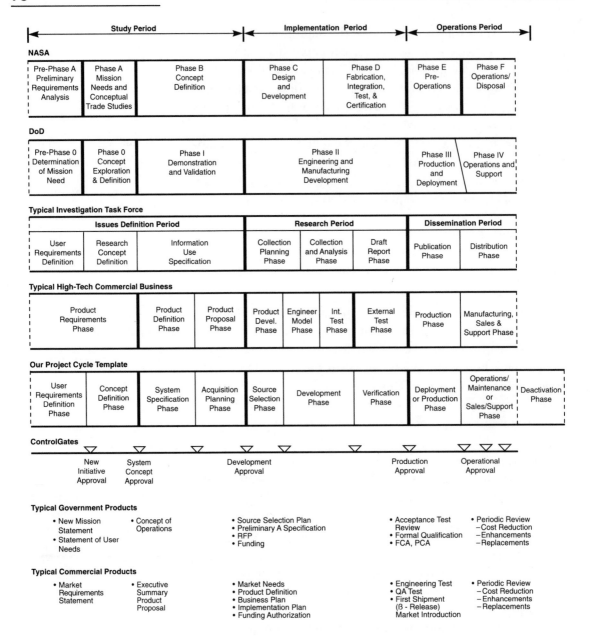

FIGURE 6.2   Project cycle templates.

In government acquisition projects and larger corporation environments, there may be two or more project teams and project managers. For example, in the case of a Department of Defense project, once a mission need is identified, a project champion is selected and a core team is formed to refine the user requirements and to produce the bidders' documents. That core team often provides the project continuity throughout the three periods. The bidders will generally form their proposal preparation team, the core of which may continue through at least the implementation period.

Larger decentralized corporations often follow the government practice of having separate customer (e.g., product marketing) and provider (e.g., product development) teams. In this example, the marketing team prepares the user requirements for the product development team.

> The project periods often represent natural boundaries to team responsibilities and composition.

Smaller commercial projects are more likely to consist of just one project manager selected as soon as the scope and nature of the project is established. Even in this case, the size and composition of the team will usually change with the transitions from one period to the next.

THE STUDY PERIOD YIELDS A HIGH RETURN ON INVESTMENT

The study period determines the scope and funding of the project (Figure 6.3) and can therefore make or break most projects. Yet important study elements are typically circumvented in the rush to implementation. High-level government panels, such as the Hearth and Packard commissions concluded that hasty study periods, resulting in flawed or incomplete requirements, are the major cause of project failure.

> Negligence during the study period is a major cause of project failure.

The project team generally must engage in considerable analysis and negotiation in order to determine the appropriate requirements. A thorough study can often prevent the time lost and the funds wasted on requirements-driven rework as illustrated in Figure 6.4.

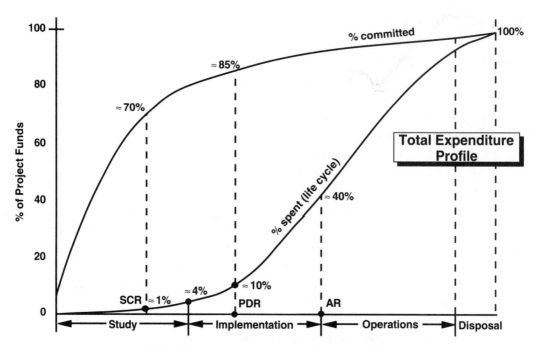

FIGURE 6.3   Typical expenditure profile.

Our project cycle template consists of four study phases: User Requirements Definition; Concept Definition; System Specification; and the Acquisition Planning Phase.

User Requirements Definition Phase

The major objective of the User Requirements Definition Phase is to determine exactly which of the user's many requirements will be included in and satisfied by the responsive project. In some cases, user requirements may be more comprehensive than can reasonably be incorporated into a single project. This phase is essential in both government and commercial projects since each is susceptible to over-specifying and grandiose expectations.

Concept Definition Phase

The objectives of the Concept Definition Phase are to select the system concept, to develop the total lifecycle budgetary cost estimate, the target schedule, and finally, to identify and address areas of high risk. During this phase, funding actions are updated.

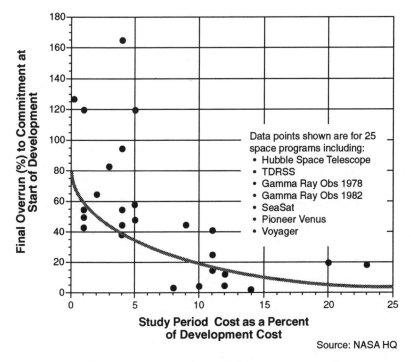

The y-axis is labeled "Final Overrun (%) to Commitment at Start of Development" and the x-axis is labeled "Study Period Cost as a Percent of Development Cost"

Data points shown are for 25 space programs including:
• Hubble Space Telescope
• TDRSS
• Gamma Ray Obs 1978
• Gamma Ray Obs 1982
• SeaSat
• Pioneer Venus
• Voyager

Source: NASA HQ

FIGURE 6.4   Twenty-five NASA program profiles.

The objective of the System Specification Definition Phase is to quantify the system and interface requirements for the selected concept, and to perform risk reduction actions in areas where technical feasibility is uncertain.

The final phase of the Study Period is used to plan and initiate the Implementation Period. It includes the schedule for acquiring or developing the proposed system and ensures the availability of funding for the project. The Acquisition Planning Phase is used to define the method of acquisition, identify participants in the acquisition process, and identify the candidate suppliers. The final step is to obtain executive approval to proceed with the project. For internal development projects, the final step in the Study Period is to present the business opportunity to executive management and secure their commitments.

System Specification Definition Phase

Acquisition Planning Phase

THE IMPLEMENTATION PERIOD IS FOR ACQUISITION OR DEVELOPMENT

The Implementation Period consists of three phases: Source Selection, System Development, and Verification. In government projects, the Implementation Period may be referred to as the Acquisition Period. It sets the contractual foundation for the project, and initiates the process of building the buyer-seller team.

Source Selection Phase

The objective of the Source Selection Phase is to choose, through fair and open competition and through the comprehensive evaluation of contractor proposals, the highest value bidder. For acquisition projects, the buyer releases the Request for Proposal, receives and evaluates bidders' proposals, and negotiates a contract with the selected contractor. For internal developments, the Implementation Period may have one or more Source Selection phases for specific elements of the system; however, theses phases often occur after the "Design to" specifications are available.

System Development Phase

In both external and internal developments, the objective of the System Development Phase is to design and build the first article or develop the service concept.

Verification Phase

The Verification Phase is used to test and verify the system or service in accordance with all specifications.

THE OPERATIONS PERIOD IS FOR FULFILLING THE USER'S NEEDS

During the Operations Period, the users' needs are fulfilled and the solution to the project challenge is realized. It consists of three phases—Deployment and Operations/Maintenance—for government acquisitions corresponding to Production and Sales/Support phases for commercial projects, and for both, the third phase is Deactivation.

In government or acquisition projects, the objectives of the Deployment Phase are to transfer the system from the contractor's facility to the operational location and to establish full operational capability. Operations and Maintenance, the second phase of the government cycle, consists of operating and maintaining the system in conformance with user requirements, and to identify system improvements for future implementation.

In commercial projects, the objective of the Production Phase is to transfer the system to manufacturing operations, often accompanied by the formation of a new project team to emphasize the production engineering function. Finally, the system is delivered to users in the marketplace and the Sales and Support Phase begins. During this time, the project team handles any design changes justified by manufacturing or by market demands.

Early planning for a deactivation phase is vital in certain projects. The NASA Skylab fell to earth in an uninhabited part of Australia. Pieces of a Russian satellite fell in Canada. Love Canal and other superfund sites are also examples of failed deactivation planning.

Deployment and Operations/Maintenance Phases

Production and Sales/Support Phases

Deactivation Phase

THE IMPORTANCE OF CONTROL GATES

We define a Control Gate as a management event in the project cycle, sufficiently important to be defined and included in the schedule by executive management, the project manager, or the customer. Control gates represent the major decision points in the project cycle. They ensure that new activities are not pursued until the previously scheduled activities, on which the new ones depend, are satisfactorily completed. The primary objectives of control gates are to:

A control gate requires formal review to evaluate status and obtain approval to proceed to the next management event according to the project plan.

- Ensure that all current phase activities and products are complete.
- Ensure that progressing to the next set of activities is based on hard evidence that the team is prepared and that the risk of proceeding is acceptable.
- Promote a synergistic team approach.

Too few control gates
allows the project to
operate out of control.

Control gates need to be defined to occur throughout the project phases to control all three aspects: budget, business, and technical. Failure to provide adequate checks along the way can set subsequent phases up for failure and is usually a major factor in cost overruns and delays. At each control gate, the decision options are:

Acceptable—proceed with project.

Acceptable with reservations—proceed and respond to identified action items.

Unacceptable—do not proceed; repeat the review.

Unsalvageable—terminate the project.

Upon successful completion of a control gate review, the appropriate agreements (usually in the form of a document—a product of a project cycle phase) will be put under configuration management, requiring buyer/seller agreement to effect any changes.

The definition of each control gate should identify the:

Each control gate's
definition should be
included in the project's
Terminology Manual.

- Purpose of the control gate.
- Host and chairperson.
- Attendees.
- Place.
- Agenda and how to be conducted.
- Evidence that is evaluated.
- Actions.
- Closure method.

A broadly employed control gate, the System Requirements Review (SRR) is held whenever needed to confirm the provider's understanding of the buyer's requirements. More specific design control reviews are held at project phase transitions.

The consequences of conducting a superficial review, omitting a critical discipline, or skipping a control gate altogether, are usually long term and costly. The executives at a leading conglomerate literally choked on their new microwave lunch bucket product when they set out to investigate its market woes. They discovered 28 product deficiencies that should have been caught early in the project cycle, well before its introduction. A few of the more obvious flaws:

- Attempting to turn the carton so as to read the heating instructions spilled the contents.
- The instructions, printed in black on a dark blue background, weren't legible, anyway.
- The specified microwave heating time was insufficient, but when doubled to heat adequately, the food migrated into the plastic container.

In another example, a late model Lincoln car design separates the seat controls, placing some of them on the dashboard. When the seat is reclined, the dashboard set is inaccessible. As in the case above, entire control gates were skipped or critical skills omitted, such as Human Factors. This could also be a result of inadequate concurrent engineering, addressed in the next chapter.

THE THREE ASPECTS OF THE PROJECT CYCLE: BUDGET, BUSINESS, AND TECHNICAL

The *Budget* aspect depicts the activities and events necessary to fuel the project with funds throughout its project cycle. The executive's budgeting challenge is in appropriately allocating the available funds among the active projects. The project manager's challenge is in securing the necessary funds for the project at hand.

All organizations, government as well as commercial, have to operate within a total budget, usually established on an annual basis. New project initiatives have to compete with ongoing projects for a share of the total budget. This reality may present

> Control gate approval must include the appropriate disciplines and be based on hard evidence of compliance.

> Some companies are gaining flexibility and responsiveness by planning their total budgets on a six-month basis rather than annually.

difficult timing constraints, especially with increasingly narrow market windows.

The budget aspect for government projects is very complex, involving both the executive and legislative branches. Whereas Congress used to focus primarily on new initiatives, deficit reduction pressures are placing increased emphasis on the cost of the implementation and operation periods of major projects.

The *Business* aspect contains the necessary business events related to the overall business management of the project and associated contract management. These include the activities necessary to solicit, select, and manage vendors for participation in the project. An important business aspect is pursuing and managing the customer, be it an in-house marketing function or an external customer.

> The Technical aspect drives the project's length and cost.

The budget activities and business management activities are overlaid on the *Technical* aspect to yield the complete project cycle. The technical events are often the most significant force driving project length and cost, and they're often the most difficult to manage. For these reasons, we will treat the technical aspect in more detail than the other two aspects. However, this does not mean that the budget and business aspects should be discounted. If the project is to succeed on both financial and technical criteria (the only true definition of success), all three aspects of the project must be skillfully balanced using value as the driver.

SYSTEM ENGINEERING IS VITALLY IMPORTANT TO THE TECHNICAL ASPECT

> System engineering is about doing the right thing right the first time.

The technical aspect starts with user needs, which are then translated into system requirements. That translation is usually the first step in the system engineering process. The System Requirements Baseline is progressively decomposed into a series of specifications. These documents systematically define all of the subsystems, assemblies, and parts. They also define the procedures both for system integration and for the verification and validation that each integration stage, including the final result, meet the user requirements. That is the essence of the system engineering process.

System engineering's role is often confused with that of system design engineering. But system engineering doesn't create the design, rather it creates a description of system parameters, documented in the set of baseline specifications. System engineering is responsible for conducting the trade-offs and creative process that lead to the specifications, starting with the System Requirements Document.

Examples of system engineering failures illustrate the distinction. In the initial B-1 bomber, the advanced electronic system and counterattack system interfered with each other—the enemy jamming system jammed the B-1 electronics—yet each system was designed (by design engineers) to meet their individual specifications. On the Blackhawk helicopter, the "fly-by-wire" system failed when exposed to radio broadcast at short range—a test flight crashed when flying over a radio station! On the commercial front (waterfront, that is), a shipping container from a British exporter, for sale in the United States, was discovered to be fully loaded with hair dryers built for 50-cycle, 220-volt power only.

The system engineering manager directs the overall process towards the optimum technical solution, including:

- System engineering plans.
- Requirements management.
- Requirements analysis.
- Requirements audit.
- Baseline management.
- Interface control.
- Risk management.
- Verification management.
- Performance management.
- Design audits.

The specification process progressively decomposes the system requirements until the lowest level of detail (e.g., hardware and/or software units) are specified. Each level of assembly represents one or more entities or Configuration Items (CIs) that make up the system at that level. A Configuration Item requires its own:

> System engineering defines what is to be done, not how to do it, the latter being a design engineering responsibility.

- Specification (functions, performance, interfaces, design constraints, quality attributes).
- Design reviews.
- Qualification testing and certification.
- Acceptance Reviews (AR).
- Operator and maintenance manuals.

A CI should be selected to facilitate management accountability and replacement capability. For example, a car and a car battery are both CIs to the consumer, because they can be readily replaced. However the battery's cells are not a CI, because they cannot readily be purchased and replaced by the consumer.

THE VEE MODEL: A TOOL FOR MANAGING THE TECHNICAL ASPECT

Referring to the Vee model illustrated in Chapter 3, System Decomposition and Definition descend down the left side of the Vee (Figure 6.5).

> The Vee model is a valuable tool for managing the system engineering process and project risk.

Decomposition: The hierarchical functional and physical partitioning of any system into hardware assemblies, software components, and operator activities that can be scheduled, budgeted, and assigned to a responsible manager.

Definition: The "design to," "build to," and "code to" documentation that defines the functional and physical content of each entity.

> Early work is to support the decision process and is not to be interpreted as out-of-phase project cycle activity.

Unlike most other system engineering models, our Vee encourages detailed work early in the cycle to reduce risk. For example, our project cycle template accommodates hardware and software requirements-understanding models and technical feasibility models in the first period. This helps clarify user requirements and ensures that the customer is not asking for an unachievable result like an anti-gravity machine. Early

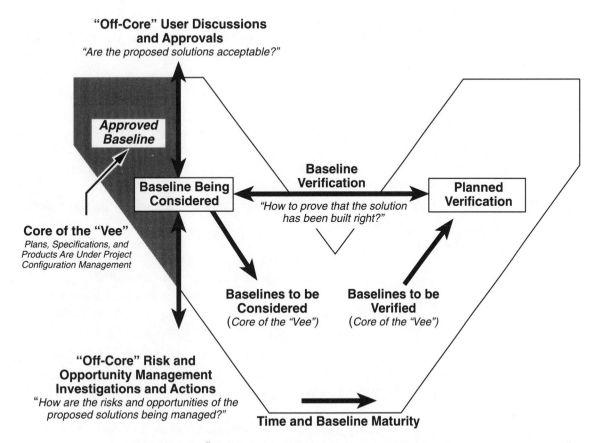

FIGURE 6.5   Vee model—decomposition and definition.

involvement of the technical and support disciplines is an essential part of this process.

As the project progresses, requirements flowdown analyses, risk identification, and risk reduction modeling continues. This is shown below by the vertical off-core activities that descend to the decomposition level necessary to satisfy the concern. For instance, if there is a question about piece part technical feasibility, the downward off-core activity will descend to the piece part level where modeling can prove that ultimate performance is achievable.

While technical feasibility decisions are made in these off-core activities, only decisions at the core of the Vee are put under configuration management at the appropriate control gates. Off-core analyses, studies, and modeling are performed to substantiate the core decisions. They ensure that risks have been mitigated or determined to be acceptable, and that opportunities have been identified and are being appropriately managed. The off-core work may not have to be formally controlled, and will be repeated at the appropriate level to prepare justification for introduction into the baseline definition.

System Integration and Verification ascend the right side of the Vee:

Integration: The successive combining and testing of system hardware assemblies, software components, and operator tasks to progressively demonstrate the performance and compatibility of subsystems, elements, and segments of the system.

Verification: The timely, methodical process of determining that the system, as it evolves, meets all specified requirements and survives its intended environment.

The method of verification to be used at each level on the right must be determined as the requirements are developed and documented at the corresponding decomposition level on the left.

The critical aspects of the integration and verification process are indicated in Figure 6.6. Note the overt distinction on the right of the core between verification and validation. Verification is the process of proving that each product meets its specifications. Validation is the process of demonstrating (as opposed to proving) that the product satisfies the user needs, regardless of what the system specifications require.

As the integration and verification process proceeds up the right leg of the Vee, any problems encountered will involve system engineering in the problem identification, risk assessment, and problem resolution. Issues which cannot be resolved at this level may require a waiver or deviation from the customer.

A complex verification process may over-drive cost and schedule and be the determining factor when considering alternative concepts.

Verification asks: "Are we building it right?"

Validation asks: "Are we building the right thing?"

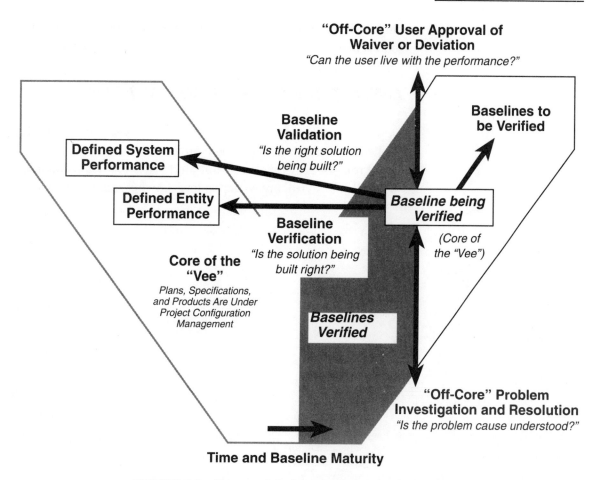

FIGURE 6.6   Vee model—integration and verification.

Time and project maturity flows from left to right on the Vee, therefore, once a control gate is passed, iteration is not possible backward. However, vertical iteration with user requirements is possible. Increased user requirements after the Preliminary Design Review should be held for the subsequent models or releases, or a schedule impact is sure to occur. If significant changes to user requirements must be made after the Preliminary Design Review, then the project should be restarted at the position, within the Vee, of the requirement impact. The repeat of much of the sequence may be faster because of previous lessons learned, but all affected phases must be repeated in view of the changed requirements.

APPLICATIONS OF THE TECHNICAL ASPECT

Depending on the development approach, the Vee process may be applied multiple times on a single project.

Projects are sometimes initiated with known technology shortfalls, or with areas dependent on emerging technology.

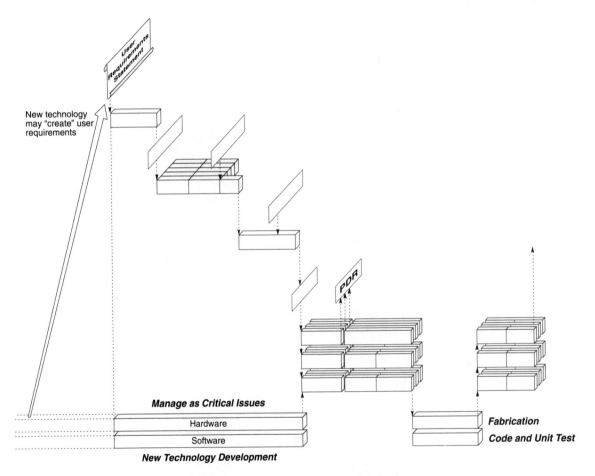

FIGURE 6.7   Technology insertion.

Technology development can be done in parallel with the project evolution, as shown in Figure 6.7, and inserted as late as the Preliminary Design Review. The technology development would be represented by a horizontal bar off the core, at the Configuration Item level (or below) where it impacts the project, and would be managed and statused by the project manager and system engineer as an activity critical to the success of the project.

If some user requirements are too vague to permit final definition at the Preliminary Design Review or if the development process itself uncovers unforeseen needs and system applications, one approach is to develop the project in evolutionary releases (like commercial software, see Figure 6.8).

Another development approach is used when all requirements can be specified up front, but incremental development is desired, resulting in either a single (Figure 6.9) or incremental delivery (Figure 6.10). This development approach is easily understood using the Vee model.[1] All increments will have a common heritage down to the first Preliminary Design Review. The balance of the project cycle has a series of displaced and

> For incremental releases, the initial version and all subsequent versions are fully functional responses to specified requirements.

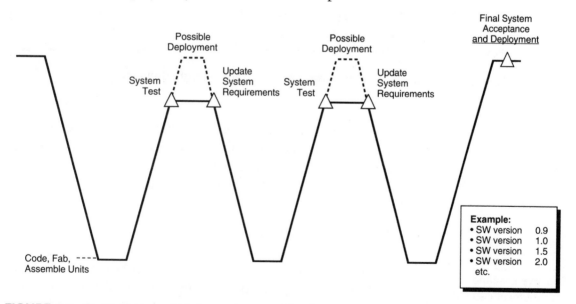

FIGURE 6.8 Evolutionary development: used for incomplete requirements—incremental releases.

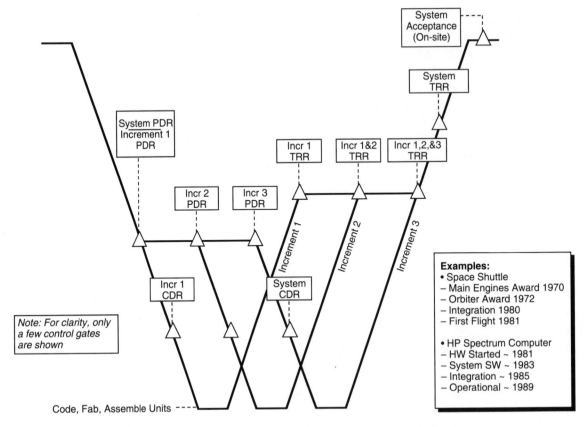

FIGURE 6.9 Incremental development—single delivery.

overlapping Vees, one for each incremental release. For the incremental delivery approach, the first release is focused on meeting a minimum set of user requirements with subsequent releases providing added functionality and performance.

BASELINE MANAGEMENT

Effective Baseline
Management depends on
complete Project Baselines.

Project baselines are the formal agreements by both the customer and provider to proceed according to the evolving documented decisions. Divided into technical baselines and business baselines, they contain all technical, cost, schedule, and deliverable

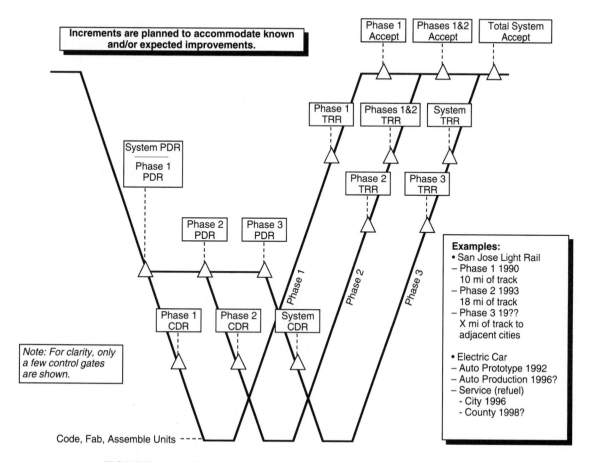

FIGURE 6.10   Incremental development—incremental delivery.

requirements that are sufficiently mature to be accepted and placed under configuration management, usually at control gates or phase transition reviews.

Baseline management is performed by configuration management through a formal change control regimen which, for each type of controlled decision document, establishes:

- The event which places that document under change control.
- The method for effecting change.
- The required approvals.

The major purpose of change control is to maintain a single knowledge base of the project design maturity. This is necessary for accurate communications with supporting technical, training, sparing, replication, and repair personnel. The change control procedure, addressed in the next chapter, is initiated by the User Requirements Document—usually the first document to be placed under formal configuration management. As the project cycle progresses, system engineering together with the contributing engineering disciplines, produce a series of technical baselines, the number directly dependent on the stage of the project. These are examples of technical baselines:

User Requirements	"Inspect-to"
System Requirements	As-Replicated (Production Release)
Concept Definition	As-Built
System Specification	As-Tested
"Design-to" and "Verify-to"	As-Deployed
"Build-to" (Pilot Product)	As-Operated

Changes to the technical or business baselines require joint action (review and approval) by the customer and the provider. In the case of commercial projects, the customer is often represented by the marketing manager or general manager. In this case, the business baseline is established by the initial agreement between executive management and marketing as to the scope, funding, and schedule for the project.

For government projects, the provider's business baseline is the contract. Business baseline changes require contract action, and funding changes may even require congressional action.

System engineering has to work closely with the business manager (both customer and provider) so that the technical requirements are congruent with business baseline provisions. When there is a reduction of funds, system engineering and the project manager have to ensure there is a commensurate reduction in technical scope.

TAILORING THE PROJECT CYCLE

A project for hosting the Olympics is unlikely to operate well on the technical project cycle tailored for developing a toothbrush that's illustrated in Figure 6.11.

Each project, or at least each project type, needs a tailored cycle. Major project types which are common to both the government and commercial environments include:

- *System Development*—create new product to meet need. Example: mobile telephone system
- *System Integration*—combine existing designs into functioning system. Example: automated manufacturing facility using commercially available equipment

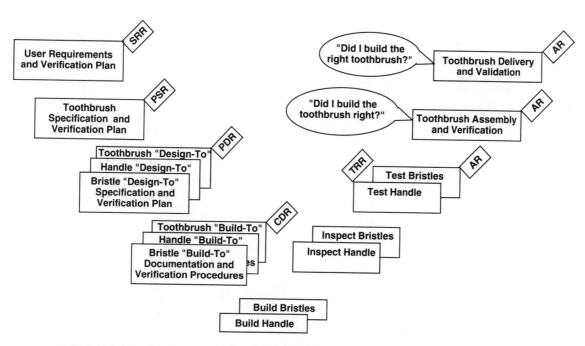

FIGURE 6.11   A technical project cycle tailored for developing a toothbrush.

- *Production*—improve product replication to existing documentation. Example: reduce cost of building computers

- *Research and Development*—discover new approach to solving a problem. Example: use biological models to increase computer capabilities

- *Facilities*—produce a new facility to meet a prescribed need. Example: Airport, hospital, wafer production facility

Each type is further characterized by its driving force and risk factors. Table 6.1 is ordered by degree of risk and management complexity, with system development projects at the high end. There are exceptions. A company depending on specialized technology research for the bulk of its income could attribute the highest risk to research projects. Some drug companies fit this category. Likewise, a company that develops very simple and predictable products, such as campaign buttons, but depends on very low cost production, will view manufacturing projects as high risk.

> Most well-known examples of failures and lessons learned come from big projects. That's because small project failures get little publicity.

The template developed by your organization needs to be adapted to each project based on the:

> Deviations from the relevant template cycle need to be substantiated with hard rationale.

- Project type, content, scope, and complexity.

- Management environment—customers, contractors, and top management.

- Mandated constraints.

TABLE 6.1 Project Types Characterized by Driving Force and Risks

Project Type	Driven By	Risk
System development	Performance	Cost, schedule
System integration	Compatibility	Equipment availability
Production	Cost	Performance, cost
Research and development	Technology	False expectations
Facility	Building codes	Performance, cost

- The management style.
- Balance between project risk and opportunity.

The customer and provider project managers should jointly define their project cycle, the content and conduct of the control gates, and the content of the required control gate documentation.

Tailoring may add or delete project cycle features as shown below:

> The tailoring process is one of the most important aspects of project planning.

Feature Modified	Example Modification
Phases	Deactivation phase added. Source selection phase deleted.
Control gates	Consent to pour concrete review added. Qualification acceptance review deleted.
Products and activities	Field test model added. On-site training deleted.

Tailoring requires foresight and good judgment on the part of everyone involved, promoted by the project manager. We recommend these tailoring steps:

- Phase selection is based on project type (development, research, product integration, production, facilities, service); content (e.g., the hardware/software balance); scope and complexity.

> Select the phases.

- Executive level control gate selection is based on the need for risk management. Control gates should always occur at phase transitions and may be mandated within some phases. Don't forget control gates that may be needed to help keep the project sold.

> Select the executive level control gates.

- Lower level control gates should be chosen to enhance opportunities and to minimize risk. Identify milestones that ensure readiness for the executive level control gates.

> Select the lower level control gates.

- Identify the products required at the control gates: Documents, Deliverables, Models, and Agreements.

> Identify control gate products and evidence.

Identify all activities.

Review appropriate
lessons learned.

Get executive concurrence.

All requirements and
standards should be
appropriate to the
reliability and risk level of
the project.

- Identify the activities necessary to produce the products required at each control gate.
- Validate the project cycle against past experience. The critique should include lessons learned from related projects and previous contract information, directly from project officials and on file.
- To obtain approval for your project cycle, be prepared to explain all deviations from the organization's template. Although changes are encouraged, they need to be justified.

Specific internal and external standards may be an explicit feature of your project cycle template. Those standards, as well as those embodied in contracts, need to be critically reviewed as part of the tailoring process. Situations that call for tailoring of standards include:

- Application of inappropriate standards.
- Blanket imposition of standards.
- Under-imposing of standards causing higher life cycle costs.
- Implementing a "no-tailoring" policy subsequent to a contract award.
- The cost versus benefits of standards implementation is ignored.
- The inappropriate imposition of high reliability or severe environmental standards.
- Standards applied arbitrarily, "just to be safe."
- Extensive and uncontrolled cross-referencing of standards.
- Inclusion of obsolete standards.
- Application of government standards where commercial practices are acceptable.

These tailoring techniques apply to standards and other formal documents, especially contract boilerplate:

- Specify exact applicable paragraphs.
- Specify requirements exempted.
- Specify tailored values for referenced standards.
- Expand on referenced standards.
- Specify exact documentation deliverables.
- Extract selected standards and include in contract documentation.
- Allow contractor choices when risk is acceptable.
- Prioritize requirements.

SHORTENING THE PROJECT CYCLE TIME

The increasing challenges imposed by time-to-market demands and technical obsolescence are familiar pressures for shorter schedules. Not only are shorter schedules less expensive, but they free up skilled personnel who may be needed on other projects.

The project cycle is the driver of subordinate project networks and, consequently, the project schedule (Figure 6.12).

Any approaches to shorten the schedule should begin at the broadest level—the project cycle. Techniques such as shortening the critical path or running multiple shifts will be addressed in the Planning and Corrective Action sections of Chapter 7.

The best way to ensure the shortest schedule is by applying a highly tuned project cycle managed by qualified and motivated personnel. You should also consider reducing the technical risks by using previously developed or previously qualified products.

> When you do it right the first time, you get there quicker.

If these approaches don't work for you, you can always make a conscious decision to gamble on short cuts such as skipping phases or eliminating risk-reduction activities, an extremely risky approach to project cycle tailoring that we recommend against. The GOES (Geostationary Operational Environment Satellite) improved weather satellite project team decided to shorten the project cycle. To reduce the predicted four-year development, the study period was deleted. The satellite was delivered nine years later.

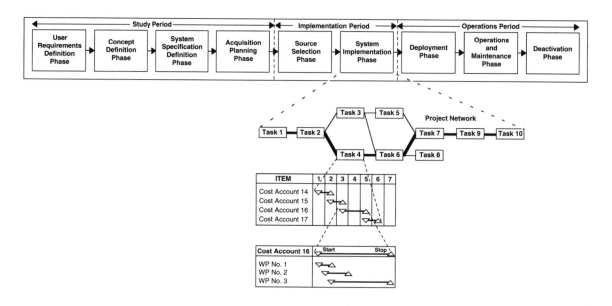

FIGURE 6.12   **The project cycle template drives the network.**

A Skunk Works may be appropriate in the case of time-critical missions or emergencies, but it often produces unexpected technical results.

Occasionally, a design team is geographically isolated from the functional organizations (such as marketing) and other "distractions" in order to maximize creativity or minimize time-to-market. To realize their potential, these so-called "Skunk Works" projects need to be staffed with highly qualified, motivated personnel. In this case, the tailored project cycle should be facilitated by a simple approval process.

Here are some inspiring examples of successful transitions to fast cycle times:

| | Implementation Period in Months | |
Product	Original	Improved
HP Computer Printer	54	22
IBM Personal Computer	48	13
Warner Clutch Brake	36	10
Ingersoll-Rand Air Grinder	40	15

7

THE PROJECT MANAGEMENT ELEMENTS

**Principles that are established should be viewed as
flexible, capable of adaptation to every need. It is the
manager's job to know how to make use of them, which is
a difficult art requiring intelligence, experience,
decisiveness, and, most important, a sense of proportion.**

Henri Fayol,
General and Industrial Management

The orthogonal model, introduced in Chapter 3, depicts the
first nine project management elements as the spokes of a
wheel (Figure 7.1), held together by its rim, Project Leadership.
This model helps to visualize the big project picture and to develop a sense of proportion and intuitive feel for the process.

"Effectiveness lies in balance," is Stephen Covey's way of
expressing the need for a sense of proportion. Too much focus, he
quips, ". . . is like a person who runs three or four hours a day,
bragging about the extra ten years of life it creates, unaware he's
spending it running."[1]

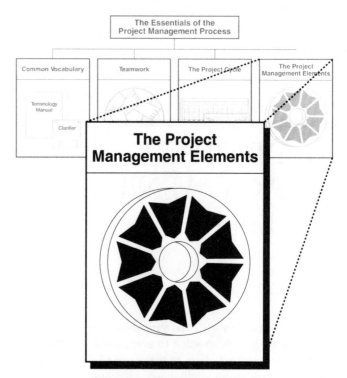

FIGURE 7.1   The project management elements.

We refer to our set of management principles as the Project Management Elements, consisting of 10 categories of management responsibilities, functions, techniques, and tools that are essential in managing:

- All types of projects.
- All phases of the Project Cycle.
- All organizations participating in the project.

This chapter is organized as 10 major sections, one for each of the elements. With the big picture in mind, we now focus on the primary techniques and tools that need to be applied daily.

1. PROJECT REQUIREMENTS

We should have a great many fewer disputes in the world if words were taken for what they are, the signs of our ideas only, and not for the things themselves.

John Locke,
"An Essay Concerning Human Understanding"

A major challenge in expressing project ideas in writing is to choose words that accurately represent the things themselves. Unfortunately, poorly chosen or missing words often create major problems. Figure 7.2 shows an excerpt from the 1907 specification for the Wright brothers' first production contract, which may be the ancestor of one of our most abused requirement cliches, the ubiquitous "user-friendly."

Project requirements start with what the user really needs (not what the provider perceives that the user needs) and end when those needs are satisfied. In the end-to-end chain of specifications, there is an ongoing danger of misunderstanding and

> Nonessential or overspecified requirements usually result in missing schedule and cost targets.

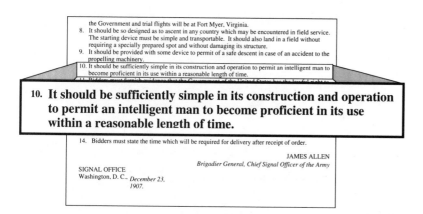

the Government and trial flights will be at Fort Myer, Virginia.

8. It should be so designed as to ascent in any country which may be encountered in field service. The starting device must be simple and transportable. It should also land in a field without requiring a specially prepared spot and without damaging its structure.

9. It should be provided with some device to permit of a safe descent in case of an accident to the propelling machinery.

10. It should be sufficiently simple in its construction and operation to permit an intelligent man to become proficient in its use within a reasonable length of time.

10. It should be sufficiently simple in its construction and operation to permit an intelligent man to become proficient in its use within a reasonable length of time.

14. Bidders must state the time which will be required for delivery after receipt of order.

JAMES ALLEN
Brigadier General, Chief Signal Officer of the Army

SIGNAL OFFICE
Washington, D. C., *December 23, 1907.*

FIGURE 7.2   Wright Brothers production contract, circa 1907.

ambiguity. This often leads to nonessential or over-specified requirements, as illustrated by Figure 7.3—a cartoon familiar to every marketing student.

The customer controls the definition of the user requirements. The provider further refines these requirements within the authorized baseline definition. User requirements are usually the first to be placed under configuration management. In practice this could be the Mission Needs Statement (DoD) or the Marketing Requirements Document (commercial) or a specific User Requirements Document embodying one or both of these. This document evolves into the full set of project requirements (Figure 7.4).

> Project requirements end only when the user needs have been satisfied.

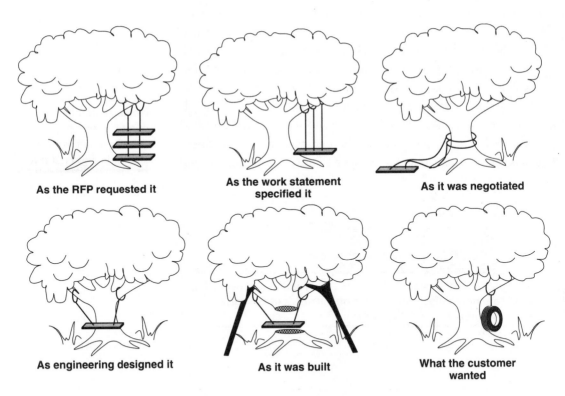

As the RFP requested it

As the work statement specified it

As it was negotiated

As engineering designed it

As it was built

What the customer wanted

FIGURE 7.3   Swings, a classic revisited.

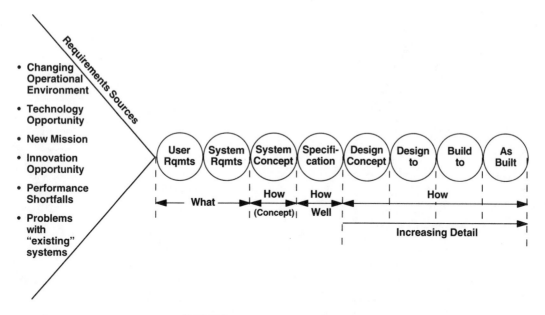

FIGURE 7.4   Document chain.

REQUIREMENTS MANAGEMENT IS THE SITUATIONAL COMPANION TO THE PROJECT CYCLE

Project requirements covers both requirement creation and management. The major documents are products of the project phases. The sequential facet of requirements creation, as represented by the core of the Vee model, is described in Chapter 6, and illustrated in Figure 7.5.

The requirements management element itself is situational since new requirements can be introduced at almost any point in the project to be managed concurrently with the maturing baselines. The two subprocesses, orthogonal to the core of the Vee, introduced in Chapter 3, may repeat many times within a phase (Figure 7.6).

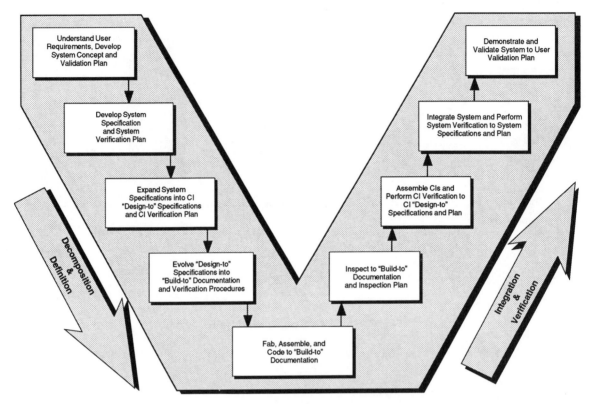

FIGURE 7.5   The basic Vee model.

THE SYSTEM ANALYSIS AND DESIGN PROCESS ENSURES USER AND STAKEHOLDER SATISFACTION

The System Analysis and Design Process (SA&D) is the framework for proactive requirements management. It is applied at each level of the Decomposition and Definition sequence and may be applied many times at a level where multiple trade-off decisions are required. This section addresses each of the major steps in the management process diagrammed in Figure 7.7.

One author's recent experience in resolving the requirements for remodeling his home illustrate the SA&D process. Furthermore, the example demonstrates the benefits of using such a

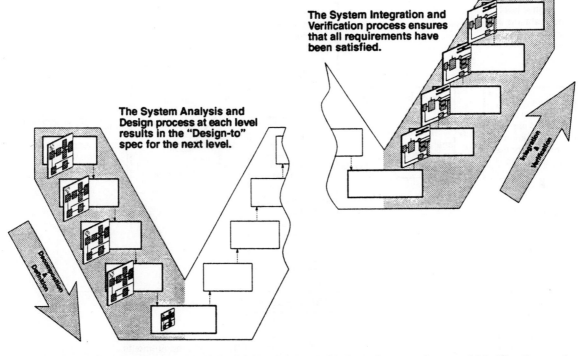

The System Integration and Verification process ensures that all requirements have been satisfied.

The System Analysis and Design process at each level results in the "Design-to" spec for the next level.

FIGURE 7.6   The System Analysis and Design and System Integration and Verification sub-processes related to the Vee model.

process—even for simple or familiar projects. In this case, the process is applied to a home-heating system. The "higher level requirements and constraints" include the better half's personal comfort zone (tighter limits than the author's), asthetics, and retained house structures. We use the margin notes to relate this example to the SA&D steps below.

The Sources and Techniques for Determining Requirements   At each level, the SA&D process is initiated by higher level requirements and constrained by approved baselines. The sources are:

- Users and other stakeholders at the system level.
- Stakeholders at every level.

The sources for remodeling requirements include contractors' and building codes, and most important, the users' comfort zones.

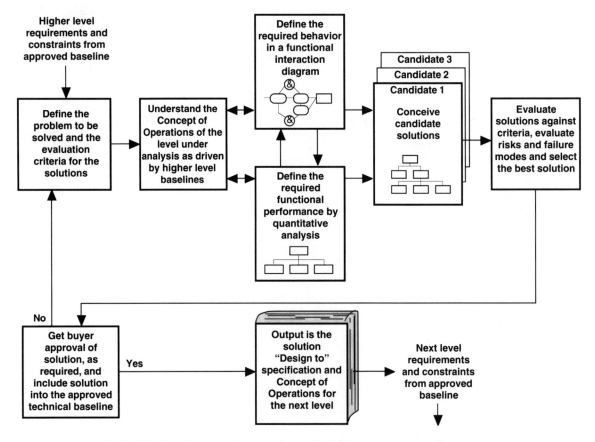

FIGURE 7.7   The System Analysis and Design process flow chart.

Establish a "check and balance" system by using multiple techniques for determining user needs:

Documentation review	Of best available records.
	Performed before interviews, if possible.
Interviews	Face-to-face discussions with selected users.
	Best conducted using a checklist.
	Document results during the interview.

Focus groups	Ask open questions to groups of 6–10 selected users.
	Use in conjunction with other techniques.
	Use to identify issues or establish expectation.
Surveys	Questionnaire distributed to all, or sample of users.
	Typically ask quantitative type questions.
	Often require statistical analysis.
	Require extensive effort to be complete and unambiguous.
Comment cards	If you have an existing product or service.
Observation	See if what users say is consistent with what they really do.

Prioritization is perhaps the most significant technique for proactively managing project requirements and is one means for preventing over-specification. The extent to which proper management discipline can be exercised by putting first things first, obviously depends on knowing and understanding priorities. If they aren't explicitly stated in contracts (and they usually are not) they must be understood by the time the user requirements and other baseline documents are placed under change control.

> In our example, budget versus comfort (temperature, noise level, dust) presented the greatest prioritization challenge.

Prioritization is usually done in two forms: *relative* criteria for trade-off among two or more specifications, and *independent* priority levels (at least three grades: Must, Want, and Wish).

Understand the Context of Implementation   The context of the implementation is usually defined by system engineering. To understand the context, you need to define the system boundaries and include all operational factors such as reliability, maintainability, availability, human factors, and security. It's often helpful to verify your understanding with a behavioral model, validated by the customer. Use brainstorming sessions to verify your understanding. Ask "dumb" questions and LISTEN.

> For example: San Francisco Bay—mild weather; no freezing, but fast changes with fog patterns; maximum outside temperature of about 85 degrees.

The problem to be solved is to maintain a comfortable home temperature under all conditions. Anything less risks marital bliss. The evaluation criteria include a fast reaction time, economical fuel, clean (low dust), low noise and fully automatic operation . . . all as measured by residents.

Defining the Problem to Be Solved and the Evaluation Criteria   At each level, the problem is defined by the specifications (e.g., user requirements, system requirements, or entity spec.). Each requirement needs to have associated evaluation criteria and measurement methods for determining that the criteria has been met.

Before proceeding further, you need to decide the risk philosophy, since the risk philosophy drives risk management. Answers to the following typical questions will help establish the risk philosophy for your project:

- What are the consequences of system failure?

   Cost, schedule, and technical. Include safety.

- What is the maturity of critical technology? Can "off-the-shelf" technology be used?

   Consequence of delivering a new, but obsolete system, versus a state-of-the-art system with no logistics infrastructure (e.g., a gas car in 1903, or an electric car in 1993, or a NeXT computer in 1994).

- What are the risks in and from the system? How will they be managed?

- What are the opportunities of and for the system? How will they be managed?

   What are the future growth expectations?

The resulting risk philosophy drives these risk decisions:

Risk Decision	*Decision Range*
Design for growth	Planned or none
New technology	High use to no use
Expendable margins	High margins to no margin
Reliability	High to low
Part de-rating	Substantial to none
Redundancy	Full to none
Inspection	100% to none

Risk Decision	Decision Range
Qualification	Required with high margins to not required
Verification	100% verification sampling to none
Certification	Full pedigree proof to no proof
Sparing	Full to none
Cost	Mandatory constraint to desirable target
Schedule	Mandatory constraint to desirable target
Other market applications	Planned to none

Define the Required Behavior and Performance   The objective is to describe the behavior of the essential system functions, for example, by a flow diagram. When characterizing the behavior, use action verbs such as *detect, process, scan,* and *analyze.*

This process is not unique. Functions can be grouped in different ways, such as grouping those that are common or in a way that minimizes interfaces.

The two methods for expanding to lower level detailed requirements are derivation (analysis) and allocation (past experience and judgment). In the derivation method, the requirements for each succeeding system level are established on the basis of quantitative analysis. Allocated requirements flow down based on experience and, therefore, must be confirmed as the design evolves.

Develop Candidate Physical or Logical Solutions   Identify solutions that satisfy the functional and performance requirements by brainstorming candidate concepts and developing system discriminators for each viable candidate. Discriminators may be technical, cost, schedule, or risk. Avoid rejecting "obvious misfits" prematurely.

- Identify top level segments for each candidate.
- Flow down functional and performance requirements. (Note that details of the lower level flow down may be different for each candidate concept)

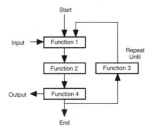

Behavior Diagram (Example)

The system behavior is to detect the difference between a temperature setting and current temperature, then to introduce heat until that difference goes to zero. The performance requires difference detection to one degree and a response to old or new settings within 10 minutes.

For this example, the candidates are electrical or hydronic baseboard, electrical radiant ceiling, hydronic-in-slab, or forced air heating.

- Identify critical system issues. (may require detail down to hardware part or software unit level)
- Use hardware and software feasibility models to determine or confirm performance values.

In our example, none of the conventional solutions meet all of the criteria. Radiant solutions are too slow; forced air is too noisy and dirty.

Select the Best Solution By using criteria previously defined, work toward selecting the *best* solution (Figure 7.8). Evaluate each candidate solution by using the criteria previously defined. This ultimately leads to rational design choices which meet the highest priority requirements.

The techniques for weighting criteria or alternatives include scoring against a fixed standard, weighting relative to the most important criterion or best alternative, and pair-wise comparison. The decision criteria may need to include subjective criteria and inputs from many individuals. These could be decided by consensus, voting (permitting multiple votes per individual), or the geometric mean of individual scores.

The selection process is not complete until the residual risks have been identified. The highest scoring candidate may not be the best choice. The final step in the tradeoff process is to evaluate the risks as follows:

The process had to be repeated by creating new solutions. One contractor, brainstorming, recommended a forced hot air system installed in the attic and suspended on shock-mounted rods from the rafters to minimize noise and ground residual vibration to the outside wall and foundation. By adding flexible fabric ducting and an electronic air filter, all criteria could be met.

- Assess risks for the highest scoring alternatives:
  —Determine consequences of identified risks.
  —Estimate probability and seriousness.
  —Define risk mitigation actions.
- Evaluate failure modes and effects for the selected alternative:
  —Determine impact on system design.
  —Define approach to mitigate effects (e.g., requirements for increased reliability, fault tolerance, or fail safe operation).
  —Incorporate in specification documentation.
- Incorporate risk mitigation actions.
- Rescore candidates.
- Identify remaining risks (residual risk).

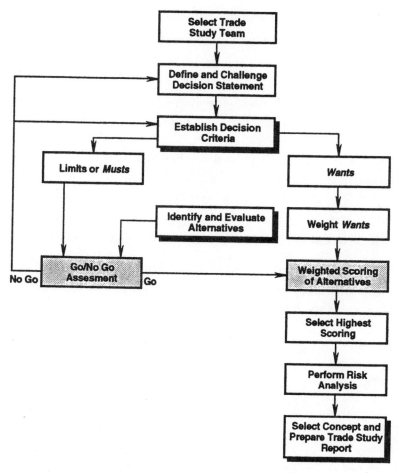

FIGURE 7.8   Selection flow chart.

The Specification for the Decision Made Completes the SA&D Process   The baseline includes the specifications and the decision-support documents such as trade-off analyses. Each specification must answer the following:

- What is the problem to be solved, and in what context?
- What must the system do? (Functional Analysis)

In our example, "forced hot air" becomes the requirement for lower level decisions like furnace room, foundation, and wall design.

- How well must the system do it? (Performance)

- Within what constraints and interfaces?

- What level of risk is acceptable (risk philosophy, e.g., redundancy, as detailed previously)?

- How will we know if the system meets the requirements (verification and validation planning)?

The result forms the approved baseline and context of implementation for the next level.

THE SYSTEM INTEGRATION AND VERIFICATION PROCESS

The counterpart of the SA&D process is the System Integration and Verification process (SI&V), an iterative process repeated throughout the integration and verification sequence (Figure 7.9).

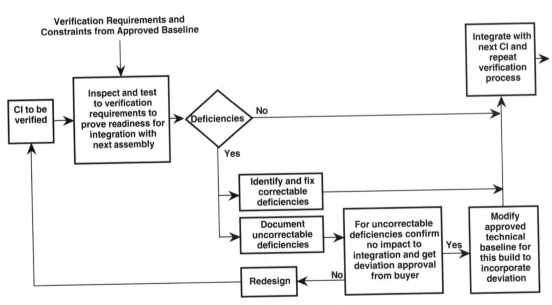

FIGURE 7.9   The System Integration and Verification process flow chart.

The SI&V process is an integral part of requirements management. It provides the framework for inspecting and testing each level of integration according to the verification criteria embodied in the requirements documents. The testing objectives are comprehensive:

The success of the SI&V process is rooted in planning and in decomposition and definition (the left side of the Vee).

Engineering	Establish feasibility and demonstrate performance in support of the design process.
Informal	Checkout tests and walk-throughs used to demonstrate readiness for formal testing.
Formal	Designed to produce "sell off" verification data. Tests are witnessed by the customer.
Qualification	Demonstrate that the design will perform in its intended environment with margin.
Acceptance	Demonstrate the deliverable is of sufficient quality to replicate the qualification item performance and will perform in the intended environment.
Environmental	Simulates the actual environment by subjecting the test article to temperature, vibration, humidity, acoustic, shocks, salt spray, radiation, etc. Can also be used to stress parts to find weaknesses.
Life	Demonstrates system life time wearout and failure modes in the actual expected environment. Accelerated Life tests may be used where compression of the time does not distort the expected results.
Reliability	Long term testing to demonstrate system failure rates and failure modes.
First article	Acceptance test of the first manufactured and coded unit to verify quality.
Nth article	Acceptance test on any subsequent manufactured and coded unit to prove quality has not degraded from the first article. Sampling plans may be used, with concurrence of the customer, when sufficient data have been gathered to provide a reliable statistical basis for doing so.

PROJECT REQUIREMENTS TRACEABILITY
AND ACCOUNTABILITY

In traceability, a child may have two or more parents.

The two methods for disseminating requirements to lower level details, derivation and allocation, were discussed earlier. The identification and management of the proper "parentage" (parent/child relationships) from the highest level system requirements to the lowest level is referred to as Requirements Traceability—a requirements management responsibility.

The parentage and dependencies for software requirements are often major planning issues.

The flowdown and parentage of software requirements depend on the project type. Where software requirements are primary, such as for information system projects, they can be determined at the beginning of the project. In this case, software development usually gets off to a good start. However in hardware-driven projects, software requirements may depend on hardware needs and often can't be determined until later in the cycle when hardware development and limitations are understood. Unfortunately, software development in such projects usually gets off to a slow start and will likely pace the project. Such dependencies need to be accommodated in the planning process.

Requirements: Accountability is to ensure that all requirements have been satisfied.

The purpose of requirements accountability is to ensure that all requirements have been incorporated and that all have been satisfied as verified by test, inspection, demonstration, and, where the foregoing are not possible, analysis. System engineering is responsible for auditing the verification results and certifying that the evidence demonstrates conclusively that the requirements have been achieved.

MANAGING TBD AND TBR REQUIREMENTS

It's naive to believe that TBDs and TBRs can be resolved with no impact to cost or schedule.

Unresolved requirements should be viewed as liens against the baseline and should be resolved as early as possible. The least defined, which cannot be priced or scheduled, are referred to as TBDs (To Be Determined). Once defined, these may the basis for

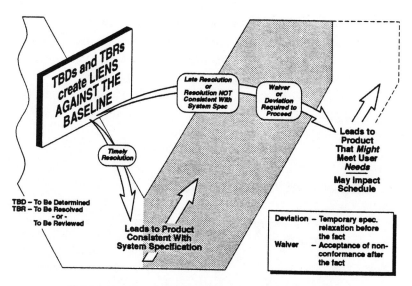

FIGURE 7.10   Resolve TBDs and TBRs early.

an engineering change. TBRs (To Be Resolved) can be estimated and, when resolved, are subject to engineering change if they're out of range. Formal work-off plans should be formalized for both TBDs and TBRs (Figure 7.10).

REQUIREMENTS MANAGEMENT TOOLS

From an information systems viewpoint, the handling of requirements data is similar to inventory control. Both involve complex, interrelated tables, cross references, and "where-used" indices. Manual tools such as card files and index tables are readily available.

General purpose database applications, many of them inexpensive desktop products such as Borland's *Paradox* and Microsoft's *Access,* can be further programmed to address a specific project or even an organization's tailored project template.

There are a growing number of software products specifically designed for management of project requirements. Two examples are *Requirements Driven Development* from Ascent Logic and *Document Director* from Jackson and Associates.

Software tools such as *Fair Witness* from Chena Software are available to handle the mechanics of weighting, scoring, and evaluating alternative concepts and designs.

2. ORGANIZATION OPTIONS

Confusion is a word we have invented for an order which is not understood.

Henry Miller,
Tropic of Capricorn

Organization: A structure through which individuals cooperate systematically to conduct business.

A great deal has been written about organizational theory—a favorite topic of industrial psychologists. The variations on form and order are limitless, as are the behavioral implications. Experience reveals that the point of confusion usually occurs when the order, though rationally structured by management, is not adequately explained to those who must operate by it—team members and others who participate in the project. This confusion is largely eliminated when individual, as well as organizational, roles and relationships are determined by a defined process. Preferably the structure itself implies much of this order, for example, the logical path to problem solving, conflict resolution, and, information. But even so, these need to be explicitly defined in the organization charter and reinforced by the project manager.

Each project presents a unique set of organizational requirements and priorities. While effective management and leadership are more important success factors than structural details, the optimum organization can contribute significantly to project performance and efficiency.

After reviewing the basic organizational forms, we will cover the major factors in selecting an organizational structure, particularly the difficult compromises that must often be made among management control, team efficiency, and technical expertise. The next section covers the Project Team, the other management element focused on building a working organization.

The organization's design should promote the team's dominant interfaces and communication channels. Its purpose is to ensure that project requirements are met, hence the importance of designing the organization after the requirements of the project are established and understood. As a practical matter, the core team (initially consisting of the project manager, systems engineering manager, and other lead positions) is probably involved during the Study Period.

> The organization should be designed after the requirements are understood.

Most projects are best served by some form of matrix organization with elements that are pure functional and others that are pure project, each addressing specific project or environmental needs. We will address the primary reasons for selecting each form after reviewing their relative strengths and weaknesses.

FUNCTIONAL ORGANIZATIONS

The functional organization is the traditional business structure. It has prevailed throughout the manufacturing-driven, industrial era. The functional organization has proved its effectiveness, with a few exceptions, for single-technology companies having these characteristics:

- One high-volume product line serving a common market, with
- A common manufacturing process, and/or
- A business segment with relatively slow or predictable technical changes.

One notable exception is a company serving a broad common market, but also having one large customer with special requirements.

A semiconductor company supplying standard parts might benefit from a separate product or project organization to serve military customers requiring ruggedized versions of the same products.

Pure Support (Functional)—Skill Centers

Strengths	*Weaknesses*
+ Skill Development	− Customer interface unclear
+ Technology Development	− Project priority unclear
+ Technology transfer	− Confused communications
+ Low talent duplication	− Schedule/cost controls are difficult
+ High personnel loyalty	

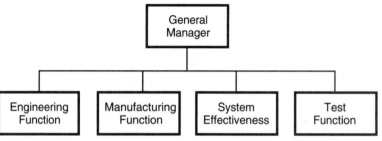

As organizations grow to multiple project/product environments with multiple markets/customers, the pure functional organization often proves ineffective. For example, one of our clients was trying to manage some 50 project/product lines through a traditional functional organization. When a customer called the salesman to find out how their project was doing, the following scenario often occurred. The salesman would refer the customer to one of the functional departments, such as engineering or production. The functional managers would pass inquiries along or respond inappropriately, being aware only of the status of their project portion. For projects that were in the design or production phase the customer might end up talking to an engineering manager or to Production Control who would give partial or misleading information, or avoid blame by revealing internal problems with other departments. This resulted in the customer calling the president for better service. The president would then raise that customer's priority to #1 causing all the other projects to suffer as the priorities in design or on the shop floor shifted. Priorities would change daily as the #1 position was given to the latest squeaky wheel!

This confusion in managing priorities and determining status usually leads to setting up product centers or divisions.

Pure Support (Functional)—Product Centers

Strengths	Weaknesses
+ Product development	− Customer interface unclear
+ Technology development	− Technology transfer hard
+ High personnel loyalty	− Project priority unclear
	− Communications confused
	− Schedule/cost controls are difficult

```
                    ┌─────────────┐
                    │   General   │
                    │   Manager   │
                    └─────────────┘
          ┌───────────┬────────┴───────┬───────────┐
   ┌────────────┐ ┌────────────┐ ┌────────────┐ ┌────────────┐
   │  Receiver  │ │  Antenna   │ │ Transmitter│ │   Power    │
   │   Group    │ │   Group    │ │   Group    │ │Supply Group│
   └────────────┘ └────────────┘ └────────────┘ └────────────┘
```

THE PURE PROJECT ORGANIZATION

The pure project organization, shown below, is composed of separate autonomous units, each being one project. They often evolve from functional or support organizations with the success of a high-priority task force as a model. Since the project manager has full line authority over the team for the project's duration, project organizations maximize the project manager's control and the clarity of the customer interface. Unfortunately, the dramatic success of a single, high-priority task force is not easily replicated when multiple projects are competing for key company resources and priority.

Pure Project Organization

Strengths	*Weaknesses*
+ Accountability clear	− Talent duplication
+ Customer interface clear	− Technology development
+ Controls strong	− Technical sharing
+ Communications strong	− Career development
+ Balances technical, cost, and schedule	− Hire/fire

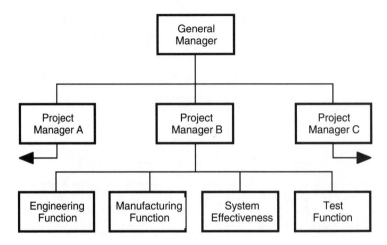

Project organizations are relatively costly because of the inability to share resources for short periods and they may cause isolation of personnel from the company's strategy and technology focus. Also there is a natural tendency for team members to be kept on the project well beyond the date that is justified. Team members are typically dedicated full-time—another contributor to the inefficiency of this organization. This is one of the reasons that some functions such as Personnel (Human Resources) and Finance are often maintained as central support departments, with specific people assigned to identified projects on an as-needed basis.

THE CONVENTIONAL MATRIX ORGANIZATION

Most organizations are a blend of functional and project structures in the form of a matrix with solid (hire/fire management) vertical lines and dotted (task assignment or borrow/return) horizontal lines. The most common form of matrix has the team members connected to project managers by dotted lines and connected to their functional managers by solid lines. We'll refer to this as the Conventional Matrix. These structures combine the best aspects of both pure forms, as demonstrated by their relative strength.

> The weaknesses of a matrix organization can usually be overcome by effective leadership.

Conventional Matrix Organization

Strengths	*Weaknesses*
+ Single point accountability	− Manager skill level high
+ Customer interface clear	− Competition for resources
+ Rapid reaction	− Employee recognition
+ Duplication reduced	− Management cooperation required
+ Technology development	
+ Career development	
+ Disbanded easily	

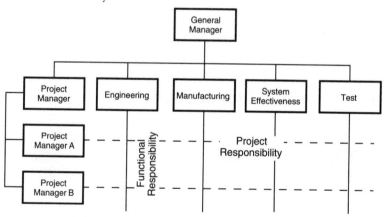

Those of you familiar with military resource deployment have seen a similar battlefield evolution brought about largely by technology. Traditional, vertically organized, functional branches (Army, Air Force, and Navy) are rapidly being "matrixed" into

> The military matrix in the field is analogous to the Conventional Matrix on the business battlefield.

battle units or task groups. This counterpart to the business task force consists of tightly coordinated resources under the direction of perhaps a tank commander, for the period of one engagement. The infantry, armor, aircraft, and even ships form a team, coupled more by computer communications than by voice. These task groups, after having carried out their mission, return to their permanent units where equipment is depoted and maintained.

Functional organizations that have evolved to product centers may transition to a matrix organization based on those product centers. While this structure does offer some of the advantages of the Conventional Matrix, it combines the disadvantages of both the matrix and the product-centered functional organization. It tends to inhibit both technology and career development and requires greater integration skills. We will therefore focus on variations of the Conventional Matrix which has proved to be effective for most projects.

Conventional Matrix organizations operate in two ways. In the first, the project manager borrows people from the support managers and provides daily supervision and funding. In the second form, the project manager "subcontracts" the work to the support manager, providing a task statement and funding. For example, a key technology may require the combined talents and synergy of a team of specialists working in close proximity This need may best be met by a small amount of time from each one of the technical specialists without disrupting their technical focus and the teamwork within their specialty.

THE COMPOUND OR COLLOCATED MATRIX ORGANIZATION

The Compound and Collocated Matrix forms offer effective compromises between the Project and Conventional Matrix structures.

Some environments may benefit from variants of the Conventional Matrix form. To compensate for structural and/or personnel shortcomings, most large projects will introduce pure functional and/or pure project sections to form a compound matrix. For example, especially critical resources (either administrative or technical) may report directly (solid line) to the project manager or, alternatively, be collocated with the project office. The latter, known as the Collocated Matrix, is shown next. It provides for maximum focus on project objectives with a corresponding disadvantage: isolating the project team from the company's overall strategic operations.

The Collocated Matrix

Strengths	Weaknesses
+ Single point accountability	− Technology development
+ Clear customer interface	− Management cooperation
+ Good control	− Technical sharing
+ Single location	− Irregular workloads
+ High personnel loyalty	− Personnel evaluation (by
+ Career development	support manager)

In highly projectized environments, such as the aerospace industry and in geographically dispersed companies, the relationships are sometimes reversed. In the Hybrid Matrix, the team members are connected to the project manager for the duration of the project by solid lines approaching a pure project organization. In this case, the functional departments are small core staffs responsible for long term technology and concept development—

The Hybrid Matrix retains the focus and most advantages of the pure Project while improving efficiency. Its technical and career aspects are also strengths.

perhaps even common component or subsystem development. For example, the corporate engineering manager typically looks for means to avoid duplication, share technology, and provide for professional development. He or she may have line/budget authority for proprietary technology development projects—some or all of which may be performed by direct reports. Another variation shares a common (typically high-tech) manufacturing operation, but assigns the Production Engineering function, usually part of the manufacturing function, to the project.

For further details of organizational theory and how the matrix organization evolved to meet the needs of projects refer to the list of references at the end of this chapter.

DESIGNING AND MAINTAINING A RELEVANT STRUCTURE

All decision criteria should be prioritized.

A single government agency or company may simultaneously use several organization options for project management. Furthermore, each project will typically experience several structures during its life cycle. The project manager and customer can significantly influence the option selected. Deciding on the initial structure involves both subjective criteria, such as prior organizations experienced, and objective criteria, such as the availability and location of resources. The guidelines that follow are for simple projects or subprojects:

- *Pure functional* organization is the best match for a single project that is relatively independent in interface or technology. Pure functional is not good for any organization that must manage multiple projects.
- *Pure project* is the best choice for projects for which schedule or product cost performance is paramount and development cost is relatively unimportant.
- *Conventional Matrix* works well if the project manager controls the funds and has defined interrelationships with the supporting managers, including formal commitments and

participation in project planning. The Matrix fails when the project manager is seen as a coordinator and the support managers operate on a "best effort" basis.

- *Collocated Matrix* should be considered for very high priority projects dependent on critical resources and/or technologies and when on-going involvement with company strategy is secondary.

INTEGRATED PROJECT TEAMS AND INTEGRATED PRODUCT TEAMS

There are many ways to develop an organizational structure. Some managers begin by assuming a starting form, say a conventional matrix, and then they modify it to resolve staffing barriers. We prefer a process that matches the organization to the requirements (as segmented into major work packages by the Work Breakdown Structure). In this process, the total project is viewed as a set of simple projects, defined by the nature of their deliverables and/or resource requirements (Figure 7.11). The terminology for this approach is Integrated Product Teams.

Matrix refinements, such as Integrated Project Teams and Integrated Product Teams, have solved entity responsibility issues; however, these forms bring a new set of issues regarding system integration and responsibility for the eternalization of the enterprise, such as technology development and sharing. The role of system engineering, always an important one, becomes crucial when integrating a system developed by multiple product teams.

As Peter Drucker commiserates, ". . . at best an organizational structure will not cause trouble."[2]

When defining the original structure, you need to plan responses to the inevitable project cycle dynamics. Without anticipating changes, you may find yourself evaluating the symptoms below and thrashing through crisis-driven reorganizations. While no organization is expected to be perfect, some may be flawed to the extent that project success is at risk. Before reorganizing, be sure it is justified. The authors of "Dynamic Project Management"[3]

> Integrated Project Teams and Integrated Product Teams instill responsibility and accountability.

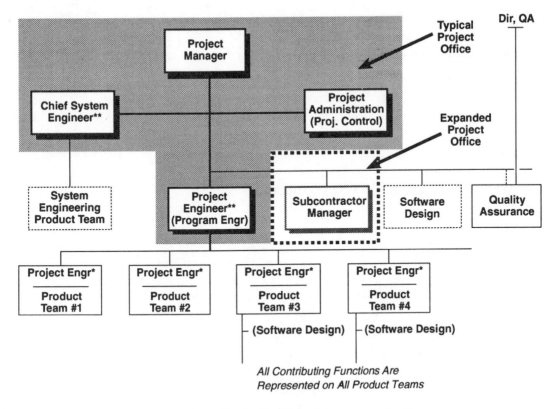

FIGURE 7.11   Typical project team organization.

offer these symptoms of an inappropriate organization to watch for:

Is there a [lack of] product pride and ownership among the team members?

Is too much attention typically given to one particular technical function, to the neglect of other technical components?

Does a great deal of finger*f*pointing exist across technical groups?

Is slippage common, while customer responsiveness is negligible?

Do project participants appear unsure of their responsibilities or of the mission or objective(s) of the project?

Are projects experiencing considerable cost overruns as a result of duplication of effort or unclear delegation of responsibilities?

Do project participants complain of a lack of job satisfaction, rewards, or recognition for project efforts?

The authors observe that "Unfortunately, when symptoms of inadequate organizing appear, some companies typically respond by applying more time, money, or resources to the already weakened and inadequate project organization. If the problem truly is an inappropriately structured project organization, simply addressing the symptoms while ignoring the basic problem itself may leave the organization and its people frustrated and demoralized, as projects continue to slip and conflict continues to grow."

On the other hand, each of these symptoms, taken separately, could have little to do with the organization and a lot to do with leadership, or the lack thereof. One has to look closely at the combinations and patterns to conclude that a reorganization is indeed needed.

The single biggest error in organization design is over-complexity or redundancy leading to confused responsibility. We've defined several complex configurations and suggested others in an effort to define the problem and provide choices. However, some configurations such as the Hybrid Matrix are suitable for only the very largest projects or for an entire multidivisional corporation.

> Complex projects should not always lead to complex structures.

3. THE PROJECT TEAM

The meeting of two personalities is like the contact of two chemical substances: if there is any reaction, both are transformed.

Carl G. Jung

In Chapter 5, we focused on instilling teamwork, a perpetual property of projects and the second Essential to successful project management. We now look at team formation, a situational process, ongoing throughout the project cycle:

> Forming the team starts with selecting the right people and defining their roles.

1. Defining the project manager's roles, responsibilities, and authority.
2. Selecting the project manager.
3. Chartering the project and confirming the project manager's authority.
4. Staffing the team.
5. Managing the major interfaces and interrelationships.

The Project Team goes beyond the traditional staffing function to define and manage the interfaces with supporting organizations, with contractors, with upper management, and with the customer (which may be the internal marketing/sales department) (Figure 7.12).

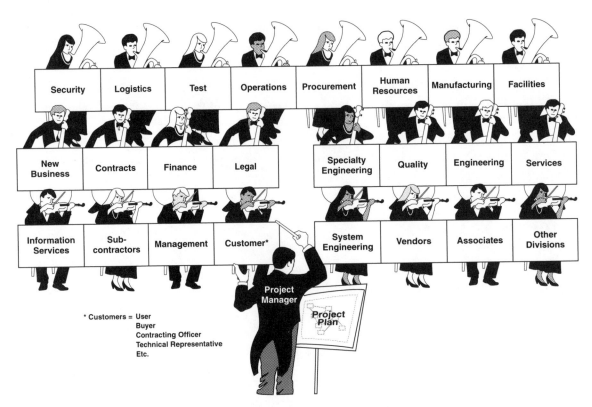

FIGURE 7.12   **The project team.**

DEFINING THE PROJECT MANAGER'S ROLES, RESPONSIBILITIES, AND AUTHORITY

The project manager's roles are broad—like those of general managers—going from administration to negotiation to leadership. But the focus is shorter range that of a line manager who must be alert to the long-term strength of the total organization. By contrast, the project manager is focused on the relatively short term results of the project.

Roles	Goals
Manage the project to the Project Cycle.	Meet an aggressive schedule.
Balance technical, schedule, and cost performance.	Implement state-of-the-art technology.
Solve problems expeditiously as they arise.	Perform within the budget by using limited funds and resources.
Inspire and motivate the entire team.	Optimize the mix of dedicated, shared, and contract personnel.

A major challenge is to make both the customer and the organization successful by leading the project team, even those who don't report directly.

Project management challenges are often exacerbated by an imbalance among:

- *Responsibility*—the duty or obligation to complete a specific act or assignment.
- *Authority*—the power to exact obedience and to make the necessary decisions to fulfill specific obligations.
- *Accountability*—the acknowledged state of being answerable for success or failure.

The project manager should have total project responsibility with maximum accountability, yet often has too little authority.

Broad responsibilities increase the need for information and lead the project manager to cut cross organizational lines, like a general manager. But without the general manager's formal authority, the project manager (equipped with implied authority) must often depend on interpersonal skills and negotiating abilities to influence others.

The project manager must have authority for resource control and must be able to start and stop work.

While the range of direct authority varies greatly, effective project management policy requires that:

- The project manager have financial control.
- The support managers view the project manager as their customer.
- A culture of "make a promise—keep a promise" exists.
- Delineation of responsibilities are documented.

Before selecting the project manager, the job responsibilities need to be documented. They should include responsibility for:

- Establishing the team and teamwork environment;
- Inspiring and motivating the team;
- Ensuring all project requirements are clearly defined and documented, and that they flow down to the lowest level;
- Ensuring the controls are in place and effective;
- Controlling baseline requirements through a change control system;
- Ensuring that the visibility techniques are in place and effective;
- Determining the frequency and the level of status that is appropriate for the project; and
- Timely execution of corrective action to recover the project to plan.

SELECTING THE PROJECT MANAGER

The manager should be selected *after* the project requirements are defined, but *before* other team members are selected.

Selecting the key person on the team is a critical matchmaking task for executive management. In too many cases, the project manager is selected before the requirements and the organizational form of the project are determined. This is backwards, and often leads to a bad match.

Selecting the right project manager is critical to project success, and for this reason must be carefully done. The project manager must fulfill the requirements of the customer or user, must answer to senior management by generating a fair return on investment, and must provide a stimulating, positive work environment for the project team, while at the same time meeting family obligations and pursuing personal goals.

Peters and Waterman[4] report a high correlation between project success and the leadership qualities and/or authority level of the project manager. In many types of projects, leadership qualities are more important than authority level. But this should never be taken for granted. It is essential that the project manager operate as a manager/leader rather than just as a coordinator/monitor. He or she must have well-defined, business-driven interrelationships with the support managers participating in the project.

When selecting any team member, it is important to have an objective basis for evaluating the most important competency factors for the specific project. The example competency model (Table 7.1) anticipates significant contract activity.

The base structure for most projects is some form of matrix, designed to take advantage of critical technical demands, to accommodate unique management strengths and weaknesses, and to balance short-term project priorities with the long term priorities of the company and/or functional organizations. They are all characterized by complex interpersonal relationships requiring that the project manager be selected more on the basis of behavioral (e.g., negotiating and leadership) skills than on technical skills. The person chosen for this challenging assignment must have the right combination of attributes and qualifications. ". . . the ideal project manager would probably have doctorates in engineering, business, and psychology, and experience with ten different companies in a variety of project positions, [yet] be about twenty-five years old."[5] In addition to the skills identified earlier, the project manager should exhibit the following capabilities:

- Leadership and team building.
- Entrepreneurial and business acumen.

> The project manager has roles in three different arenas, the customer's, executive management's, and the project team's.

> Our experience shows that strong leadership can compensate for a lower authority level.

TABLE 7.1   Example Competency Model

Rating Factor	Basic	Score	Advanced	Score	Expert	Score
Project Management Training	Has had some project management training		Has had the company's or equivalent project management training		Has had the company's, PMI[1], or equivalent certification in project management	
Project Management Experience	Has served as a deputy or assistant project manager		Has been a successful project manager		Has managed several successful programs	
Contracting and Negotiating	Is knowledgeable of types and applications of the relevant contract types		Has participated in developing contract negotiation strategies		Has considerable experience in contract negotiation strategy and participating in negotiations.	
Subcontracting	Is knowledgeable in the difference between purchasing and subcontracting		Has participated in the selection and award of subcontracts		Has successfully managed subcontractors	
Decision Analysis	Is aware of the importance and practice of Analytical Decision Analysis[2]		Has been trained in Analytical Decision Analysis[2]		Has been trained and routinely practices Analytical Decision Analysis[2]	

[1] PMI (Project Management Institute) certification as a Project Management Professional is based on a comprehensive eight-hour examination.

[2] Analytical Decision Analysis was originated by Kepner Tregoe Associates (Princeton, NJ).

- Balance between technical and business interest and abilities (generalist).
- Planning, organizing, and administration abilities.

Team members will naturally resist some of the vital project management techniques. The project manager will have to "sell" those techniques in the face of this resistance. How well the project manager handles this difficult task will be a significant factor in the success or failure of the project.

CHARTERING THE PROJECT AND CONFIRMING THE PROJECT MANAGER'S AUTHORITY

The first step in gaining recognition for a new project and team is to formally charter the project manager and project office. High-level authorizing of the project's charter mitigates the historical handicap mentioned earlier: project management responsibility without commensurate authority. Harold Kerzner[6] offers this sage advice: "Generally speaking, a project manager should have more authority than his responsibility calls for, the exact amount of authority usually depending upon the amount of risk that the project manager must take. The greater the risk, the greater the amount of authority."

The project manager's authority should be documented when the project is chartered. The project's charter represented by the sample letter in Figure 7.13, performs several key functions:

> Document the charter and get your management to sign it.

- Identifies the project and its importance to the organization.
- Appoints the project manager and other key personnel.
- Establishes top level responsibilities and authority.
- Refers to the support organizations in delegating project authority.
- Places subcontractors in a service relationship.
- Acknowledges the project team.
- Establishes the funding control.
- Confirms that the cognizant executive started the project and chose the manager.

Figure 7.13 sets the tone for teamwork by accepting personal accountability for the proposal made by the team. This may seem like an obvious gesture, but even though accountability, unlike authority, can never be delegated, not all senior managers publicly acknowledge their accountability for the team's efforts. Posting such memoranda on bulletin boards is useful.

MEMORANDUM

Date:

To: All Functional Managers; President's Office; List

From: Vice President, Special Projects

Re: Establishment of the Advanced Systems
                Development Project

I'm pleased to announce that, after tough competition, we have been selected
by the customer as the prime contractor for the Advanced System
Development. We have pursued this prestigious opportunity aggressively and
we are now committed to providing this state-of-the-art system.

To carry out this critical project, I am establishing the ASD Project Office
with Fred Jones as Project Manger, reporting directly to me. I have delegated
to Mr. Jones the authority to manage all activities necessary to fulfill our
contractual obligations by working directly with our key subcontractors. Mr.
Jones will be held fully responsible and accountable for the technical,
schedule, and financial success of this project.

Others with key responsibilities for the ASD project are: Joan Wait as System
Engineering Manager, Jim Wu as Business Manager, and Mary Fay as
Contract Administrator.

The Program Implementation Review will be held 30 days from today with
the primary objective of executive approval of the total Project Plan. At that
time, I expect to approve the necessary funding, under Mr. Jone's control, for
the next period of the project.

Congratulations to all of you who contributed to this important win! I am
asking for your full support for Mr. Jones and his team in this most important
business opportunity.

Our customer is counting on us to perform and, in turn, I am counting on you
to deliver as we have promised in our proposal.

/signed/
Vice President,
Special Projects

FIGURE 7.13   The project team charter.

The project manager's authority needs to be confirmed and maintained on a daily basis. Authority is a way of thinking that starts by delegation at the top, to be accepted and seized by the project manager. Continuing authority is based on acknowledgment by the organization's culture that needs to be reinforced by executive management in daily decisions and demonstrated by the project manager's consistent actions. As Kerzner[7] observes,

> Authority can be delegated from one's superiors. [Personal] power, on the other hand, is granted to an individual by his subordinates and is a measure of their respect for him. A manager's authority is a combination of his power and influence such that subordinates, peers, and associates willingly accept his judgment.
>
> In the traditional structure, the power spectrum is realized through the hierarchy, whereas in the project structure, power comes from credibility, expertise, or being a sound decision-maker.

The organization's culture should view the project manager as a customer.

While the proper chartering is necessary for establishing the project manager's authority, it is far from sufficient.

STAFFING THE TEAM

The stages of staffing correspond to the project phases and funding milestones, beginning with selection of the core team. We frequently refer to just the project manager when discussing management responsibilities, authority, and accountabilities, but there are three distinct roles which comprise the project office (Figure 7.14).

The *system engineer/manager*—second only to the project manager in responsibility and accountability—is responsible for the technical integrity of the project while meeting the cost and performance objectives of project requirements. The system engineer is a key participant in the planning process and provides technical management of the system engineering process directed at achieving the optimum technical solution. To ensure the appropriate balance between technical and business factors, it is highly desirable to have a system engineering manager specifically responsible for the technical aspects of the project:

For small projects, two or three roles of the triad may be performed by the project manager.

- Requirements management, analysis, and audit.
- Orchestrating technical players in timing and intensity.
- Baseline, risk, verification, and performance management.
- Interface control and design audits.
- Alerting the project manager to technical risk and required risk management.

The *business manager* is responsible for all business aspects of the project including planning, scheduling, contractual matters, as well as legal, moral, and ethics issues. The business manager also assists the project manager in implementing planning, control, visibility, statusing, and corrective action systems.

Before selections occur, the required functions and related skills should be determined. The nature of the project will dictate

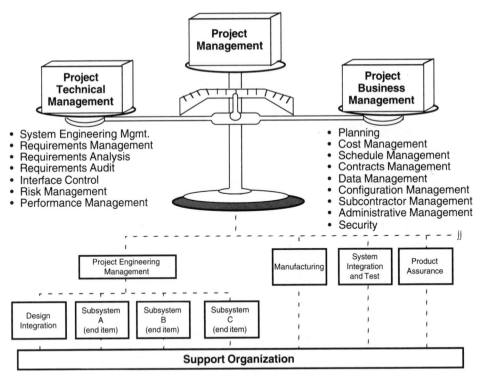

FIGURE 7.14 The project office triad.

the core team, for which the project manager should prepare formal job descriptions. Most job descriptions can be based on the task descriptions provided by the Work Breakdown Structure. These job descriptions are not only important in the selection process, but they are also a vital tool for successful negotiations with the support managers.

Staff selection for the independent project environment is influenced more by personal attitudes than are the functional positions that normally require less teamwork. There are three selection categories that need to be consciously balanced:

- Functional skills required by the project.
- Skill inventory of the candidate.
- Personal attributes of the candidate.

Those who thrive in the project environment will typically be adaptable and interdependent as well as independent and results-driven. To paraphrase Stephen Covey,[8] independent thinking alone is not suited to the interdependent project reality. "Independent people who do not have the maturity to think and act interdependently may be good individual producers, but they won't be good leaders or team players."

While all team members are selected on the basis of both skills and personal attributes, it is particularly important that the core team have previous project experience, preferably at the task or project management level.

As each member is added to the team, it is a wise, proactive practice for new members to define their roles and to have these roles acknowledged by the rest of the team, beginning with the project manager. Doing this early affords the opportunity to make adjustments, as appropriate, to create synergy and minimize discord. Until the detailed planning is done, roles and responsibilities may have to be defined in general terms with later refinement consistent with the planning results.

Outsourcing is an increasingly popular alternative to staffing. Subcontractors, vendors, and consultants can be a very

People who are attracted by project assignments are generally motivated by intangible factors such as the work itself, rather than position or title.

cost effective way to obtain a critical skill or fulfill a specific project requirement outside the organization's functional repertoire. However, you should be just as diligent in selecting an outside source as you are in selecting a staff member, including reference checks, facility tours, and key person clauses.

THE IMPORTANCE OF CONCURRENT ENGINEERING

> Concurrent Engineering is the concept that all stakeholders need to be considered throughout the project cycle in order to produce the best product.

The project team needs to include and consider, *from the outset,* all elements of the product life cycle. This extended breadth of the team to include all stakeholders in the development process is known as Concurrent Engineering (Figure 7.15). For example, airline pilots should participate in the concept definition of a new plane to properly influence the operational aspects of the system. Likewise, the baggage handlers should influence that part of the system design pertinent to their operations. Similarly, recent

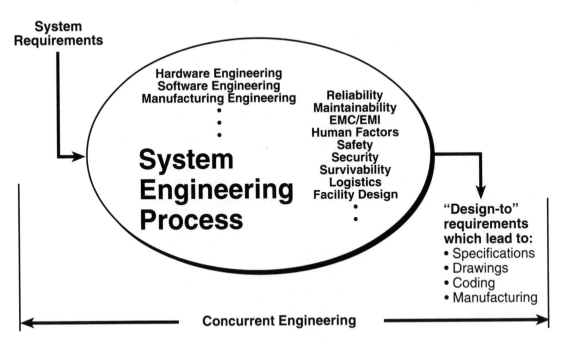

FIGURE 7.15   **Concurrent engineering is a form of system engineering.**

generations of computer architecture have benefited greatly from having software engineers involved in the hardware design.

System engineering is responsible for involving the key personnel (to address human factors, safety, producibility, inspectibility, reliability, maintainability, logistics, etc.) at each step, starting with early risk analyses and feasibility studies in the Concept Definition Phase. This does not require a dedicated team of specialists. However, it does require a proactive system engineer who can ensure that appropriate expert advice and detailed assistance is applied to all areas of project risk.

> System engineering must ensure the timely involvement of all disciplines.

MANAGING THE MAJOR INTERFACES AND INTERRELATIONSHIPS

The authors of *Dynamic Project Management*[9] have likened matrix interactions to those of a marketplace. "Negotiations concerning assignments, priorities, equipment, facilities, and people are constant. Matrix team members often complain of the continuous meetings, but it is through such meetings that the characteristic decentralized decision making occurs."

The complex relationships and confusing lines of authority in the project/functional lattice demands thoughtful planning. As illustrated in Figure 7.16, the project manager identifies what is to be done, primarily by means of the project requirements (or the work authorizing agreements or MBOs derived from the requirements). The functional organizations are responsible for defining and negotiating with the project manager how the requirements are to be achieved and then implementing them. In this structure, it is especially important for the project manager to have financial control and to be able to start and stop work.

Both project and support management responsibilities are assigned by executive management. The project manager ensures that project objectives are achieved on schedule and at the lowest cost compatible with user/ contractual requirements. The support managers ensure the performance of specific project requirements as defined and authorized by the project managers. As the

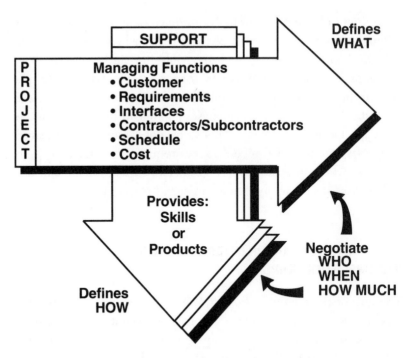

FIGURE 7.16   Matrix functions chart.

advocate for technical excellence, each support manager is responsible to:

- Perform for executive management in support of all projects.
- Perform as agreed with each project manager.
- Maintain personnel expertise at the leading edge of technology.
- Recommend means within the function to meet project objectives.
- Provide that function's cost, schedule, and technical risk assessment.
- Assign skilled personnel to support identified projects.
- Actively participate in problem solving and conflict resolution.

One of the most significant techniques for minimizing confusion and avoiding excessive interaction is to anticipate critical project functions where conflict in authority and function are likely to take place in order to clarify roles and responsibilities. The critical functions that should be documented include:

- Project direction, objectives, priorities, planning, reviews, status, and controls.
- Assuring project effectiveness and customer commitments.
- Proposal preparation, contract negotiations, and contract management status.
- Technical, schedule, budget, and make versus buy decisions.
- Assignment of key personnel and establishment of employee objectives.
- Communications, correspondence, and data requirements.
- Point of contact for customer, upper management, and support interfaces.

A technique for managing any form of matrix organization is the Project Work Authorizing Agreement or an equivalent method for defining tasks and responsibilities. The PWAA is a contract between the project office and the supporting organizations. As illustrated in the next section on Planning, it contains task definition, budget, schedule, performer's commitment, and project office authorization. Companies or organizations which have a formal, quantified, and measurable Management By Objectives (MBO) program can make use of that system to supplement, or in the case of simple projects, substitute for the more formal PWAA. These methods are addressed in the sections on planning and statusing.

These are common expectations of executive management, the customer, and the team members:

- *Timely, accurate information*—for teams to work well, information and ideas have to flow smoothly.

Teams rarely go wrong by themselves—more often they suffer from lack of direction and false assumptions.

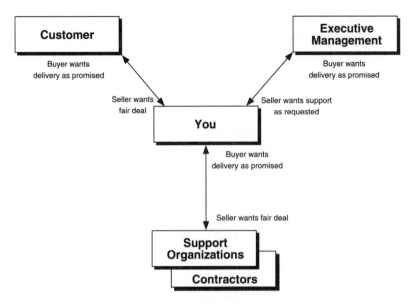

FIGURE 7.17   The buyer/seller viewpoints.

- *No surprises*—for cooperation to grow, communication must be complete and candid. There is no place on a project team for a problem withholder.
- *Credit given where credit deserved*—the rewards must match the risks and recognition given for both individual and team efforts.

Matrix operations depend on their project manager being viewed as a buyer of services provided by the support managers (Figure 7.17).

4. PROJECT PLANNING

"Would you tell me please, which way I ought to go from here?"

"That depends a good deal on where you want to get to," said the cat.

"I don't much care where—," said Alice.

"Then it doesn't matter which way you go," said the cat.

Lewis Carroll's,
Alice's Adventures in Wonderland

A PROJECT CANNOT GET ANYWHERE WITHOUT A VALID PLAN

A valid plan has:

- Compatible tasks, schedules, and budgets.
- Defined and acceptable risks.
- Agreement and commitment by the team.

The alternative to planning ahead is to plunge ahead. Harold Kerzner's[10] scenario below may resemble some projects you've suffered through. It suggests that the alternative to planning may be to end up at the beginning:

1. Project initiation.
2. Wild enthusiasm.
3. Disillusionment.
4. Chaos.
5. Search for the guilty.
6. Punishment of the innocent.
7. Promotion of the nonparticipants.
8. Definition of the requirements.

To achieve a commitment to the planning process as well as to the resulting plan, the issues need to be resolved beforehand.

> A poor planning environment inevitably results in a lack of team commitment and in failure.

Examples of a Problem Planning Environment	Possible Solutions
Lack of team involvement and interaction:	*Off-site, collocated team:*
– a separate planning organization developed the plan.	+ all the players are present
– key players were not involved	
– team members were not involved in the planning until schedules were set.	
– poor communication existed between participants	
The planning process was not structured: systematic, and consistent:	*Proved planning process:*
– planning activities were not integrated	+ participants are trained in the process
– plans were not updated to reflect major technology shifts.	+ participants have authority to make decisions and commitments
– inappropriate organizational structure was used.	
– company goals were not understood or reconciled with project goals	+ team includes people with appropriate experience
– cost and schedule estimates were based on poor assumptions or insufficient data such as: availability of critical skills not being verified, lack of standards, historical data, or experience.	
Insufficient time for planning:	*Plan to plan:*
– near-term distractions were given a higher priority	+ no interruptions
Result: Inadequate commitment to planning and the resulting plan.	*Result:* Strong commitment to planning and the resulting plan.

Planning is performed in each project cycle phase to prepare for the subsequent phases.

We define planning as the process which determines beforehand the activities necessary to complete the project. Planning evolves as the project progresses sequentially through the phases of the project cycle. A plan contains at least:

- *What* is to be done.
- *When* it should be done.
- *Who* is responsible for doing it.

At the highest, total-project level, planning is performed in each project cycle phase to prepare for the subsequent phases. The lowest level of iteration occurs within each step—such as iterating through network development and task schedules to determine and shorten the critical path. While the emphasis, level of detail, and risk factors change from one phase to the next, the process defined here is relevant to each project phase. Some aspects will require only minor updates as a new phase is entered.

The project plan (Figure 7.18) is usually composed of separate plans for each period and for major phases of the project. Some plans, such as the Acquisition Plan and the Source Selection Plan may not occur in all projects. The Implementation Plan is

> Project planning is an iterative process on several levels, as well as an ongoing one.

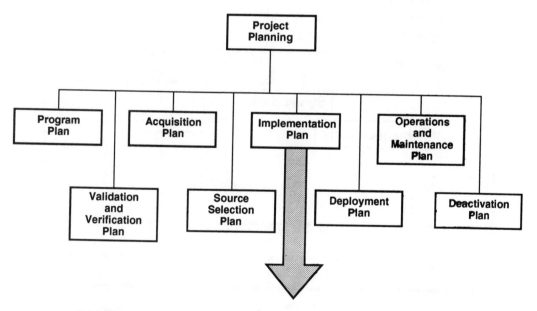

FIGURE 7.18 The total project plan evolves from several plans.

common to all projects and will be used to illustrate the overall planning process.

IMPLEMENTATION PLANNING IS TURNING THE REQUIREMENTS INTO ORDERLY WORK

We define implementation planning as the process of converting all project requirements into a logically sequenced set of negotiated work authorizing agreements, as illustrated by Figure 7.19, and subcontracts.

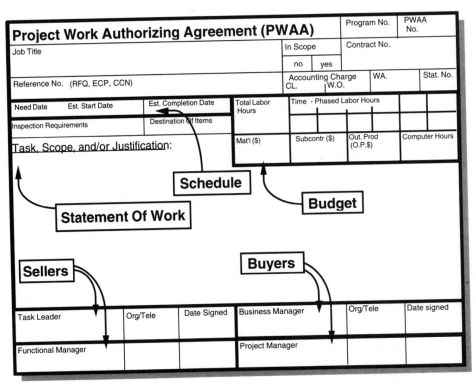

FIGURE 7.19 The project work authorizing agreement (PWAA).

Project Work Authorizing Agreements are internal contracts containing:

- Task description.
- Schedule for deliverables.
- Time-phased budgets.
- Agreement by the implementer.
- Agreement by the project manager.

Subcontracts are external contracts containing all of the above plus:

- Contract terms and conditions.
- Legal authority to perform.
- Conditions for default.

THE PLANNING PROCESS IS SIMULATING THE PROJECT

An overview of the plan development is depicted in Figure 7.20. It highlights the role of the project manager in integrating the customer objectives with those of the management, and it emphasizes a major reason projects fail: lack of team interaction. Productive interaction helps motivate and commit the team. But it has to be a true interactive process. The most difficult project objectives offer the best team brainstorming opportunities. When the team members resolve strategies to achieve the objectives and impact the plan, their investment skyrockets—they're committed to attaining success.

A significant contributor to planning failures is lack of a systematic and structured process. As emphasized in Chapter 2, to test for a sensible plan, it is important to be able to envision it—to be able to decompose it into deliverables and then simulate the

Implementation planning is driven by the objectives and the need to obtain agreements and commitments.

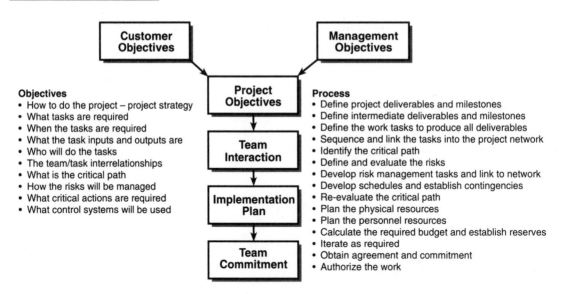

Objectives
- How to do the project – project strategy
- What tasks are required
- When the tasks are required
- What the task inputs and outputs are
- Who will do the tasks
- The team/task interrelationships
- What is the critical path
- How the risks will be managed
- What critical actions are required
- What control systems will be used

Process
- Define project deliverables and milestones
- Define intermediate deliverables and milestones
- Define the work tasks to produce all deliverables
- Sequence and link the tasks into the project network
- Identify the critical path
- Define and evaluate the risks
- Develop risk management tasks and link to network
- Develop schedules and establish contingencies
- Re-evaluate the critical path
- Plan the physical resources
- Plan the personnel resources
- Calculate the required budget and establish reserves
- Iterate as required
- Obtain agreement and commitment
- Authorize the work

FIGURE 7.20 Planning objectives, process, and drivers.

The project manager reviews the project requirements to eliminate any fuzziness, ambiguity, or inconsistency with the project objectives.

work flow in a visual walk-through. Our planning process steps converge on a Cards-on-the-Wall (COW) networking technique that provides this visualization. The main process elements are listed in Table 7.2.

These planning techniques, as flowcharted in Figure 7.21, offer a systematic way to transform the project activities into a baseline plan suitable for both proactive and reactive management. In the remainder of the planning section, we will address each flowchart element in detail.

The goal of planning parrots the project goal: ensuring that all commitments to the customer are met. To get there, we start the planning with the project requirements which include the Statement of Work (SOW), the milestone schedule (Master Schedule), cost targets, and definition of all deliverables. The Master Schedule identifies the overall start and stop dates and all major milestones.

TABLE 7.2   The Planning Process: Major Elements and Techniques

Key Element	Process	Primary Technique
Products	*Decomposing* the deliverables into their hierarchical structure—all the way from the project requirements down to the lowest level internal and external deliverables.	Project Product List and Fact Sheets
Tasks	*Defining the tasks* needed to complete each deliverable.	Work Breakdown Structure
Strategy	*Identifying the risks* and opportunities and the customer-compatible risk and opportunity strategy with preventive, causative, and contingent action plans.	Lessons Learned
Network	*Logically arranging* the required tasks to portray the best delivery approach.	Cards-on-the-Wall network, followed by a computerized network and critical path determination.
Schedules	*Scheduling* each task then refining and shortening the project's overall critical path through iterative steps.	Scheduling software
Resources	*Establishing* resources (personnel, equipment, finances) needed to accomplish each task on schedule.	Spread sheets and cost estimating models
Commitments	*Committing* the necessary resources and funds for each task as determined from the schedule and task definition.	Project Work Authorizing Agreements

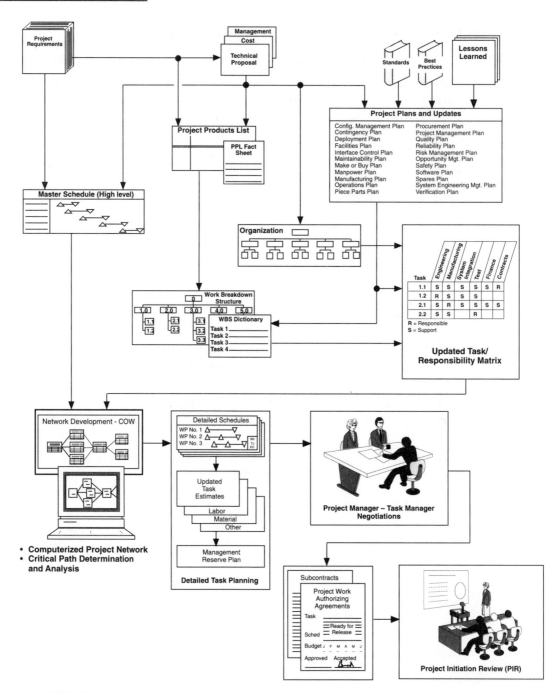

FIGURE 7.21   The planning process: From problem solving to commitment.

DETERMINING THE PROJECT DELIVERABLES

One of the first planning steps is to determine all of the project deliverables and to provide a narrative description of each. The Project Products List (PPL) is derived from system decomposition and definition and is a list of all contract deliverables and internal deliverables, in all forms produced, with the quantities required. Examples of the different forms of products that could be produced are:

- Drafts.
- Simulations.
- Models (user requirements understanding, technical feasibility, physical fit, field test, preproduction. etc.).
- Qualification units.
- Deliverables.
- Spares.

An example of a hardware PPL and a software PPL are shown in Figure 7.22. Other PPLs would include support equipment, documentation, and services.

A Project Product List Fact Sheet should accompany each PPL (Figure 7.23). Its purpose is to provide a description and use for each item. It is usually written by the most knowledgeable expert available, whether they are to work on the project or not.

DEFINING THE TASKS AND THE WORK BREAKDOWN STRUCTURE

The Work Breakdown Structure (WBS) is used to decompose the system by assemblies, subassemblies and components rather than by discipline or functional organization (such as hardware, software, engineering, etc.). The WBS is depicted graphically or in an indented list (Figure 7.24), and illustrates the way the project will be integrated, assigned, and statused. The WBS is mandatory for

> The Project Products List and Fact Sheets are techniques that facilitate this step.

> As the keystone of the plan, the WBS depicts each task and organizes all tasks into their hierarchical relationships to the products and system.

Project Products List — Title: **Propulsion System Dual Tank Configuration (WBS 11.01.02)** — Project Office Approval — Organ No. — Name: — Date — Revision — Page 1 Of 2

Legend — Status: N = New, M = Modified, E = Existing

"Category": TF – Technical Feasibility Model; PF – Physical Fit Model; TS – Thermal Simulation Model; SI – System Integration Model; FT – Field Test Model; Q – Qualification Unit; DV – Development Vehicle; F – Flight; S – Spares

Item no	Nomenclature and WBS Number	Drawing Number (or similar to)	Make or buy	Des	Hdwe	TF	PF	TS	SI	FT	Q	DV	F	S	Remarks
1	Propulsion Module (10.01.02 .19)		M	N	N						1	2			Assemble, Install & Test
2	Propellant Tank (10.01.02.07)	8160485 - X (2P64002)	B	M	N				2		1	2	4	1	Spherical Version Of 2P64002 (cylindrical)
3	Reaction Engine Module (10.01.02.06)	8160481 -X (2P64000 - 13)	B	M	N			14	16	1	2	2	32	2	RRC Intelsat V 0.5 LBF Thruster Mounted In Pairs On An REM
4	Latching Solenoid Valve (11.01.02.11)	2P60481 - 3 or equivalent	B	E	N				4	1		4	8	1	
5	Service Valve (11.01.02.11)	2P60483 - X	B	E	N				3			3	6	1	
6	PR XDucer (11.01.02.15)	8111210 - X	B	M	N	1			4	1	1	4	8	1	Modify To Increase Shielding For New Radiation Environment
7	Filter (11.01.02.10)	8103465 - 15	B	E	N				4			4	8	1	

Also software

Also support equipment

Also documentation

Also services

PROJECT PRODUCTS LIST — Software

LEGEND — STATUS: N - New, M - Modified, E - Existing

PRODUCT LEVEL: CSCI – Computer Software Configuration Item; CSC – Computer Software Component

WBS NO. 1.3.7.1 — SUBSYSTEM Data Compression — WORK PKG NO. 1.3.7.1.0

Date June 12 — Revision 1.2 — Page 1

NOMENCLATURE	MNEMONIC	CI	CSC	User Rqmt's Model	Technical Feasibility Mdl	-01	-02	MAKE (M) OR BUY (B)	SOFTW. DESIGN	PROGR. CODING	EST. LINES OF CODE	SECURITY CLASSIF.	REMARKS
Data Base Core	RDMS	X		X	X	X		M	M	N	125K	Uncl	Convert to Ada
Report Writer	WRIT		X	X		X		M	N	N	87K	Uncl	
Graphics	GRAF		X			X		B	N	N	42K	Uncl	
Dictionary	DICT		X				X	M	N	N	65K	Uncl	

FIGURE 7.22   Project product list examples.

Item:	Pressure transducer
Part No:	8111210 - 503
Source:	Electromech, Inc.
WBS No:	11.01.02.15
Description:	This transducer is identical electrically to existing part no. 8111210-501. The envelope is to be modified to increase heat survivability. The shield concept must be proven by tests of the development model. The shielding design must be qualified by selected qualification tests per the test plan.

FIGURE 7.23 PPL fact sheet example.

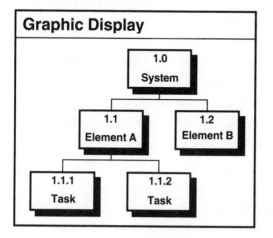
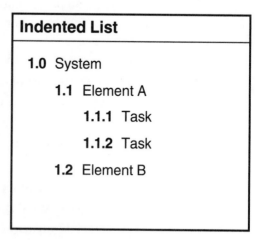

FIGURE 7.24 The work breakdown structure.

project planning because it is the basis for work assignments, budgeting, scheduling, risk assessment, cost collection, and performance statusing.

Figure 7.25 illustrates how the Work Breakdown Structure relates the work to produce the individual components (from the Product Breakdown Structure) to the work to integrate those components into the system.

The WBS has been successfully employed by government agencies such as the DoD and NASA, and is fast becoming an important planning technique for commercial projects as well. For government projects, the Request for Proposal usually provides a top level WBS with which the project WBS must interface. MIL-STD-881A (government WBS standard) embodies WBS requirements as well as examples. Helpful for planning commercial projects, it provides a system management structure for:

- System decomposition.
- Specifications and drawings.
- Configuration management.
- Budgeting.
- Scheduling.
- Responsibility.

The following guidelines (Figure 7.26) refer to the WBS examples of hardware and software subprojects, and reflect our experience in refining this planning technique:

- Structure the WBS by product and elements of the product.
- Include all authorized tasks.
- Cost collection is usually one level below budget performance reporting to facilitate problem cause identification.
- Identifiers for like tasks should be similar.
- All tasks for an element should be collected with the element identifier.
- WBS depth (number of levels) depends on the risk to be managed and reported. The level-of-effort tasks are usually at the second level, which may include project management, system engineering, system integration, and system-level

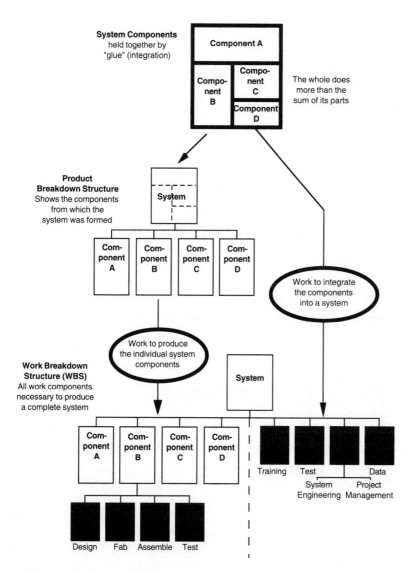

FIGURE 7.25   The work breakdown structure related to system and products.

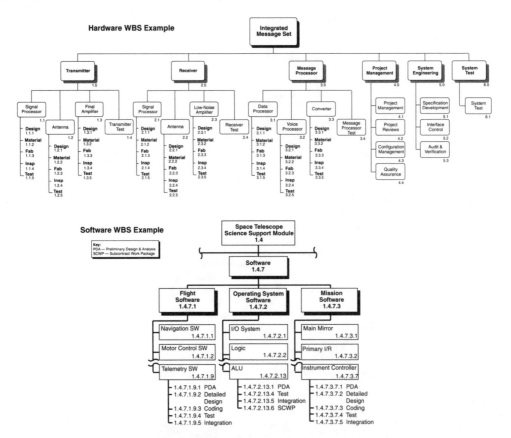

FIGURE 7.26 Hardware and software work breakdown structure example.

testing. For each element, system decomposition should proceed to the level necessary to manage the risk associated with the development of that entity. The task level should employ the relevant action verbs such as "design," "fabricate," "code," "assemble," and "test."

The WBS is supported by the *WBS Dictionary,* which links the WBS elements to the final technique in the task definition—work packages. As Figure 7.27 shows, the *WBS Dictionary* is a narrative description of each work task identified in the WBS. This document drives task estimating and supports task assignment.

Component Test

This task consists of preparing test procedures, test facility, test personnel, and test conduct including documentation and resolution of all test discrepancies. The output from the task is a satisfactorily completed test, resolution of all test anomalies, and the final test report.

FIGURE 7.27   Work breakdown structure dictionary excerpt.

The work package is a complete description for each task, including what, when, how, by whom, and the budget for each task to be performed. It may incorporate the *WBS Dictionary* entry or reference it. The work package represents another important link in the plan—the connection between the WBS and the functional organization or contractor assigned to the task, which is accomplished by the Work Authorization Agreement.

> A work package is prepared for each element at its lowest level in the WBS.

DEVELOPING THE PROJECT NETWORK AND SCHEDULES

There are three types of schedules to resolve: performance, personnel, and budget. This section deals primarily with performance schedules, bounded by the start and stop dates for each task. They form the basis for the other schedules. Personnel schedules identify the timing for specific personnel involvement and facilitate resource planning. Cost schedules define the planned allocation and spending for each task as a function of time. Their primary purposes are to plan the budgets and subsequently, to be the reference for budget management.

Scheduling usually involves more iterations than any other stage in the planning process. This is partially due to the tradeoffs which must be made among the constraints of time, cost, technical requirements, available personnel, and risk. Another complicating factor is that many interdependencies among tasks may not be obvious when scheduling is performed at the task level.

The WBS tasks are the foundation for the project network and schedule as shown in Figure 7.28.

The scheduling process iterates through these steps:

- Combine the tasks to form a project network.
- Define and evaluate the risks.
- Develop risk mitigation actions and add to the network.
- Factor in task duration time.
- Determine the critical path.
- Shorten the critical path.
- Commit to performing to the task schedules.

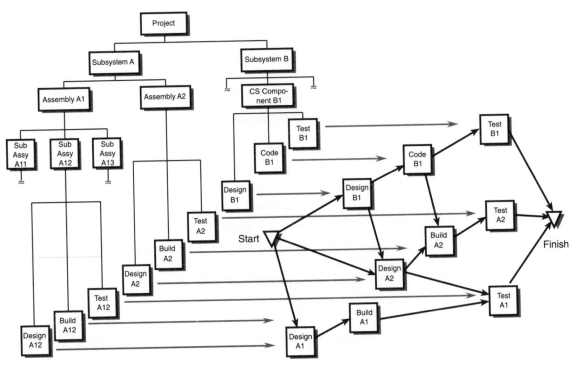

FIGURE 7.28 **The work breakdown structure tasks are the foundation for the project network and schedule.**

Historically, there have been two principal methods for constructing network diagrams, the Program Evaluation and Review Technique (PERT) and the Critical Path Method (CPM). Rosenau[11] characterizes these methods as follows:

> PERT and CPM emerged in different ways in the late 1950s. PERT is event oriented (that is, the labels go in the nodes of the diagram) and has typically been used for aerospace and research and development (R and D) projects for which the time for each activity is uncertain. CPM is activity oriented (that is, the activity label is placed on the arrow) and has been applied to the construction industry, in which there is typically a controllable time for each activity. There are now many hybrid forms of network diagrams that provide the best features of PERT and CPM. The network purist undoubtedly cares about the distinctions between these two, but in reality they are not very important.

PERT or CPM afford very limited opportunity for team interaction during network construction. Computer-based network construction, regardless of the specific software, is usually automated from work packages input by a single person working at the keyboard and viewing the network on the computer screen. The problem with using a computer at this stage is that the team is not building the network. Not being able to get a team interacting around a small display, you rely on one person's expertise. We prefer a more interactive network diagramming technique that begins with a method we have dubbed Cards-on-the-Wall. In this method, the team literally hangs each work package on the wall, by project phase, and interconnects them to reflect the interdependencies (Figure 7.29). We prefer the wall because it allows the whole team to cluster around the equivalent of an 8-foot by 20-foot display screen. We use "wetware" (the brains of the team) for creating the network, and software for capturing that network and computing the critical path. We've devised a form for creating the network, as shown on a section of the network wall in Figure 7.29.

Technically, the Cards-on-the-Wall result is similar to PERT, but the process is much more visual and interactive, leading to more reliable schedules.

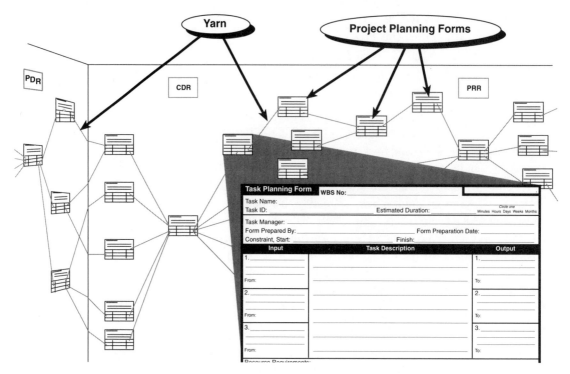

FIGURE 7.29   **The cards-on-the-wall method.**

Our Cards-on-the Wall process uses:

- A 5″ × 8″ project planning form for each task,
- Yarn or string for interconnecting the cards, and
- Ample walls to hang and arrange the cards.

The Cards-on-the-Wall method consists of interconnecting the tasks (cards) to reflect the optimum order of events and the interdependencies. Among the benefits of this interactive, visual procedure are:

- Participative decision-making.
- Fewer "I forgots."
- Shared risks.

- Shared concessions.
- Quality results.
- *And most important:* team ownership of the plan.

In a recent planning session, someone commented that it was a shame that the walls weren't magnetic. "But they are," said the leader, looking at the cluster of people over at the wall discussing how to shorten a link in a critical path, "they attract human flesh." We've never seen people crowd around a computer terminal talking about how to move tasks, but we've seen lots of groups cluster around a wall draped with cards and yarn, moving "logic" around to make a tight schedule work.

Schedules at the task level usually employ a linear format or bar chart such as the Gantt chart. Figure 7.30 shows the relationship between the project network and the task schedules.

The next step after network construction is determining the critical path—the task sequence that paces the project. When asked to identify his project's critical path, one rather defensive project manager we encountered asserted, "This project has no critical path, if it does, we will eliminate it." We define the Critical Path as the sequence of project activities for which there is minimum or zero slack. The critical path for preparing to go on vacation is shown in bold in Figure 7.31.

After adding contingency and risk management tasks, the critical path needs to be re-evaluated. Analyzing resource requirements for concurrent activities, using the critical path as the time scale, will usually reveal sub-optimal lumping of personnel resources. At the same time, these tasks are considered for leveling or smoothing with concurrent and/or contiguous tasks, the following actions to reduce the critical path need to be considered:

- Eliminate or shorten tasks on the critical path.
- Re-plan serial paths to be parallel.
- Overlap sequential tasks.
- Increase the number of work days or work hours.

The critical path paces the project schedule.

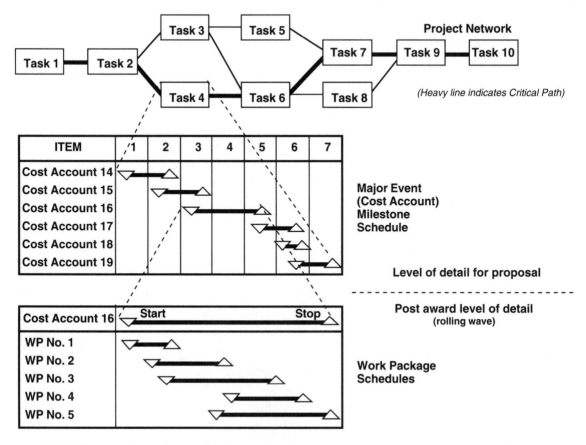

FIGURE 7.30 The relationship between the project network and the task schedules.

- Shorten tasks; the best candidates are those:
    —That are early, long, or easy.
    —For which you have available resources.
    —That cost the least to speed up.
    —That your own organization controls.

Each action to shorten the critical path should be justified.

Actions taken to shorten the critical path usually have other impacts. Using the vacation preparation example above, the critical path could be shortened by having the hitch installed while the car is being fixed, or you could rent a car to pick up supplies

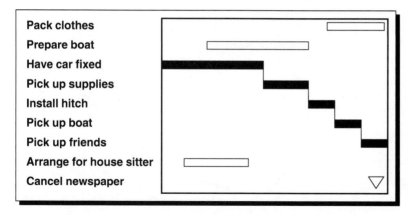

FIGURE 7.31   Critical path example: Vacation preparation.

while the car is being fixed. In the first case, if the car is having the fuel injection system repaired, the mechanic may not have the skill to install the hitch, hence a risk would be added. In the second case, renting a car adds cost. In each case you must ask yourself, "Is it worth it to shorten the schedule?"

Sometimes risk reductions and critical path reductions are synergistic. You can expect to identify parallel, lower risk tasks off the critical path which can contribute needed resources to the higher risk tasks, thereby reducing the critical path and/or the risk. The optimum balance is achieved when both sets of tasks end up on the new, shorter critical path.

Next, resource leveling and optimization can be performed. These steps can best be performed with the help of computers, once the network is constructed and described in either an activity-on-arrow or activity-on-node format. Reducing the critical path and optimizing resource allocation can significantly affect a task's cost as illustrated graphically. Shortening a task schedule below the optimum point usually leads to a sharp increase in its cost (Figure 7.32). On the other hand, optimization at the network level consists of offsetting a relatively small increase in task cost with a savings at the project level. For example, the incremental cost associated with compressing one task may result in equivalent overhead savings for the total project.

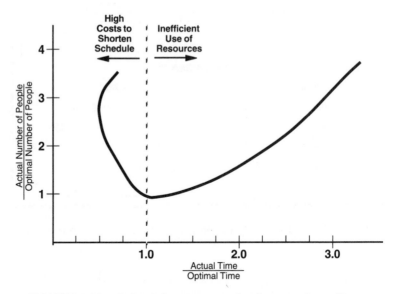

FIGURE 7.32 Schedule compression/expansion effects.

PLANNING THE RESOURCES

While this section focuses on the two limiting resources in most projects, personnel and funds, occasionally a unique physical resource can impact the schedule. Take nothing for granted. Just when you need a special piece of test equipment, covered with dust, which hasn't been used for six months, you can be sure Murphy will need it too. And Murphy's team reserved the equipment when they planned their project. Another property issue to plan for in government projects is the use of government furnished equipment, services, and material.

To illustrate the time-phased requirements for task, personnel category, and total project levels, Gantt charts are useful. They are derived from the PERT/CPM network, but are easier for the team to understand. Having already adjusted some tasks to smooth resource requirements or reduce risks and/or the critical path, the next step is to return to the task level and identify the personnel schedules in more detail.

The WBS is the basis for identifying task responsibilities. As a checklist, the Task Responsibility Matrix (Figure 7.33) is useful

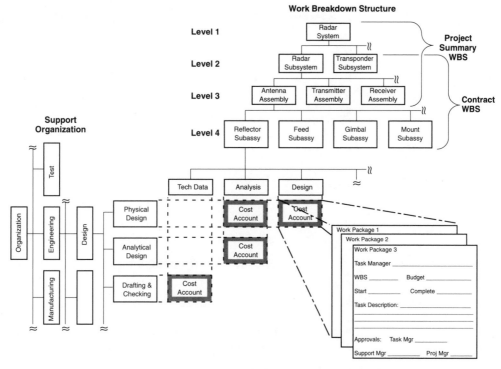

FIGURE 7.33a   Relationship between WBS and organization.

	Engineering	Manufacturing	System Integration	Test	Finance	Contracts
Task						
1	S	S	S	S	S	R
2	R	S	S	S		
3	S	R	S	S	S	S
4	S	S		R		

R = Responsible
S = Support

FIGURE 7.33b   Individual task responsibility matrix.

Organization Task Estimate		MFG No.		Contract		CCN No.	Doing Org. Name			No.
		Date Of RFP		Program			Responsible Org. Name			No.
WBS No:		Subject/Title of Task								
Work Package No:		Time - Phased Labor Hours								

Yr	Jan	Feb	Mar	Apr	May	Jun	Jul	Aug	Sep	Oct	Nov	Dec

Material description	$		Computer HRS		Other
Task description			Skill Mix		
			Basis of Estimate		

Prepared By	Doing Org. Manager's Signature	Responsible Org. Manager's Signature	Control
	——————Date———	——————Date———	17633

FIGURE 7.34   Resource planning form.

in summarizing who and which organizations have been assigned primary and support responsibilities for each task, and who will participate in the Cards-on-the Wall process. Figure 7.34 is an example of a planning form that extracts the monthly personnel needs from the task Gantt chart at the functional organization level and combines that with other resource requirements.

OBTAINING THE COMMITMENTS AND INITIATING THE WORK

Authorization Agreements and Subcontracts authorize the project work and, collectively, represent the Project Plan.

The payoff for all of the detailed planning and scheduling is in securing full support and commitment on the part of the team, functional organizations, subcontractors, general management, and the customer or user. The key negotiations, made easier by detailed scheduling, are those with the functional managers. The resulting agreement should be documented in the form of a Project Work Authorizing Agreement (PWAA) shown earlier. The PWAA contains task definition, budget, schedule, performer's commitment, and project office authorization. Subcontracts also contain terms and conditions clauses. The approved PWAA results from having:

- Open and direct negotiations.
- Tasks understood.
- Milestones agreed to.
- Budgets accepted.
- Contingencies identified.
- Caveats documented.

Our project cycle template includes a Project Initiation Review. The objectives are to secure executive management approval of the implementation plan and to obtain corporate commitment of resources. The items to review include: contract and incentives; project strategy; project plan; risks, opportunities, and actions; functional organization commitments; and resources required.

KEEPING THE PLAN CURRENT

The project manager is responsible for:

The harder it is to plan, the more you need to plan!

- Assuring that all plans are consistent with current strategy, constraints, and project environment.
- Establishing the methods, tools, and techniques used in planning.
- Using the tools and techniques to update the plan.

The techniques and tools, especially software applications, that support these responsibilities are constantly improving. Before committing to a new software tool which may come up short as the project grows, you may do well to heed the following precautions:

- Beware of nonstandard data input and output formats.
- Some products are conceived and promoted as a full management tool, but only provide a scheduling algorithm.
- Test run the software.
- Talk to users who manage projects similar to yours.

- Set up operating procedures and standards.
- Insist that the standards be used.

5. RISKS AND OPPORTUNITIES

Problems are only opportunities in work clothes.
                                              Henry J. Kaiser,
                                                        Maxim

Risks, as well as opportunities, are endemic to the project environment. However well-planned a project may be, there will always be risk elements. Projects without risk are like ships in a harbor—they're safe. But ". . . that's not what ships are built for."

In the heat of project battle, it is easy for risks or opportunities to slip in (or by) inadvertently. It is the project manager's responsibility to maintain a high level of awareness among all project participants, especially during:

- Concept trade-offs in early phases.
- Development of system documentation.
- Project definition.
- Detailed planning.
- Change evaluation.
- Manufacturing preparation.
- Test preparation.
- Shipping/Handling.
- Deployment.

There is no simple way to prevent disasters. Nothing short of a systematic, detailed process will work.

Reporting on a $1 billion overrun on the space station program, a *Washington Post* article[12] quoted a NASA official as admitting: "I wish I could say with certainty that we understood how the cost growth occurred and have found a simple way to prevent this from reoccurring." The reasons cited by others included ". . . an increase in aerospace contractor overhead rates charged to NASA as a result of declining business coming to those companies from the defense industry." Over-optimism also occurred, particularly on the part of software developers who ". . . overestimated how efficiently they could write and deliver the station's enormous requirement for a million-plus lines of custom-tailored 'man-rated' software code."

Over-optimism is one of the toughest elements to determine. Very large projects justify independent estimates or audits of major subprojects. Estimating the efficiency of software development is a major planning issue. In the case just cited, the number of source lines had been estimated, but optimistic productivity factors were used. The increased overhead charges could have been anticipated from awareness of broad trends such as fewer defense contracts—a national news item. The consequences of this trend were ignored in this case. By the time the overrun had reached $1 billion, proactive management was no longer possible.

Regarding the career-limiting effect of under-estimating future risks, March and Shapira[13] have articulated this management dichotomy:

> Society values risk taking but not gambling, and what is meant by gambling is risk taking that turns out badly . . . Thus, risky choices that turn out badly are seen, after the fact, to have been mistakes. The warning signs that were ignored seem clearer than they were; the courses that were followed seem unambiguously misguided.

This section is about maximizing opportunities and dealing directly with the inevitability of risks—the foreseeable ones as well as the "unknown unknowns" that occur throughout the project. Risks are chances of injury, damage, or loss. In project management, risks are the chances of not achieving the results as planned. Opportunities are chances for progress or advancement. In project management, opportunities are the chances of improving the value of the project results.

We focus on methods for clarifying and prioritizing the warning signs— unambiguously.

Ours is a value driven approach to managing both risks and opportunities, meaning that the relative merits of mitigating each risk and exploiting each opportunity is carefully evaluated using the appropriate tools. You make that kind of evaluation in your personal life every time you decide what insurance to carry and what size of deductible. And while most car manufacturers and consumers don't question the relative value of carrying a spare tire, we seldom carry other spares, such as certain failure-prone engine parts, because of the space required and the expertise or special tools needed to replace them. The latter is given by one RV manufacturer as the reason for pricing a spare tire as an option.

We define risk and opportunity management to be the methodical process used to reduce the risks and enhance the opportunities by:

- *Identifying* potential risks and opportunities.
- *Assessing* associated probabilities of occurrence and the impact (consequence or benefit) of the occurrence.
- *Deciding* to:

Do nothing	OR	Take preventive action for risk, causative action for opportunity	OR	Take contingent action later based on an identified trigger

Risk management objectives are driven by the desire to succeed, while opportunity management objectives are driven by the desire to excel. The major driving forces for each are shown in Figures 7.35 and 7.36.

Risk management depends on a good foundation of planning and proactive project management:

- Develop (and use) an Implementation Plan:
  —Developed by and committed to by the project team.
  —Keep implementation plans current.

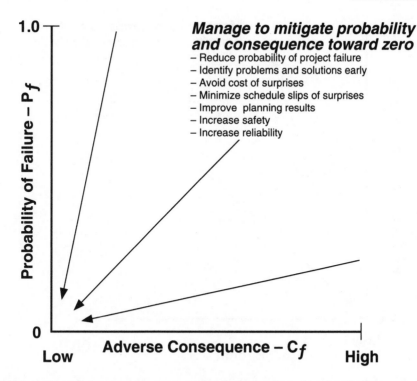

Manage to mitigate probability and consequence toward zero
– Reduce probability of project failure
– Identify problems and solutions early
– Avoid cost of surprises
– Minimize schedule slips of surprises
– Improve planning results
– Increase safety
– Increase reliability

FIGURE 7.35   Risk management objectives—driven by the desire to succeed.

- Use proven processes tailored to your project:
    —System engineering methodology.
    —Software development methodology.
    —Hardware development methodology.
    —Reliability and quality methodology.
- Manage the business and technical baselines:
    —Keep participants informed as the baseline evolves.

Just completing a careful planning session (and being anxious to get to work) can lull a project team into feeling secure that all uncertainty has been wrung out of their project. Their up-front requirements analysis led to contingency tasks covering all the risks they identified—mostly from recent project history. They

> Not only is it impossible to eliminate all risks up front, it is also impractical to identify all of them early.

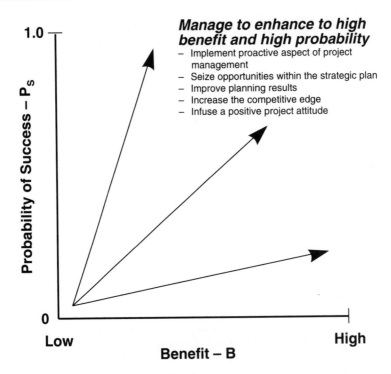

FIGURE 7.36   Opportunity management objectives—driven by the desire to excel.

Each risk or opportunity needs to be evaluated as a whole, taking into account relative probabilities and offsetting benefits and consequences.

---

may feel they have already "managed" the risks. But risk management is ongoing—it evolves as the project proceeds. Plans need to be updated as new risks and opportunities are identified and the impacts are evaluated.

In a global sense, opportunities and risks are interrelated and use similar techniques. We have structured a process which separates the uncertainties themselves and their analysis, from the management actions and decisions. This risk and opportunity management process takes specific steps to make overt, conscious decisions with justifiable rationale:

1. Identify the risks and opportunities:

   —What could go wrong? What opportunities are available?

—Use "If . . . , Then . . ." statement.

—Group by like categories.

2. Assess both probability and impact. Forecast the expected outcome.

3. Compare expected outcomes and prioritize.

4. Develop feasible management actions to enhance opportunities and mitigate risks.

5. Estimate the cost of proposed immediate and contingent actions.

6. Compare resultant changes to weighted value against action costs.

7. Decide on actions required, and obtain concurrence.

8. Document and incorporate decisions in all planning.

Some project managers and executives make a distinction between eliminating versus insuring against a risk (such as liability insurance), or deciding on an action versus planning a contingency. In our view, these are simply alternative cases of risk and opportunity management and need to be evaluated as such. For example, we consider insurance as one possible mitigating action for product liability risks. The examples that follow demonstrate techniques that are unique to risk and opportunity management.

> Risk and opportunity management is essential to, and performed concurrently with, the planning process, but uses separate and unique techniques.

IDENTIFY THE RISKS AND OPPORTUNITIES

One of the biggest problems a project manager faces is motivating team members to identify risks. You want to make everyone risk conscious. However, there is often that hesitancy to surface risks, lest one be labeled a worrier or negative thinker. It's partly a problem that messengers are in fact often shot or at least put down by their management (the problem with a risk being identified is that you have to do something about it) and partly a failure to realize the real value of risk identification (you can't mitigate it if you don't know it's there so its better to anticipate a lot of problems, some of which won't happen, than too few and miss the "project-killers"). It's easier with opportunities because everyone wants to be a hero and find ways to do it better, quicker, cheaper, etc. and that suggests some strategies. The simplest is to reward risk identifiers. The best (and cheapest) one we've seen is a listing outside a manager's door of all the risks anybody had identified on her project together with the name of the identifier. A brief statement of what actions were to be taken (or if no action was to be taken, why not), and who had the action. The listing had powerful effects:

- It said the manager wasn't afraid to identity risks.
- It rewarded risk identifiers (printed recognition is an effective, inexpensive reward).
- It stimulated others to think of risks by listing those already identified.
- It precluded people from coming in with the same risk over and over again.
- It allowed others to offer suggestions for how to mitigate identified risks.

The manager wasn't concerned with who got the credit as long as the project succeeded—a good leadership and teamwork technique as well.

It can be helpful to break the myriad of possible risk and opportunity sources into several categories. Two categories of project risk, Implementation and Product, are summarized in Figure 7.37, together with the most common development risk categories. This is only a representative list—all relevant areas must be considered.

Figure 7.38 shows the two major categories of project opportunities.

Identify the risks and opportunities for each cycle phase by systematically applying the appropriate techniques based on analysis, planning, and history.

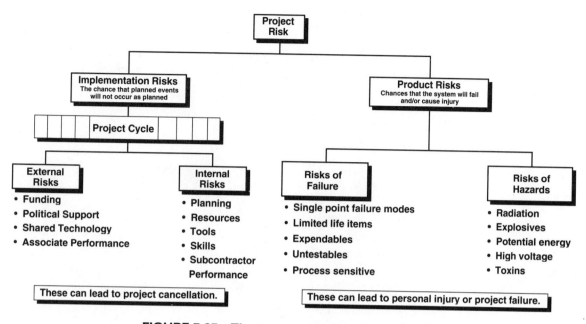

FIGURE 7.37   The two categories of project risk.

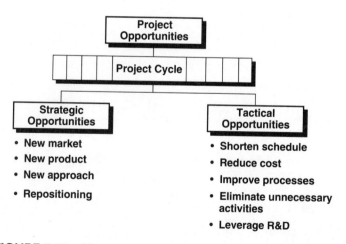

FIGURE 7.38   The two categories of project opportunities.

Techniques based on analysis include:

- Risk and opportunity checklists (the categories and lists in Figures 7.37 and 7.38 offer a beginning checklist).
- Rules of thumb/standards of performance.
- System decomposition and critical items (off-core studies).
- Hazard analysis.
- Failure modes analysis.
- Interviews with experts.

Hazard Analysis is used to ensure all system hazards have been identified and anticipated. Once identified, all hazards to personnel and to the system are either accepted, reduced by design, or contained by design. For example, a high pressure gas hazard could be reduced by designing with a large safety factor or contained by placing sand bags between the hazard and personnel.

Failure Modes and Effects Analysis (FMEA) is a risk management tool used to ensure all failure modes have been identified and planned for. This tool employs the following method:

- Select a ranking technique for project failure modes concern and attention.
- Identify all single point failure modes.
- Analyze failure modes and the resultant mission effect.
- Determine those requiring correction: redundancy and/or increased reliability.
- Implement the corrective action decision.

A technique based on planning—Scenario planning—is a "low-tech" technique for visualizing risks or opportunities, is useful in the realms of judgment and project planning. It consists of querying:

- What if . . . ? followed by . . . then what?
- What could go wrong?
- What opportunities might become available?

This technique can be used to build a decision tree based on broad market and economic trends: If the economy does this, I do that . . . . These scenarios can often identify important assumptions that traditional forecasting tends to miss. It represents another systematic way to consider future possibilities. Planning techniques also include:

- Project network interactions.
- Critical Path.
- Schedule slack.

Techniques based on history are the most natural to apply. They include:

- Similar efforts and lessons learned.
- Technical surveys.
- Development test results.

Generalized historical templates can work well in some industries. For example, construction projects are highly repetitive, compared with research and development. Since the work patterns of one project may be similar to selected ones from the past, the same types of risks are likely to occur.

On the other hand, misperceptions or misinterpretations about prior projects will sometimes lead project teams to overestimate their ability to control future risks or to exploit future opportunities. It has often been left up to project leaders to identify risk based on their own experiences and perception of the situation. Such projects were at the mercy of whatever their experiences and perceptions were. As one engineer put it, "The alligator that was the closest to you was the one you worried about the most. You didn't look at the other gators in the swamp, even though they were bigger and meaner." A common misperception is that successful experiences with simpler projects scale to complex ones. Every new project has to be analyzed in detail to understand those unique properties which distinguish it from its

> Not only is each project unique, but that uniqueness is often related to its particular risk factors.

predecessors. This needs to be an ongoing team effort and rely heavily on lessons learned.

ASSESS BOTH PROBABILITY AND IMPACT

The Weighted Value (WV) provides a tool for quantitatively comparing both risks and opportunities. It provides the project manager with a measure for sizing management reserves. The Weighted Value of risk and opportunity is equal to the probability of occurrence multiplied by the impact, for example:

Probability of occurrence of an opportunity $= 0.6$

Benefit of the opportunity $= \$720{,}000$ if it does occur

Therefore: $WV = (0.6) \times (\$720{,}000)$

$= \$432{,}000$

A goal of identifying and anticipating *all* risks would usually be doomed to failure. The result of anticipating every possible risk could bury the team in questionable information and turn the project into a hand-wringing exercise. This dramatizes the importance of setting priorities.

Weighted Value provides a tool for quantitatively comparing both risks and opportunities. The primary use of Weighted Value is to prioritize actions. When applying WV, be sure to use consistent units. For the purposes of prioritizing, "burn rate" (usually expressed as daily expense rate) may be used to measure schedule impact in dollars. Here's an example prioritization of two risks.

When applying Weighted Value, common sense and good judgment are required since the calculations, usually based on subjective information, have low precision.

Risk 1 Weighted Value

$(0.8) \times (\$100{,}000) = \$80{,}000$

Risk 2 Weighted Value

$(0.4) \times (\$60{,}000) + (0.4) \times (45$-day slip$) = \$24{,}000$ (cost) plus 18-days (schedule)

Applying a \$2000/day burn rate, a 45-day slip would cost \$90,000.

Weighted Value, on a cost basis, $= \$24{,}000 + (0.4) \times (\$90{,}000) = \$60{,}000$.

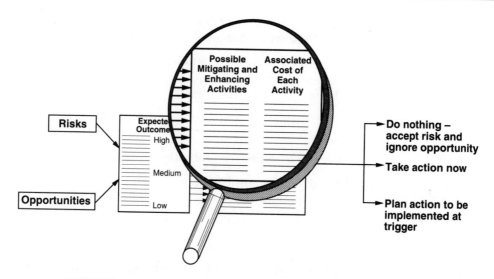

FIGURE 7.39   Management of risk and opportunity actions.

On the basis of this analysis, Risk 1 should be of higher priority than Risk 2. Risk and opportunity can be managed by influencing the *probability* of occurrence and/or the *impact* of the outcome.

A complete listing of the possible influencing activities with their associated costs should be developed (Figure 7.39). From this, you can decide on the appropriate actions. There are basically two types of actions to consider: preventive and contingent. Contingent actions are the same as preventive actions, except no action is taken other than planning, until a predetermined trigger event occurs.

Examples of Preventive Actions:	*Examples of Contingencies:*
Redundancy to eliminate single point failure modes	Red line limits in test procedures (terminate test if exceeded)
Higher quality to increase reliability	Establish thresholds for variance analysis and corrective action (triggers focused review)
Increased margins to improve safety	Planned strategies contingent on competitor's performance

Examples of *Preventive Actions:*	*Examples of Contingencies:*
Enforced use of common software language and standards across subcontractor and prime team.	Unsolicited proposal based on associate's poor performance.
Expert review to ensure best approach	
Overtime to shorten critical path	
Over-design for possible future growth (pre-planned product improvement)	

The cost effectiveness of candidate actions can be evaluated using mitigation leverage (ML) or enhancement leverage (EL) factors defined as follows:

$$ML = \frac{\text{WV before} - \text{WV after}}{\text{Risk mitigation cost}}$$

$$EL = \frac{\text{WV after} - \text{WV before}}{\text{Benefit enhancement cost}}$$

The leverage values can be used for comparison and as an aid in the selection process.

DECIDE ON ACTIONS REQUIRED AND INCORPORATE THEM IN THE PLAN

It is often impractical to accurately estimate the probabilities of occurrence and impacts of potential events. In these cases, decisions may be based on a qualitative assessment for both the probability of occurrence and the consequence or benefit. In the sample risk decision matrix in Figure 7.40, based on qualitative assessments, carrying a spare ignition key in your wallet or purse is a high-impact, low probability instance (for some, a high-probability instance).

All risk mitigation actions must be incorporated into the project plan and kept current (Figure 7.41). Carrying a spare key

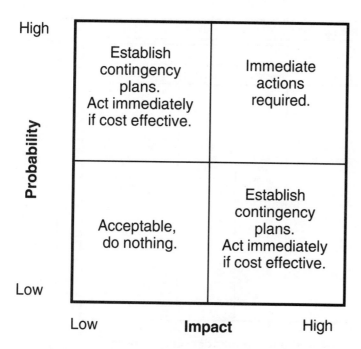

FIGURE 7.40 Sample risk decision matrix.

for the car you sold two years ago is an example of a good risk management decision that, through neglect, turned bad (what's worse, you believe you're secure until that first time you discover you are locked out).

On cost reimbursable contracts, get customer concurrence with risk and opportunity management actions, since the customer will be paying for them.

To be effective, this management process should occur throughout the project and at all levels in the system decomposition and project organization. The management actions must:

- Result from overt, conscious decisions;
- Have justifiable rationale;
- Be incorporated in the plan; and
- Be implemented through work authorizations and subcontracts.

Opportunity Decision Record

Risk Decision Record

"If..."	"Then..."	Probability	Impact	Actions
List major worries (i.e., what could go wrong?)	Describe consequences	High, Med, or Low	High, Med, or Low	Acceptable risk, Preventive actions, or Contingent actions with identified triggers

FIGURE 7.41   Risk and opportunity decision records.

RELATING RISKS AND OPPORTUNITIES TO THE PROJECT CYCLE

As we emphasized earlier, risk management is ongoing—it evolves as the project proceeds. The sources and nature of risks and opportunities vary from period to period and from phase to phase. For example, the major risks during the Study Period may be the stability of the requirements, understanding of the user problem, and project funding, whereas, training and logistics may loom large during the Implementation Period.

The Vee model[14] of the technical aspect provides a visual basis for identifying and managing risks and opportunities during system decomposition and definition. We used Figure 6.5 in Chapter 6 to introduce the idea of using off-core activities for risk identification and risk reduction.

Figure 7.42 lists critical issues to be studied off-core during the user requirements understanding phase, since users (or the

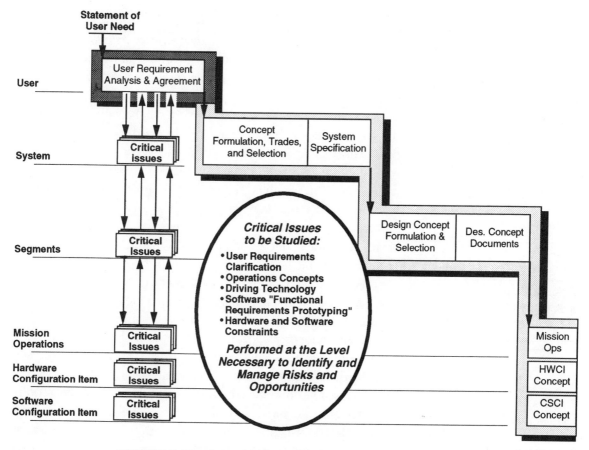

FIGURE 7.42   Critical issues for user requirements phase.

organization representing the user) often do not have a clear understanding of their needs. This diagram details the first part of the core of the Vee, starting with the statement of user need. Until concepts, and even lower level details are defined, the user requirements statement may continue to evolve. Off-core studies can provide the necessary user requirements clarification and understanding.

A major objective of off-core studies is to identify areas of risk, including unfulfilled user expectations, and to identify areas of opportunity. Opportunities include innovations which extend the life cycle through planned technology upgrades or value enhancements which reduce the cost and/or broaden the market. An example of the latter occurred several years ago on a client's project to develop a new calculator for the U.S. financial community. As part of the off-core user's requirements clarification, a meeting was held with a group of financial analysts. The users requested that a button be added to the keyboard which divided the current display by 365, the U.S. standard for interest-bearing days. This feature was an opportunity for a competitive edge and was adopted. Still another opportunity occurred soon thereafter which more than doubled the market. A development team member suggested reconfiguring the keyboard to accommodate the 360-day European standard. The change was easily accomplished at this early stage, but would have had a major impact after coding or manufacturing had started.

> Off-core studies do not seek a final solution, but rather a demonstration that one is feasible.

The off-core studies begin at the earliest point in the project and may be very simple explorations requiring only a few hours to ensure that risks are acceptable. However, if the solution is challenging the state of the art, the studies themselves can be very involved projects requiring years of effort (the Reagan-era "Star Wars" space defense initiative is an example).

> Projects that fall short of user expectations, even though they surpass the state of the art, are not likely to succeed.

The studies may be analytical in nature, or they may require development of a software or hardware model to resolve system capabilities, constraints, and technology or integration issues. These models may need to go to the lowest level of detail in selected areas. For example, creating a software algorithm to prove that a data search of a large, distributed data base can be performed within a specified period. The authors were involved in developing a database management system that could perform a complex search of six-million entries in three seconds. The off-core feasibility studies focused on functionality rather than performance, resulting in an algorithm that was successfully tested on 100,000 entries. Unfortunately the project failed when the fully-implemented system required up to one minute to perform a complete search (even though the typical search met the three-second limit).

The core of the Vee extends to the lowest level of hardware parts and processes and computer software units. Figure 7.43

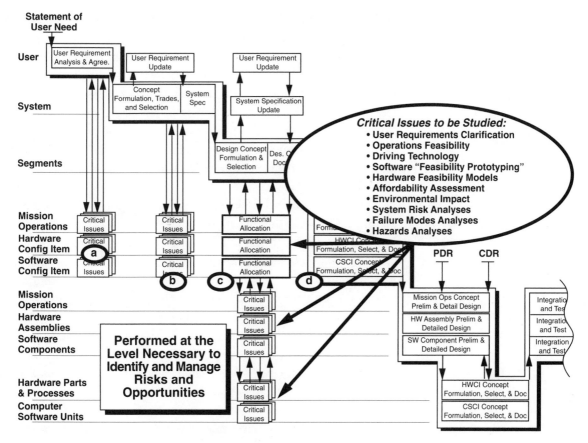

FIGURE 7.43   Off-core alternatives.

illustrates a six-level hierarchy. The number of levels on a given project depends on the system complexity and the system integration approach.

Even though the first phases of the project have ostensibly been completed, it is often necessary to revisit the decisions as external events change, or as new insights are discovered through off-core studies in lower level detail. The revisiting process does not occur by going back up the core of the Vee, but rather, by moving vertically to the system specification update, concept update, or user requirements update, as shown.

Upward iteration with the user is often needed to manage the risks (and take advantage of the opportunities) in the continuous process of user requirements clarification.

The functionality that the user expects must be flowed down to components within the system. In order to complete those components, piece parts and lines of code must be provided. At each of the subtier levels there may be critical issues that should be explored to minimize the risk that, when these details are finally designed and verified, they fall short of the expected functionality or performance. Other critical issues include the expansion of risk and opportunity evaluation to include affordability assessment, environmental impact, system risk, failure modes, and hazard analysis.

The upward and downward risk and opportunity iterations continue through the preliminary and critical design reviews. During the decomposition and definition process major areas of risk are identified and approaches are developed to manage them. As shown in Figure 7.43, it is not necessary that the same solution to a given problem be followed throughout. As the project moves from phase to phase, a new and better approach may be conceived. Thus the solution at step (b) in the diagram could be superior to the solution at step (a). In fact, step (a) may be a hardware solution, while step (b) may be a software solution. Furthermore, step (b) and (c) may represent widely varying approaches with no evolutionary path between them. For this example, the final configuration item must be developed at step (d) which may evolve from (c) or be distinctly different. The only necessity is that a feasible solution be proved at each step and then baselined at its level of decomposition within the Vee.

6. PROJECT CONTROL

A good system of control helps prevent undesirable surprises; it provides for turning the 'lemon' into lemonade.

Henri Fayol,
General and Industrial Management

Fayol goes on to say, "Control activities provide an opportunity for people to take the initiative in planning against deviations, to head off forces that might cause a deviation, to make corrections very quickly when a deviation does occur, and finally, to redirect the firm to capitalize on a deviation when correction is less feasible." Fayol referred to the final alternative as "making lemonade."

PROJECT CONTROL IS PROCESS CONTROL

Project control is not monitoring or tracking of cost and performance data. While this kind of tracking, carried out by an organization or function typically called Project Control or Program Control, may alert the project manager to problems, the data are rarely current. Tracking tends to shift the focus from proactive "planning against deviations" to reactive "make corrections."

> A tracking function is not a control function and can lead to project failure by giving the false impression that project controls are in place.

We define project control as *process* control, a dual system designed and implemented to reduce risk:

Baseline Control	*Performance Control*
Proactive control of the Project Plan and changes to the plan.	*Reactive* control of Variances in Performance to the Project Plan
Management techniques that help ensure that events happen as planned, and that events not planned do not happen.	Corrective action taken when unplanned events do happen.

This section deals with the functions of *defining* and *establishing* five essential elements of the control process. Like planning, these functions focus on the project's objectives by building the project's process control path and staying on it. These are the five essential elements in our control process:

1. *Things to Be Controlled.* The function that must be controlled to a standard of performance.
2. *Control Standard.* The acceptable standard of performance.
3. *Control Authority.* The person or organization that imposes the standard and can grant exceptions.

4. *Control Mechanism.* The forum or device that measures and controls conformance to the standard.

5. *Variance Detection.* The identification of deviations of the control process or violations of the standard.

Typical things to be controlled:

Project baselines: business, cost, and technical

Environment

Funding

Manufacturing process

Materials

Parts

Personnel conduct

Quality

Reliability

Safety, both product and personnel

Security

Test

Time recording

Work standards

Examples within the business baseline include schedule, funding, changes, personnel quality, headcount level, key personnel, work practices, ethical conduct.

Personnel Safety examples include high pressure, radiation, toxins, high voltage, slippery surfaces, sharp edges, overhead clearance, stair risers, air quality.

Even an ideal process control implementation may not anticipate events such as accidents or technology surprises—the good ones as well as the bad. Variance control (Figure 7.44) is the detection and correction of surprises and practices or performance considered substandard. Variances could result from poorly implemented standards or deviations from the application of standards. This reactive factor relies on the management elements of visibility, statusing, and corrective action to close the process control loop. We address each of these elements in separate sections.

Process controls are needed at every level and in all project activities. Without appropriate process controls, details get lost or overlooked. The lost detail is always the costliest one (all lost details are costly in terms of budget, schedule, etc.). Smaller

	Activity	+	Visibility	+	Project Plan	=	Status	+	Corrective Action	=	Reactive Project Control
Case 1: No Visibility	?		No		?		No		No		No
Case 2: No Plan	Yes		Yes		No		No		No		No
Case 3: No Corrective Action	Yes		Yes		Yes		Yes		No		No
Case 4: Desired Approach	Yes		Yes		Yes		Yes		Yes		Yes

FIGURE 7.44   Reactive control of variances.

projects are often more vulnerable due to overconfidence that the details can be informally "kept in mind."

- Large projects have complex communication paths—details get lost or overlooked.
- Geographically dispersed projects have inefficient communication paths—details get lost or overlooked.
- High reliability projects must be built to exacting standards—details get lost or overlooked.
- Long duration projects have personnel turnover—details get lost or overlooked.
- Projects with subcontractors have long communications and geographic paths—details get lost or overlooked.

It follows that large, long, high-reliability projects using subcontractors need the ultimate system of process control. In short, projects with inadequate process controls usually fail. Projects having the appropriate process controls have a good chance for success. But what is the "appropriate" level of control?

TOWARDS ACHIEVING THE APPROPRIATE LEVEL OF CONTROL

The appropriate level of control is achieved by pursuing the optimal balance between formality and discretionary freedom. It reflects and accommodates the need for change by managing those changes with formal, trackable procedures. Configuration management, discussed next, is perhaps the best example of an optimally-designed control procedure.

As Leonard Kazmier[15] observes:

> Ultimately, the success of a control system is determined by its effectiveness in getting people to make the necessary modifications in their own performance. Although the classical approach to control systems assumes that people will automatically act to correct their own behavior when directed to do so, this does not necessarily happen. Individuals may resist formal control systems for a variety of reasons, some of which are discussed below.

Stated another way:

- Controls disrupt a person's self-image (they highlight things a person has done poorly).
- People tend to avoid unpleasant involvement (such as behavioral changes).
- Goals of the control system may not have been accepted.
- Standards of expected performance are too high.
- The controls are irrelevant or lack completeness.
- An outside staff is administering the controls.
- Informal team norms may conflict with, or be outside of company norms.

One of the most pervasive reasons for resistance is the equating of project controls with a lack of freedom. Controls therefore should never be arbitrary—they should make sense. But even the most logical controls may encounter resistance. We are increasingly scripted in a "zero sum" concept of personal freedom and control—the more we're controlled, the less we are free. Experienced managers know however, that appropriate controls enhance rather than inhibit creativity. Such controls free the project team to be creative in finding solutions, rather than being distracted by the day-to-day confusion of deciding what the project activity should be. Since this may not be the initial perception, particularly for inexperienced team members, it is the responsibility of the senior team members to gain general acceptance for the process control system. To accomplish this, the team needs to be intimately involved in: process control definition and implementation; the control activities and decisions; and access to relevant information at the lowest organizational levels.

Some team members may still have to be sold on the potential benefits to gain their acceptance and to maintain a high level of teamwork. In this regard, the productivity and quality improvements that accrue from designing, selecting, and tuning the controls through team consensus, can be particularly convincing.

Peter Drucker[16] stresses the importance of *congruency:*

Meaningful control systems . . . are discernible and appropriate for the complexity of the tasks being assessed and the size of the project effort. They are timely, simple to employ, and congruent with the events being measured.

In summary, both proactive and reactive process controls should be:

- *Relevant.* Controls should never be arbitrary. Their purpose, rationale, and benefits should be documented. The controls should be designed and selected to match the complexity of the project. In general, the more visible and larger the commitment of resources and the greater the human risk, the greater the managerial attention and control expended.

- *Efficient.* While selecting the controls, determine the minimum information needed by the team to measure project performance. Measure primary variables that impact results.

Avoid the tendency to measure and report marginally significant items just because they're readily available (such data tend to mask and divert attention from more important items). Tailor the information to the needs of the team members who will be interpreting the data and taking action. Summarize and use graphics wherever possible.

- *Simple.* To maximize their use and utility, keep the controls as simple as possible.

- *Timely.* The controls need to be in place and tested before they're actually needed on a critical task. The process should produce timely information to facilitate corrective action. This means determining the proper "sampling rate" to avoid obscured visibility at one extreme and information overload at the other.

To be effective, project control systems must be in place before the project is underway, and the use of the controls must be tailored to each situation, with due consideration for the nature, size and/or complexity of the project. As relayed below, one of the author's recent experience demonstrates just how important the appropriate controls are and how critical the timing can be.

The incident occurred on vacation while I was driving a 24-foot motor home, towing a two-ton jeep. The primary control to slow the vehicle down is the brakes, but in mountainous country another even more powerful control is the compression of the engine. By shifting to a lower gear, a safe vehicle speed can be maintained on a steep incline. On the highway between Flaming Gorge in Northern Utah to the town of Vernal, Utah, there is a twenty mile stretch of an 8 percent grade, with accompanying precipitous cliffs along the roadside. Going down this hill I used the primary or standard control (brakes). The car ahead of me was proceeding rather slowly, and judging by the tail lights, was using the brakes frequently. In fact, we could actually smell the overheated brakes. I had to use my brakes fairly frequently since it was a no-passing zone, and I decided to stop to take some photographs to put some distance between us and the slow vehicle. After I started downhill again, I tried to use the brakes to slow the vehicle at about 30 mph. But due to brake fade, the brake pedal went to the floor with no effect on the vehicle speed. I immediately shifted to low gear but the vehicle would not slow down because the automatic transmission would not downshift from second to first at speeds above 25 mph. We continued to accelerate. A hairpin turn loomed ominously less than a half-mile ahead, with a drop of considerable depth very close to the road. Rather than go over the 300 foot cliff, I chose to run the motor home and jeep straight up a rocky embankment on the right just before the hairpin turn. The impact slowed the vehicle to a stop with less than 100 feet to spare to the cliff edge. Miraculously, there was no damage as a result of the impact.

Because of the failed brakes, the motor home could not be driven, and was towed by truck down the same steep grade of 8 percent with exactly the same engine and brakes as the motor home. This journey was made without incident because the tow truck driver started in low gear and the engine compression kept the speed of the vehicles at a safe 20 mph.

The significance of this story is that powerful control processes are available to us, but are ineffective if they are not engaged at the proper time. The entire journey down the steep grade from Flaming Gorge to Vernal could have been made in low gear without requiring use of the brakes, but only if the choice was made before the descent was begun. The same thing is true in a project environment. There are many powerful controls such as configuration management or earned value performance measurement, that can be very effective if implemented at an appropriate time. It is also important to recognize that there are situations when these tools are not appropriate. There are small projects for which more simple tools are entirely adequate, and the more sophisticated approaches are not needed. In driving a car down a steep incline, it is appropriate to use low gear as the primary control, but even the most ardent controls enthusiast would not advocate driving all the way across the United States using low gear. That ardent control enthusiast would, however, have at least suspected that the strong hot brake smell could be coming from the motor home brakes rather than the vehicle in front, and would have responded promptly to the warning signs.

GENERAL CONTROL TECHNIQUES

Guidelines

General

> One person should be placed in charge of specific areas, for example:
>
>> Project Manager: Overall Project Requirements
>>
>> Chief System Engineer: Technical Requirements and Technical Baseline
>>
>> Business Manager: Contracts and Business Baseline
>
> Approved documents must be readily accessible. This is best accomplished by establishing a Project Information Center with a responsible information manager. This subject is addressed in the section on Visibility.

Technical

> One person must control each task
>
> There must be a controlled work release system
>
> There must be an audit for compliance with Project Requirements
>
> Deviations must be negotiated with the project manager

Cost

> Team leaders must control their budget
>
> Deviations must be negotiated with the project manager

Schedule

> All team leaders must sign off on integrated schedule and Project Work Authorizing Agreements
>
> Deviations must be negotiated with the project manager

Contract Control The buyer controls the seller through standards set by contract types and incentives:

Type:	*Application:*
Fixed price	Reliable prior cost experience
Cost reimbursement	Research or development with advancing technology
Cost sharing	Seller shares cost in return for use of technology
Time and material	Not possible to estimate the task beforehand
Labor hour	Like time and material, but labor only
Indefinite quantity	Establishes price of deliverable when quantity and schedule are uncertain
Letter	Limited project start without completed negotiations

Data Control A Data Manager should be designated to control all supplier contract data and supplier-approved baseline data. Typical tools include a Project Library and a computer-based document management system.

Self-Control Operates at the most personal level. This kind of control is infectious.

"Setting a good example" includes:

Being on time to work and to meetings.

Demonstrating high personal standards.

Reacting appropriately to stress.

and controlling the pen by:

Authoring strawman documents.

Proposing agendas.

Recording action items.

Reviewing and signing letters.

Management by Objectives Can be a supplement, or in some cases a substitute for, the Project Work Authorizing Agreements (PWAA) introduced earlier as planning techniques.

Conversely, managing with definitive PWAAs can be thought of as MBO in its most effective form. In either approach, the corporate accounting system must provide cost accounting down to the task level in order to measure cost performance against the PWAA/MBO commitment and to provide early, in-process warning of potential problems.

In the absence of a WBS/PWAA system, a rigorous MBO system can accomplish many of their control functions. MBO is also a useful supplement to WBS/PWAA at a more detailed and shorter range, that is, the level of detail associated with monthly schedules and/or the first and second levels of the organization.

Many companies and government organizations have developed comprehensive MBO systems. Among their primary benefits, MBOs align individual contributions with the broadening objectives at each level of the organizational hierarchy, starting with the top strategic goals. In that environment, project teams can benefit substantially by using the same MBO structure to align project team goals with functional unit goals and with individual team member goals as well.

For an MBO system to be effective and self-motivating for the user, objectives need to be thoroughly documented (typically on a quarterly schedule) and reviewed/revised regularly (usually weekly) and in detail. An effective system is characterized by objectives that are:

- Specific, clear and unambiguous.
- Realistic, measurable, and verifiable.
- Consistent with available resources.
- Consistent with company policies.

The best results are usually obtained by starting at the top levels. Every manager and all individual contributors draft their own objectives to fit with the level above while adding more detail and assumptions to represent their specific contributions. Each objective needs to include assumptions, measurement means, and verification methods. Joint commitments should be negotiated among the parties to arrive at identical objective statements. Team

Because of the time invested and the impression given of having working controls, a loosely constructed MBO system is worse than none at all.

objectives are best negotiated with the team leader in a joint session resulting in consensus.

CONFIGURATION MANAGEMENT AND CHANGE CONTROL

As illustrated in Figure 7.45, Configuration Management is used to maintain the project baselines after their approval. A vital element of Configuration management, the Change Control Board (CCB), controls changes to the baselines, viewing them as an integrated whole. Configuration management recognizes the inevitability of changes in the configuration of hardware and software. It assures that changes are adequately accounted for as they reverberate through the baselines, impacting technical performance, budgets, schedules, etc. Each time the project successfully passes a major milestone (a point of consensus among seller and buyer—a control gate), the approved baselines which result are subject to formal control.

Change control is intended to manage changes—not to prevent them.

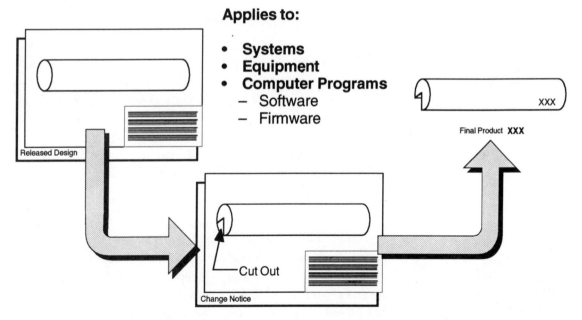

FIGURE 7.45   Configuration management.

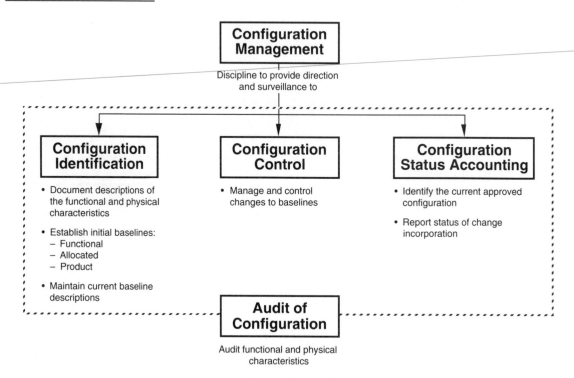

FIGURE 7.46   Key elements of configuration management.

The purpose of Configuration Management (Figure 7.46) is to control the physical and functional characteristics of the elements of a system to ensure that total system integrity is maintained through:

- Identification of physical and functional characteristics.
- Control of changes.
- Identification and reporting of changes.

The change process usually begins with an Engineering Change Request (ECR) which documents the scope of the change including the budget and schedule impact. The ECR precipitates a Change Control Board (CCB) review (Figure 7.47). The participants include the managers of each affected organization. The project manager chairs the CCB and is responsible for ensuring that:

- The decision is informed and objective.
- Each change is logged for traceability to the work package level of the WBS.
- All affected parties are notified of baseline changes.
- Upper management and the customer are officially informed of all baseline changes.

The CCB Agenda needs to include the following issues which must be thoroughly understood before an informed decision can be made.

Usually the impact on people is the trickiest to assess objectively. For this reason, the customer impact and customer position are two different items.

- The details of the change and the need for it.
- What is the impact of the change on the: performance, design, cost, schedule, support equipment, spares, contract, customer, project team?
- What is the impact of making the change versus *not* making the change?
- What is the change effectivity (e.g., date, versions and units to be modified)?
- What documentation is affected by the change?
- What is the customer's position?

The project manager needs to factor the customer's situation into the decision process. Likewise, secondary impacts on the project team need to be accounted for in schedules. For example, the disruption resulting from redesigns are often underestimated. Conversely, a substitution or alternative could relieve a source of conflict or risk and motivate the team to recover the schedule.

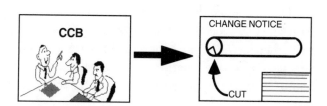

FIGURE 7.47   The change control board.

NASA, Intelsat Discuss Shuttle Rescue Of Satellite Stranded In Useless Orbit

NASA and Intelsat have begun planning a space shuttle rescue mission to either retrieve or reconfigure the $157-million Intelsat 6 spacecraft that was stranded in a useless orbit Mar. 14 by a malfunction in its Titan 3 booster.

Martin Marietta has traced the failure to a design error in the wiring associated with the separation electronics on its Commercial Titan...

When the core vehicle of the Titan's second stage shut down after a normal launch from a propulsion point of view, the vehicle's computer sent a spacecraft separation command. But the mismatch between the software and the wiring resulted in a signal being sent to the wrong wiring position, and the satellite stayed locked atop the booster.

According to Martin Marietta managers, the hardware engineers were supposed to go through a formal engineering change procedure to communicate any hardware changes to the software engineers.

"The hardware guys thought they had communicated that change to the software side of the house," a Martin Marietta official said. But the communication breakdown occurred because an established change procedure was not used, the official said.

The same communications breakdown allowed the same wiring mistake to occur on the next Titan being prepared for an Intelsat launch. That vehicle is being rewired.

— Aviation Week & Space Technology; March 26, 1990

FIGURE 7.48   Ineffective change control.

Many—in some case, all—of the PWAAs must be updated to effect a change. Recognizing that a large project generates many PWAAs, requiring a great amount of time to reissue them, it is the ounce of prevention that avoids having some people working to an incorrect project plan. That ounce often comes in the form of communication, as demonstrated by Figure 7.48. Use telephones or some other speedy method to notify all affected parties that a change is forthcoming. Many organizations are now using e-mail to perform this expediting and coordinating function of the CCB.

QUALITY CONTROLS AND TECHNIQUES

The basic quality challenge is to produce specifications that result in a product that satisfies the customer's desires.

We define "Quality" as conformance to the project's requirements. Quality is ultimately judged by the customer, not just the project manager or other provider personnel. In this case, the "customer" may be any person or organization in the complete provider-customer chain extending from those internal to the project to the intended user.

It is that final user viewpoint that determines product or service quality, that is, fitness for use. That viewpoint encompasses ease of learning, usability, serviceability, reliability, durability, and documentation effectiveness.

Traditional Quality Assurance The traditional approach to controlling quality (Figure 7.49) focuses on the results of manufacturing operations where quality is most visible. For example, product Quality Assurance consists of a separate organization that screens the product (perhaps at several points in the manufacturing process) for adherence to its specifications (Figure 7.50). The faulty material is rejected and dispositioned for scrap or rework— whichever is the least costly. Eventually, most design or process defects are recognized and addressed by a change control procedure.

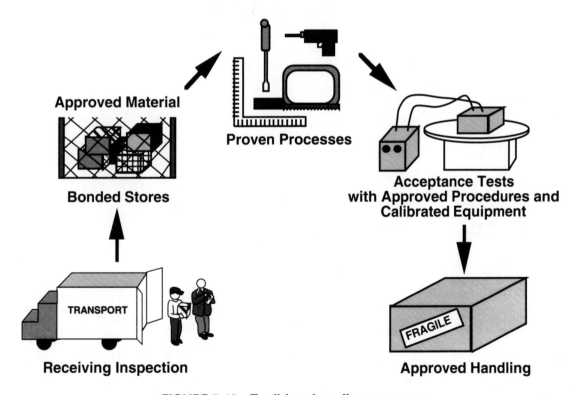

FIGURE 7.49   Traditional quality assurance.

Provisions:

**There should be a
quality organization.**

**High in the
reporting structure**

**Quality's functions
should include:**

- Quality Engineering
- Standards Control
- Process Control

- Inspection
- Audits

**There should be a
system for handling
discrepancies.**

Scrap

Rework

FIGURE 7.50   MIL-STD 9858A: A sensible standard for all industries.

A sensible standard for all industries is illustrated in Figure 7.50.

In most industries, quality is considered the top competitive success factor.

Total Quality Management (TQM) The need for improving profitability and to respond to increasing global competition in recent years has motivated both product and service industries to broaden the scope of Quality Assurance in order to reach the entire organization at all stages of the process.

Total Quality Management is:

- Required from project initiation to completion.
- Required of everyone.
- Applied to every process and transaction.

The quest for higher quality has been embodied in two closely related practices: Total Quality Management (TQM) and Continuous Quality Improvement (CQI). Total Quality Management is a concept that is founded on the following fundamentals:

1. Everything that people can do can be described as a process which can constantly be improved. This concept, known as Continuous Quality Improvement (CQI), emphasizes the process—the *system* for doing things—rather than the results themselves.

2. In order to produce satisfactory results, each individual must have clearly defined expectations.

3. The person you deliver your output to is your customer and deserves to be satisfied. Every user has the right to reject any unsatisfactory deliverable.

Most people are unaware of their own process and therefore do not consciously attempt to improve it for the customer's benefit, as well as for their own. Creating this awareness and motivation is part of the leadership responsibility of both the project manager and the system engineering manager.

Attention to TQM principles can enhance other control techniques, notably Management By Objectives (MBO). The two concepts are complementary in the sense that TQM/CQI stresses the process while MBO stresses results.

Software Quality Assurance   The Software Quality Assurance (SQA) function is responsible for auditing software development for compliance to the SQA plan. The availability of an audit trail, from automatically generated software configurations mentioned above, greatly enhances the efficiency of this audit which:

- Verifies process adequacy.
- Assures that prescribed standards, procedures, and methods are being followed.
- Alerts the project manager to deficiencies.

> To the extent that the project team is aware of and accepts these fundamentals, and conscientiously applies them:
>
> -Project output rises.
>
> -Failure rates decline.
>
> -Efficiency improves.

TECHNICAL CONTROLS AND TECHNIQUES

The following controls supplement the basic control techniques described earlier. The *major* selection criterion is the risk associated with each technical area, regardless of the proportion of project resources it represents. In general, the value of each technique below depends on the project type, the risk associated with the technologies involved, and the project complexity.

> ***Controls Unique to Software***   Software-intensive projects have historically been difficult to manage. We hear excuses like "I didn't change that section, so there's no need to test it." (invariably, "that section" fails because of a change in another section that was tested independently.) Worse yet is the assurance, "I only changed a few lines of code, so it was easy to verify manually."

An incident that received national attention in June 1991 provides a graphic example of the consequences of such "leaky" manual controls. The telephone service in Los Angeles and Pittsburgh was temporarily shut down. The reason turned out to be poor software change and verification controls. A computer programmer, not understanding the potential consequences of his action, changed a few lines of code. Since only a few lines were changed, performance verification tests required by the company policy were omitted. The thirteen changed lines of software inadvertently caused the program to generate a repetitive message saying that the system required maintenance. Soon the system was swamped with such messages, blocking all calls.

Part of the problem is the intangibility of software until the code is highly functional. Other factors include the rapid change in development tools and technology, coupled with the explosive growth in size and complexity of software products. Although details of the conventions, techniques, and controls needed to manage the design process is beyond the scope of this book, the following techniques are common to most software development projects, regardless of size.

Before development is started, choices must be made among the myriad software development environments. False starts can

Having the development environment critiqued by an expert can avoid expensive false starts.

sometimes be avoided by having this environment critiqued by an experienced expert. A Computer Resources Working Group is a name given to a panel established to judge the adequacy of the software development environment before it is implemented and at major conversions or ports.

Two major areas for improvement in software change controls are integration and automation. Integration refers to the combination of all source, executables, objects, graphics, documents, and other applications that are related. This Software Development Library is a controlled collection of software, documentation, test data, and associated tools that include global resources common to the entire project as well as product modules. By adding automatic generation capability, the development system supports the regeneration of any level or version. This level of automation is capable of facilitating an automated audit trail as well, fulfilling an important Quality Assurance audit requirement.

The Software Engineering Institute's Capability Maturity Model (CMM) can be used for internal and external evaluation of your software process, or that of a subcontractor. The CMM appraises the software process maturity of an organization at one of five distinct levels. This is discussed in more detail in Chapter 8.

Design Controls and Design Drawing Controls   Design drawings can best be formally controlled through a subprocess of baseline controls whereby all affected disciplines approve initial releases and design changes. It is also vital that affected disciplines be involved in the design process itself. Known as concurrent engineering, this process was discussed in the section on the Project Team.

Design controls occur at several organizational levels with commensurate formality. Technical supervision overviews and audits provide the most flexible and informal control. Supervisors, being familiar with the designer and the design work on a daily basis, can adjust review depth and frequency to match the situation. Other informal reviews are discussed next. Formal design reviews are addressed in the section on Control Gates.

We strongly recommend peer review on even short memos.

Peer reviews vary in rate and formality, from informal walk-throughs and chalk talks, to formal peer group presentations. With planning and preparation, peer reviews can be highly effective. They provide the additional benefit of cross training.

Expert reviews usually draw on experts outside the project—often outside the organization. They occur less frequently than peer reviews but in greater depth. They demand heavy preparation on the part of both reviewers and presenters. The customer may also conduct expert reviews—usually required by government contracts.

THE CONDUCT AND RESOLUTION OF CONTROL GATE REVIEWS

We defined Control Gates in Chapter 6 and discussed their role in managing the project cycle. Their primary control objective is to ensure that the project team has completed all scheduled activities so as to avoid progressing to an activity for which the team is unprepared.

The conduct of control gate reviews should lead to confidence in the project's progress by being:

Honest	Constructive in challenges
Open and interactive	Mutually beneficial
Helpful and supportive	Synergistic

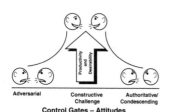

Control Gates – Attitudes

The method of resolution should be an explicit part of each control gate's definition and should identify the:

Purpose of the control gate	Agenda and how to be conducted
Host and chairperson	Evidence that is evaluated
Attendees	Actions
Place	Closure method

The control gate decision options are:

- *Acceptable*—proceed with project.
- *Acceptable with reservations*—proceed and respond to identified action items.

- *Unacceptable*—do not proceed; repeat the review.
- *Unsalvageable*—terminate the project.

Upon successful completion of a control gate review, the appropriate agreements (usually in the form of a document—a product of a project cycle phase) will be put under configuration control.

7. PROJECT VISIBILITY

Not only is there but one way of doing things rightly, but there is only one way of seeing them, and that is, seeing the whole of them.

John Ruskin,
The Two Paths

The lack of total visibility is obscurity, referred to by Robert A. Heinlein as the "refuge of incompetence" and by Vauve-Nargues as the "realm of error." In the project environment it is both, and consequently, a major cause of project failure.

Project visibility as diagrammed in Figure 7.51 is the means by which project personnel and management are made aware of project activity to facilitate timely statusing and effective corrective action. While its main purpose is to lead directly to reactive management, good visibility also supports proactive management. Visibility objectives are to:

Project Visibility is *how* you and your team know what's going on.

- Determine activity:
  —Planned tasks.
  —Unplanned tasks.
  —Work habits.
  —Control process.
- Communicate.
- Verify status.
- Determine and influence morale and team spirit.

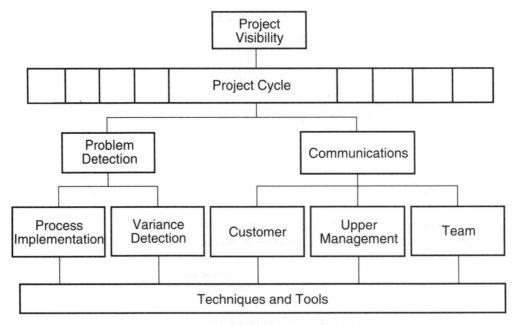

FIGURE 7.51   Project visibility decomposition.

Project visibility is the implementation of information gathering techniques such as:

Meetings	Glance Management
Reports	Project Information Center
Tiger Teams	Top-Ten Problem List.

These techniques are driven by the timing, critical need, and geographic location of the required data. They change as the project progresses through the project cycle.

GLANCE MANAGEMENT

Glance Management encompasses Management-By-Walking-Around (MBWA) and other informal techniques used for follow-up and daily awareness by an appropriate project member, particularly the project manager, chief system engineer, or specialists. We chose the name to reflect a major visibility lesson learned. Far too many project failures from fatal problems or omissions could have been detected by a follow-up "glance" by the cognizant supervisor or expert. Small, yet critical, details or delegated tasks are particularly vulnerable. They are rarely subjected to formal review—except as a part of a larger unit—which may obscure subtle deficiencies and delay their visibility to a much later event.

Glance management involves periodic sampling of work in progress by:

- Casual questions about a project detail . . . perhaps in a chance hallway meeting or in the parking lot.
- Engaging in conversations before or after meetings, or at group functions.
- Skip-level meetings—sitting in on a lower level meeting.
- Quick scans of FYI copies of routine correspondence for key phrases.
- Maintaining a reputation for an open door and an open mind.
- MBWA—walking through the project area and actively observing.

Management-by-Walking-Around is an important leadership and team building technique as well as a visibility technique. Even though its primary purpose is to improve visibility, it is useful for assessing morale and for obtaining general information. The MBWA method consists of stopping to talk while taking different routes through the project area. To promote openness, it is important to give direct answers to any questions that may be asked and to encourage follow-up. But be sure to diffuse political situations and to avoid immediate problem solutions. Be careful not to usurp the authority you have delegated to those supporting you. Here are some MBWA guidelines and protocol:

- Go where the action is.
- See and be seen.
- Talk to your project personnel.

- Make plant tours—your own facility and contractor/ subcontractor facilities.
- Observe, but do not direct.
- Be careful how you use the information gathered.
- Verify status—spot check details and look for evidence of work in progress (drawings completed, software in test, parts machined).
- Use this opportunity for team building:
  —Show interest and ask people to tell you what they are doing.
  —Confirm that team members understand their part in the process.

MBWA can be especially effective when two or three work shifts are operating. The second and third shifts often feel left out of the mainstream: "Hardly anybody from day shift ever comes in." On one such project, the project manager and marketing manager, separately, made periodic visits to the work areas during second and third shift. They were surprised by the number of valuable inputs they received. Even more surprising was the general morale improvement that even carried over to the day shift.

All glance management techniques share a common risk— giving the impression of invasive scrutiny. Everyone dislikes being interrogated or watched too closely. This is where leadership techniques come in to play. Glance management, especially MBWA, works best when visibility is both ways—when it includes recognition, praise, and casual advice—as well as questions.

THE PROJECT INFORMATION CENTER

A visibility system should include a project information center—a dedicated area that displays the current status of all project activities against the plan (Figure 7.52). The use of a name like Short Cycle Room conveys its own message and is a constant reminder to project personnel of the importance of schedule.

FIGURE 7.52 A dedicated project information center.

The main benefactors of the information center are project personnel with schedule and budget responsibility and/or interest. All users benefit from this total visibility at a glance. It also provides a means for making the project more visible to stakeholders and others who may miss, or not be included in, scheduled meetings. By posting notices and selected correspondence, the observer can quickly scan for pertinent new information.

An alternative implementation method is by use of electronic mail (e-mail). An e-mail system can include elaborate means for searching and screening subject matter for personalized categories. However, it lacks the opportunity for motivation, interaction, and cheerleading provided by a dedicated physical area. The project information center is an ideal location for all-hands and project managers reviews. On small projects, it can be the project manager's office or a conference room.

> Beware of stale data! The information center must be kept current, otherwise it is of little or even negative value.

TIGER TEAMS TROUBLESHOOT PROBLEM AREAS

To maximize chances for success, the project team must be educated by the project manager on the purpose, methods, and expected use of Tiger Teams.

Tiger Teams are focused on specific areas of concern. Usually composed of technical experts and/or experienced troubleshooters, their purpose is to objectively identify the problem sources and to recommend solutions. While anybody can suggest the need for a Tiger Team, they are usually initiated by the project manager, upper management, customer, or functional managers.

Areas of Concern:

    Design approach

    Interface compatibility

    Software approach

    Schedule approach

    Failure history

    Management techniques

    Quality performance

    Any other major project issue

Participants

Tiger team members should be experts and "quick studies."

Project personnel and invited experts with a demonstrated ability to accumulate the facts rapidly, objectively evaluate the status and impartially report their findings. Participants may include:

        Seller and/or buyer personnel

        Outside consultants

        Customer experts

Benefits

        Objective visibility on an area of concern

        Focused approach to improve performance

        Third party assistance in securing increased resources

        Tiger team follow-up on success of recommendations

Precautions

- Expected non-adversarial use of tiger teams should be publicized by project management at the outset and during the course of the project.
- Tiger teams must operate in a team (not adversary) relationship with the project.
- Tiger teams must have "free rein."
- Project manager must stay aware and support both project and tiger team personnel.

Tiger teams are for fixing problems, NOT for fixing blame (fixing the blame doesn't fix anything).

MEETINGS—THE PROJECT MANAGER'S DILEMMA

A rich variety of meeting formats can be effective, but it does complicate the management task. You need to select the best format and implement it well. For meetings to be effective, they must serve a specific, well-defined purpose. Too many meetings, or poorly conceived or poorly executed ones, can be a major demotivator. When considering whether or not to hold a meeting, ask yourself:

Some informational objectives can be handled better through other visibility techniques or tools, such as informal discussion, a telephone call, or a memo.

- What is the objective of the meeting?
- Is there a better way to achieve the objective?
- Is this meeting really necessary?
- What would be the consequences of not holding it?

Whether one-on-one or involving the entire project, meetings are the manager's major technique for orchestration, gathering, and disseminating information. As such they can easily consume 40% to 60% of a project manager's time. Meetings are the major vehicle for performing many management roles:

Informational	Interpersonal	Decisional
Gathering	Motivating	Investigating
Disseminating	Inspiring	Consensus making
Clarifying	Praising	Evaluating
Training	Committing	Decision making

We will return to the interpersonal and decisional meeting aspects in the section on Leadership, along with the "how" to ensure meeting productivity. In the meantime, here's a summary of recommended conduct:

- Distribute an agenda well before the meeting.
- Invite only those required.
- State the purpose of the meeting and stick to it:
  —Exchange information.
  —Determine status.
  —Solve a problem.
  —Make a decision.
- Start on time—don't wait for late people.
- Keep the meeting on track and control the progress.
- Summarize the results and assign action items.
- Follow-up on action items.
- Ensure that other meetings are summarized.

Informational Meetings   An informational meeting is the opportunity to update the team's collective knowledge and to inform other stakeholders. This knowledge includes perceptions

---

Douglas Speeds MD-11 Production With New Management System

The Douglas Aircraft Co. expects to be producing the MD-11 transport at a rate of one aircraft per week by the end of this month, with the aid of an aggressive new production management system for the trijet program.

The highly structured system, which emphasizes strict accountability through detailed planning and daily oversight, has decreased the production span time for the MD-11 from 400 to 260 days, according to program officials....

DAILY REPORTING—Six days a week, supervisors report to their production and engineering, quality and parts managers between 6–8 a.m. on a range of subjects, such as what they plan to accomplish that day, issues to be resolved and the critical paths that must receive priority attention on each aircraft.

At 8 a.m., those managers relay that information in 10 simultaneous meetings to their general managers. They each have five production managers and three managers for engineering, quality and parts reporting to them. The 10 general managers, in turn, meet with Jack Hayden, the MD-11 program Douglas vice president responsible for trijet production operations, at 9:30—when requirements are set—and again at 4 p.m. to recap the day's work....

— *Aviation Week and Space Technology, September 16, 1991*

FIGURE 7.53   "Just-in-time" information.

and experiences as well as facts. As with traditional staff meetings, a series of smaller, nested meetings such as those reported in Figure 7.53 can be effective in matching the information range and depth of detail to the particular group. Examples of informational meetings are:

Type	Frequency	Typical Duration
News Flash	daily	10 to 15 minutes
All-hands	as required	several minutes to 20 minutes
One-on-One	weekly	one hour
Plan Violators	weekly	less than 30 minutes
Project Manager's Review	weekly	two hours
Executive Review	monthly or quarterly	one to two hours
Customer Review	monthly	varies widely

News Flash Meetings   News flash meetings are used to maintain a high profile for fast-moving developments and critical issues. Problems requiring immediate follow-up can be scheduled for a separate review or one-on-one meeting. News flash meetings work best with a small group—usually the direct reports to the project manager or a separate task group. Some managers prefer that all participants remain standing throughout to instill urgency and discourage long-winded discussions. Others prefer to assign seats, making it easier to know who, or what organizations, are unrepresented.

News flash meetings are most effective when conducted daily at the start of each shift or a few minutes before the lunch break.

All-Hands Meetings   All-hands meetings involve a larger group—usually the entire project team. Attendance by key personnel is mandatory. They are typically convened to announce a major development such as a new contract or a technical breakthrough. They offer a good opportunity for team building.

One-on-One Meetings   One-on-one meetings should be held weekly by every supervisor with each direct report to exchange information and deal with personal issues. They are most effective when limited to one hour. Therefore, the employee needs to prepare a priority list to ensure that the high priority items get addressed before the hour is over.

Plan Violator Meetings   Plan violator meetings are held to gain visibility and determine corrective action. They are attended by the managers that, for the prior week, are off their schedule, headcount, or budget plan. Upon the first violation of the plan for a manager, the cause and proposed recovery are reviewed. Subsequent meetings update the recovery process. The business manager sets the threshold for a violation. The major benefits are:

- Forces task managers to pay attention to the plan.
- Provides review of previous week's headcount and schedule performance immediately following completion of work week.
- Provides for rapid response to new problems.
- Keeps budget and schedule plans current.
- Keeps management knowledgeable.
- Lets support management know that you are watching and that you really care.

Project Manager's Weekly Review   The Project Manager's Weekly Review meeting extends beyond visibility to active statusing and corrective action. It involves all key project and functional support personnel. This meeting should be open to executive management as well as customer personnel. The agenda includes a thorough review of the status of the total project to surface conflict, areas of inaction, items awaiting disposition, and areas requiring special attention. The results include decisive actions by project management. The benefits include:

- Overall view of the project.
- Forum for organizational interaction to resolve project issues.
- Insight for support managers into project needs.

Headcount deviation is often the earliest indicator of a more serious problem.

- Visibility into top project issues, concerns, and problems for all key participants.

Executive Management Review   The Executive Management Review is to provide upper management visibility into the status of the project. It usually consists of a presentation by the project management on the overall health of the project. The format emphasizes accomplishments, particularly regarding contract requirements, and the efficient use of resources. This review is the opportunity for the project manager to alert executive management to bad news, potential risks, contingency plans, or corrective action and any additional resources required.

Customer Review   The purpose of the Customer Review is to provide the customer an opportunity for constructive challenge of the progress against plan. This applies equally well to government contracts or to internal customers—namely, marketing. This review can be avoided altogether, or reduced in content, by including the customer in the weekly Project Manager's Review. As with the Executive Review, key project team members presents status against plan, analysis and recovery actions for problems, and seek concurrence from the customer. Well-run projects routinely generate the type of data needed for this meeting, in which case little new material needs to be prepared for this review.

TECHNIQUES FOR ENHANCING VISIBILITY

Top-Ten Problem List   The Top-Ten Problem List heightens the visibility of the most important concerns expressed by the customer, project manager, functional managers, and task managers. These problems need to be coded as:

> Publicize names of Top-Ten problem owners. It will help them get the priority they need.

- Minor—I'm in control.
- Major—I need help.
- Showstopper—emergency action required.

All problems on the Top-Ten list need to be statused daily by the responsible individual. The list is initiated by the group leaders to the project manager and propagates upward. The project manager's list should include majors and showstoppers that reach his level as well as pertinent items from the customer's list.

Use the Walls   Use the walls for documentation review (RFP, proposals, user manuals, etc.) or design drawings. Use color paper to indicate maturity (e.g., white for first draft, yellow for second, blue for third). This technique has several benefits:

- Entire team has visibility.
- Helps identify inconsistencies, overlap, etc.
- Highlights missing sections.
- Vividly illustrates document maturity.

Project Coordinators   Project Coordinators augment the project manager's visibility for larger projects. A coordinator is chartered as a representative of the project manager that proactively ensures future events will occur as planned. They signal problem areas and recommend solutions. Project Coordinators:

- Know how the organization "works."
- Provide expediting help to project and support organizations.
- Provide independent assessment of project information and status to the project manager.
- Ensure planning and milestones are satisfied.
- Ensure control procedures are being adhered to.

Customer Inplant Representatives   Customer inplant representatives provide two-way visibility because they:

- Understand customer expectations, needs, and capabilities.
- Provide continuous visibility into supplier and subcontractor activity and status.

The latter is accomplished by attending all inplant visibility meetings and by other techniques. The techniques of glance management are particularly pertinent to customer visibility. An inplant representative can address items that require guidance from the customer by immediately notifying customer personnel. A secondary benefit of having an inplant representative is for escorting and debriefing project visitors and their contacts.

TWENTY-FIRST CENTURY VISIBILITY TOOLS

Visibility tools include traditional devices and services such as:

Telephone	Cellular phone
Teleconferencing	Video conferencing
Electronic Mail	Fax
Courier services	Mail

The personal computer, together with local, wide-area networks, and the Internet have grown into powerful visibility tools.

WHEN DESIGNING YOUR VISIBILITY SYSTEM . . .

Keep an open door and an open mind. The concept of visibility cannot coexist with significant secrecy, avoidance, or exclusion. Yet these can take root and grow—particularly in the absence of strong leadership. The project manager needs to set an example by being open and willing to seek and accept expert advice, as well as bad news.

> Visibility is only the beginning. The visibility system needs to lead to somewhere. It must facilitate statusing and timely corrective action.

Avoid information overload. While it is better to be over-informed rather than under-informed, carried to the extreme, too much information causes overload and missed details.

Be selective. A visibility system can incorporate many techniques and tools. You need to determine the timing, critical need, and geographic location of the required data before selecting and implementing the techniques you will use. These factors, and therefore the techniques, will generally change as the project progresses through its stages. It is important to carefully select the most cost-effective techniques and tools that get the job done.

Too many meetings, for example, or proliferating devices, have a way of becoming ends in themselves.

8. PROJECT STATUS

Nothing is good or bad but by comparison.

Thomas Fuller,
Gnomologia

STATUS IS MEASUREMENT AGAINST THE PLAN

Statusing must accurately reflect reality against the plan—not how busy the project is.

Project Statusing is the timely and comprehensive measurement of project progress against the plan to determine the potential seriousness of any variances left uncorrected. The main objective is to identify variances that require corrective action in order to recover to plan. To initiate the most suitable corrective action quickly when deviations occur, the measurements must be:

- Relevant.
- Timely.
- Accurate.
- Comprehensive.
- Compared to the plan.

In practice, many "status" reports merely recount activity, in which the intensity of the work reported is confused with progress.

Project activity without comparison to the plan may well be irrelevant, or even diversionary, to determining the need for corrective action. For example, the project manager may proclaim the team's long work hours and describe their dedicated efforts—even detailed work activities. Such reporting is "tracking" the project, often confused with statusing. It contributes to the major weakness in many statusing systems—information overload. An effective statusing process:

- Collects essential information only—matched to project complexity.
- Measures primary variables that impact results.

- Tailors information to the needs of the team members interpreting it.

Status should be continuously known by task managers and their management—by all levels of project management. Anyone else that can affect project success, such as customers, subcontractors, and vendors, should be statused at the appropriate events or intervals.

STATUS MEANS SCHEDULE, TECHNICAL, COST, AND BUSINESS—COMBINED

Schedule, Technical, Cost, and Business factors should be evaluated together. The following lists are representative of the key metrics to be included for each of the four factors:

> Conducting independent cost reviews is meaningless and can even be counterproductive.

Schedule	*Technical*
Progress summary	Development results
Master Schedule	Design release
Milestone accomplishments	Technical review (closure on action items)
Earned value	
Assemblies and modules	Technical Performance Measurements
Tasks	Interface control
Subcontractors	Quality
Parts and material	Design change rate

Cost	*Business*
Actuals versus budget	Contract change process
Headcount	Actions to/from customers
Earned value vs. expenditures	Actions to/from management
Burn rate and overtime ratio	Actions to/from contractors
Estimate to completion	Funding
Estimate at completion	Top-ten problems
Profit	Security clearances
Dispersion ratio°	Project manager's assessment

°Dispersion ratio refers to the number of individuals charging to the project divided by equivalent full-time people.

	Project Manager	Customer	Executive
General announcements	✓	✓	✓
Awards	✓		✓
Past and future meetings	✓	✓	✓
Organization (optional)		✓	✓
System concept overview (optional)		✓	✓
Action items from the customer	✓	✓	✓
Action items from upper management	✓		✓
Internal project action items	✓		
Master schedule with dateline and status	✓	✓	✓
Project milestone status	✓	✓	✓
Major accomplishments since last review	✓	✓	✓
Major customer-directed change status	✓	✓	✓
Engineering change request status	✓	✓	✓
Items awaiting customer disposition	✓	✓	✓
Top ten problem review	✓	✓	✓
Interface control action item status	✓	✓	✓
System engineering detailed status	✓	✓	
Technical Performance Measurement status	✓	✓	✓
Engineering release status	✓	✓	✓
Subsystem detailed status	✓	✓	
—component by component status			
—milestones accomplished vs. plan			
—funds expended versus plan			
Contractor/Subcontractor technical status	✓	✓	✓
Contractor/Subcontractor key milestones	✓	✓	✓
Contractor/Subcontractor detailed status by item	✓		
—Budget, EAC, Variance			
Top level cost performance vs. budget	✓	✓	✓
Financial status—top level	✓	✓	✓
—Budget, EAC, Variance			
Plan for handling the reported variances		✓	✓
Manpower status vs. plan—top level	✓	✓	✓
Funding status		✓	✓
Management reserve			✓
Profit analysis		if internal	✓
Summary of new action items	✓	✓	✓
Key milestones for next 6 months	✓	✓	✓
Calendar of planned meetings	✓	✓	✓
Future business opportunities	✓	if internal	✓
Project manager's assessment		✓	✓
Customer's closing comments		✓	

FIGURE 7.54 Typical status agenda checklist.

CONDUCTING THE MAJOR REVIEWS

This section addresses the details of format and agenda for the three reviews that facilitate the bulk of reactive management decisions. Detailed statusing does occur in smaller meetings—even one-on-ones—where corrective actions are sometimes decided. However the Project Manager's Review is the best opportunity for all relevant stones to be overturned and assumptions to be challenged. The Executive and Customer Reviews have two purposes: to aid visibility and provide a forum for corrective actions that need higher level or customer concurrence. Figure 7.54 provides a checklist for conducting these meetings.

The typical symbols used for operating schedule status are shown in Figure 7.55.

The three major reviews represent a significant expenditure of team time and effort. They should be working meetings and avoid wasting time, particularly the rehashing of carefully rehearsed scenarios.

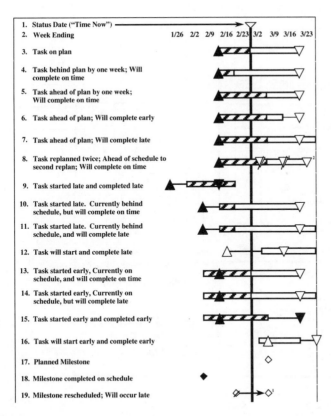

FIGURE 7.55 Typical symbols for reporting schedule status.

STATUSING IS IDENTIFYING VARIANCES

The quantity of milestones can be used as a schedule performance metric (Figure 7.56). The Milestone Deficiency Report (Figure 7.57) should include an Estimated Completion Date (ECD) and a recommended corrective action for each milestone that is past due. This way of highlighting exceptions, problems, and actions is very effective for most status measurements.

The Configuration Item Status Report (Figure 7.58) demonstrates the utility of pulling together and focusing on the tasks related to each deliverable. Again, statusing consists of reporting exceptions and actions, not activities.

Material shortages represent another critical item to status, shown here as a summary only. A separate sheet should be devoted to each problem that needs to be detailed (Figure 7.59). This should include a recap of prior progress on the previously defined corrective actions.

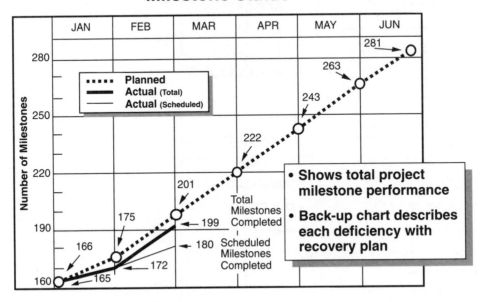

FIGURE 7.56   Milestone status report.

Milestone Deficiencies

Date Due	Project	M.S. No.	M.S. Title	Responsible	ECD	Plan
26 June	AJAX	SE-011	Release of Sys/ Segment Design Document	R. Smith	3 Aug	Revisit trade studies per action item 1072
27 June	AJAX	SE-012	Interface Spec.	H. James	10 Jul	Close TBDs from Associate

FIGURE 7.57   Milestone Deficiency Report.

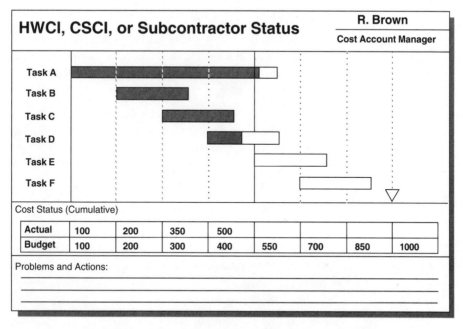

FIGURE 7.58   Configuration Item Status Report.

Part Number	Part Type	Quantity	Vendor	Next Assembly	Need Date	Prom Date	Resp. Individ.	Action
103-231	Elect.	42	Viking	1040	26 Sep	10 Oct	Fred H.	Visit vendor factory to pick up parts in person; daily phone calls to verify progress of tab and test of parts
621-040	Firm-ware	1	S/W Creations	7131	26 Sep	15 Oct	Jenny C.	Firmware coding requirements clarification to be delivered to vendor by 10 Sept. Check out tests to be witnessed by our QA and engineering at vendor facility.

The last part in paces the project.

FIGURE 7.59   Material shortage list.

Before we cover several comprehensive metrics for statusing project cost, we will look at a simple headcount cost indicator for payroll-intensive projects (Figure 7.60). As with other areas, there are several formats and metrics for statusing headcount. Typical parameters include part-time headcount ratios, on-loan, and specific skill levels.

In this example, the project manager can use Total and Experienced headcount metrics to anticipate efficiency, cost, and schedule problems, because:

- Total personnel are exceeding plan.
- Experienced personnel are under plan.

With these expectations, the project manager needs to rebalance personnel through the functional managers and/or experienced contract resources.

The Top-Ten Problem Summary (Figure 7.61) offers a means to highlight major problems which may result from a combination of factors. The summary should include the estimated

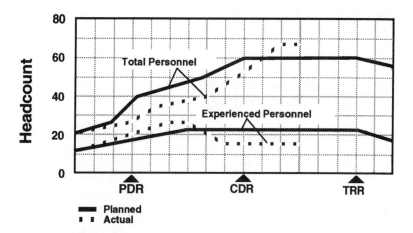

FIGURE 7.60   Headcount variance report.

Top Ten Problem Summary

No.	Problem Identification	Description	ECD	No. Weeks on list	Action/ Responsibility
71.	Update Project Products List (PPL)	Incorporate the changes from Rev A drawing release into the PPL	~~6/17,~~ ~~6/29,~~ ~~7/3,~~ 8/4	4	Frank A.
84.	Compatibility of SW with Rev A mechanical design	Ensure that software control system functions properly with Rev A mechanical modifications	8/1	1	Rich B.

Detail Chart for each problem

FIGURE 7.61   Top ten problem summary.

completion date (ECD), the number of weeks on the list, and identify who is responsible for each action.

PERFORMANCE MEASUREMENT SYSTEMS QUANTIFY THE SERIOUSNESS OF THE VARIANCES

The poor carpenter blames his tools . . . and waits too long to fix them. Meaningful statusing depends on accurate and complete information.

Garbage in—Garbage out. Meaningful statusing depends on good planning. Poorly planned projects simply cannot be statused.

Performance Measurement Systems quantify the problems you should have known about and acted on much earlier. Performance measurement systems vary widely, depending on the organization's management information system and the tools and techniques available to the project. In rapid growth years, many companies—especially technology startups—use very crude, informal systems. Figure 7.62 illustrates a cost status chart that fails to provide enough detail to decide on a corrective action.

As competition increases and profit margins shrink, most organizations recognize the need to refine their performance measurements. Successful companies today use a system similar in framework to the one we describe here. This type of system

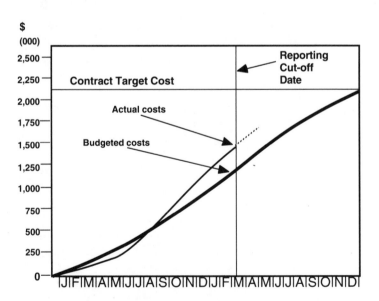

FIGURE 7.62   Superfical cost status.

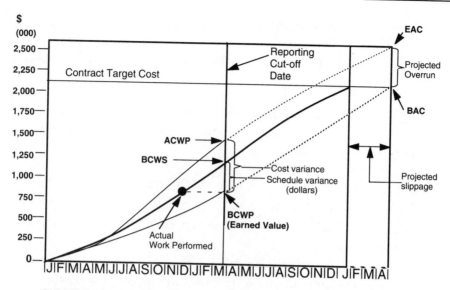

FIGURE 7.63 Performance measurement system elements.

requires detailed planning to establish and maintain. The insight provided is worth the effort, if the data are constructively used. In our experience, they've proved their value on projects with a budget as small as $200K.

The performance measurement system elements shown in Figure 7.63 are defined as:

BCWS	Budgeted Cost of Work Scheduled	The planned budget for the scheduled tasks.
BCWP	Budgeted Cost of Work Performed	The planned budget for the tasks that were actually completed. This is also referred to as the Earned Value.
ACWP	Actual Cost of Work Performed	Actual costs of performing the completed tasks.
BAC	Budget At Completion	The planned budget (a management reserve is often subtracted from the contracted or committed funding to arrive at a project budget).

EAC	Estimate At Completion.	Estimated total cost upon completion
ETC	Estimate To Complete.	Estimated remaining costs to completion

Cost and Schedule variances can both be expressed as dollars or percentage. Using the definitions below, negative indicates an overrun.

	In Dollars	*In Percent*
Cost variance	BCWP—ACWP	(BCWP—ACWP)/BCWP $\times$ 100
Schedule variance	BCWP—BCWS	(BCWP—BCWS)/BCWS $\times$ 100

Estimating the cost of the completed the project can be done in one of several ways, depending on the situation at the time the estimates are made. The alternative methods for ETC (Estimate To Complete) and EAC (Estimate At Completion) are:

Performance projections

Managerial judgment

Bottom up (grass roots)

Statistical projections

Performance projections assume that performance will continue at the same rate:

$$ETC = (BAC\text{-}BCWP) \times (ACWP/BCWP)$$

$$EAC = ACWP + ETC$$

Managerial projections for ETC are a matter of judgment. Typical methods are:

- Original plan to go (if original plan is valid).
- Burn rate multiplied by the estimated time to complete (if these factors are reliable).

- (Burn rate multiplied by schedule slip) plus the original plan roll-off.

- Performance factor multiplied by the original plan to go (if efficiency rate will continue).

- New bottom-up quote (scrubbed) (if above assumptions are invalid).

- The EAC (Estimate At Completion) is determined by adding the ETC to ACWP (Actual Cost of Work Performed).

There are several negotiable options for measuring work progress, expressed as the Earned Value (BCWP) by task. Four common definitions are listed below:

Option	Amount of Task BCWP (earned value)
0–100	Zero until task completion (For this method, Work Packages should be less than 200 hours.)
50–50	One-half of Task BAC at start; final one-half is earned at completion.
Percentage	Percentage of Task BAC based on interim milestones or task leader's estimate. (BCWP at completion = Task BAC) (For this method Work Packages should be less than 600 hours.)
Level-of-Effort	BWCP is earned as effort is expended. (BCWP = BCWS at any time) Used in labor hour contracts and services.

These examples (Figure 7.64) of using the 0–100 and Percentage Earned Value are shown here for the same three tasks. The Earned Value of the 0–100 option is distorted, since the second task is incomplete at the status date. The task Earned Value being zero makes the total look like bad news. In reality, the news is good. For the 0–100 method to be properly applied, the task authorizations should start and end within the reporting period.

The Percentage example shows a more accurate status. With this method, the data reliability depends on the task leader's ability to accurately assess status of work progress.

The 0–100 method is most effective for small work packages.

In all methods, interim milestones increase the measurement accuracy.

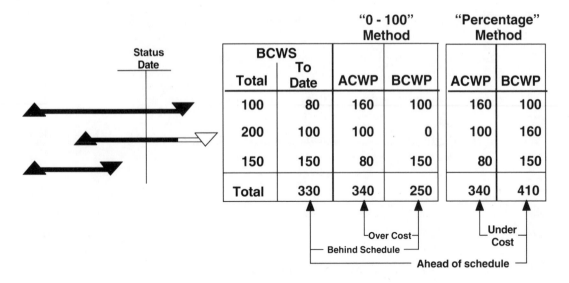

FIGURE 7.64   **The 0–100 and percentage methods compared.**

INTERPRETING THE TRENDS

In the previous sections, we selected charts that exemplify the key factors to status. These illustrations also provide a template which is adaptable to most projects. But status shouldn't be static. You need to pay careful attention to the trends, such as those in Figure 7.65, which can be leading indicators of trouble.

Two helpful indicators for trend analysis are CPI and SPI:

- CPI (Cost Performance Index) = BCWP/ACWP.
- SPI (Schedule Performance Index) = BCWP/BCWS.

These are interpreted in eight separate performance trend situations in Figure 7.66.

Timely, comprehensive project status information is important because it enables you to identify variances and quantify their seriousness. Differences between planned and actual

---

If you can't measure it, you can't manage it!

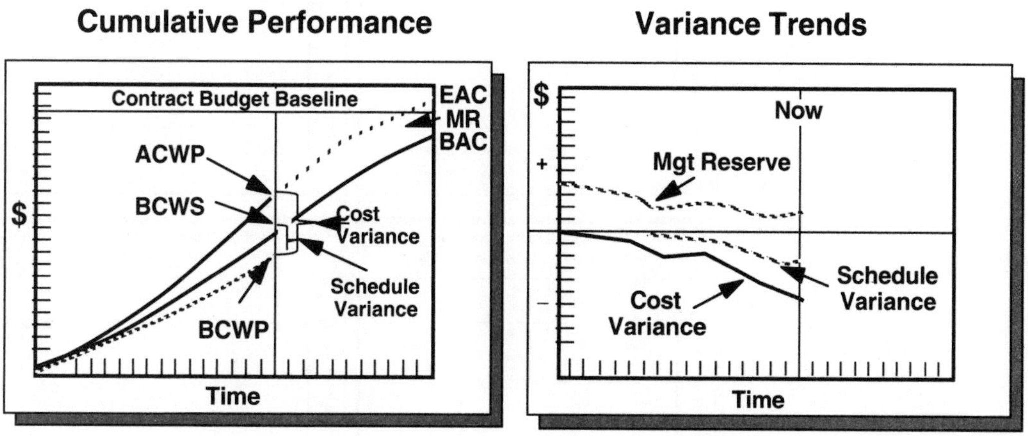

Cumulative Performance

Variance Trends

FIGURE 7.65   Trends provide leading indicators.

results need to be reviewed on at least a monthly basis for most projects. Variances that exceed predetermined thresholds should be analyzed further to determine the reasons and the actions required to improve performance and recover to plan. The thresholds depend on the specific metrics and the project. Example thresholds are:

±20% and ±$20K for the current period

±10% and ±$40K for cumulative amounts

Variance analysis reports need to be as specific as possible. The excerpt in Figure 7.67 illustrates the status for specific tasks, together with the recovery actions, the subject of the next section

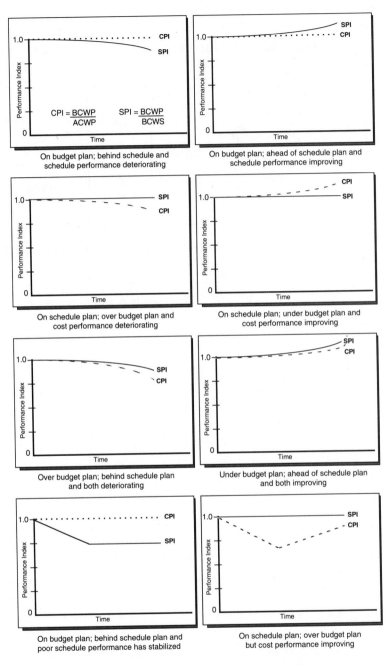

FIGURE 7.66   CPI and SPI trend analyses.

9. CORRECTIVE ACTION

> A thought which does not result in an action is nothing much, and an action which does not proceed from a thought is nothing at all.
>
> **Georges Bernanos,**
> **France Before the World of Tomorrow**

CORRECTIVE ACTIONS ARE TAKEN TO RECOVER THE PROJECT TO PLAN

Corrective Actions are the reactive management steps taken to recover the project to plan when unacceptable variances are detected (usually through statusing techniques) (Figure 7.67). Status without following through with corrective action is meaningless. Therefore, the process described in this section—deciding on corrective actions—usually takes place during statusing, or shortly thereafter.

Statusing is comparing current performance to the plan—corrective action is doing something about the difference.

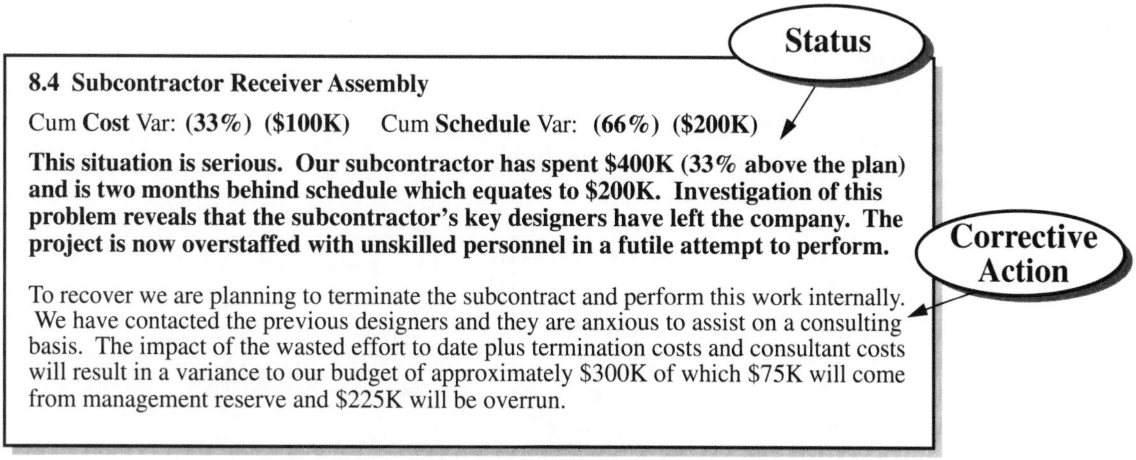

Status

8.4 Subcontractor Receiver Assembly

Cum **Cost** Var: **(33%) ($100K)**   Cum **Schedule** Var: **(66%) ($200K)**

This situation is serious. Our subcontractor has spent $400K (33% above the plan) and is two months behind schedule which equates to $200K. Investigation of this problem reveals that the subcontractor's key designers have left the company. The project is now overstaffed with unskilled personnel in a futile attempt to perform.

Corrective Action

To recover we are planning to terminate the subcontract and perform this work internally. We have contacted the previous designers and they are anxious to assist on a consulting basis. The impact of the wasted effort to date plus termination costs and consultant costs will result in a variance to our budget of approximately $300K of which $75K will come from management reserve and $225K will be overrun.

FIGURE 7.67   Status report example.

In theory, if there is a sound visibility system in place and a solid plan, the only time a project status meeting is required is when corrective action is necessary, as determined by the continuously available status system. Generally, those team members who are on plan would not attend such meetings. In practice, however, periodic status meetings with key team members are essential, even if visibility and status systems appear to be sound and the project is right on plan. Status meetings allow the team to see the project as a whole, and omissions—in project integration, for instance—can be identified and corrected early.

The effective use of reactive management must consider many of the same attributes as does an automatic control system or servomechanism (depicted in Figure 7.68):

- Fidelity   —accuracy of the status data.
- Disturbances   —surprises.
- Noise level   —rumors.
- Time lag   —timely statusing.
- Lead time   —analyze trends; predict, anticipate.
- Gain vs. stability   —too much gain can produce less than the required results.

Budget underruns may be more critical than overruns.

Corrective Action begins with variance analysis, conducted periodically, to identify significant differences (the period depends on the project and the metric). Therefore, significant differences which require analysis, need to be defined by setting trigger

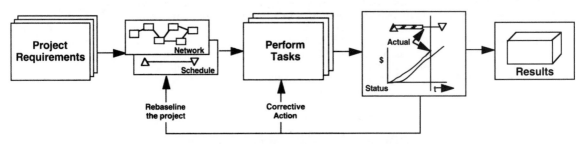

FIGURE 7.68   Corrective action closes the control loop.

thresholds. Cost thresholds should be expressed in both percentage and absolute terms—say, for example, 20 percent or $20,000 for current periods and 10 percent or $40,000 for cumulative measurements.

Schedule thresholds could vary widely, depending on the time remaining and whether the task is on the critical path, a low-slack path, or a high-slack path. One week slip is a representative threshold for a critical milestone with one-year remaining on the project.

> Repeated schedule slips require special attention, lest they become the critical path.

DETERMINING THE CORRECTIVE ACTION

The steps to corrective action are:

1. Analyze each problem:
   —The current impact.
   —The impact growth if no action is taken.
2. Prioritize project problems from the most serious to the least serious.
3. Determine the best approach using analytical decision analysis.

Before you can properly analyze the problem, you must define it—together with confirming the desire to do something about it. (It is not a problem if you don't care—it is only a situation.) The analysis needs to quantify the rate of impact growth as well as the current impact and should also identify the causes:

> Frequently, problems have several underlying causes.

- What has changed?
- Were expectations unreasonable?
- Was the plan wrong?
- Were requirements ill-defined?
- Were resources insufficient?
- Was there a lack of interest?
- Was there conflicting direction?
- Did communications breakdown?

For a corrective action to be effective, it must be: sufficiently imaginative to consider all viable options and applied decisively and vigorously.

Technical variances, as well as cost and schedule variances (Figures 7.69 and 7.70), lead to the corrective action options below.

Cost corrective actions seek to *reduce:*

- Requirements.
- Labor rates and/or hours.
- Overtime.
- Project length.

More imaginative cost options are to:

- Develop a more producible design.
- Install more efficient processes.
- Eliminate waste or superfluous tasks.
- Assign work to lower labor rate areas.

Schedule corrective actions *add:*

- Work shifts and/or overtime.
- Longer work shifts.
- Personnel.

and *improve:*

- Tools.
- Processes.

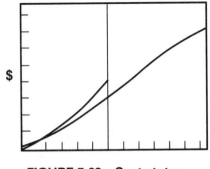

FIGURE 7.69   Cost status.

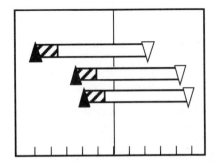

FIGURE 7.70   Schedule status.

More imaginative schedule options are to:

- Overlap tasks.
- Use more highly skilled personnel.
- Send work to high-efficiency specialty shops.

Technical corrective actions seek to resolve shortcomings:

- Use tiger team of experts.
- Challenge and narrow requirements.
- Reduce quantity.
- Add skilled talent.
- Add more capable tools.
- Improve supplier(s).
- Add training.

Business corrective actions seek to escalate, to improve the business process, and eliminate bureaucracy. They involve:

- Experts.
- Consultants.
- Executive management.
- Customer (start with one-on-one basis).

The process for evaluating alternatives, like any comprehensive decision process, may require an objective scoring system for complex trade-offs. First, establish evaluation criteria (musts and wants). Then assign relative weighting factors and score the alternatives. Figure 7.71 shows a tabular approach for scoring schedule recovery alternatives.

> Decision analysis should produce the highest value solution.

The tentative choice is usually the highest scoring alternative. However, the evaluation criteria and weighting factors, being somewhat subjective, may lead to a close or controversial decision. An effective technique is to assess the adverse consequences of implementing the tentative choice and to compare it more rigorously with the closest alternative(s). The final decision should

> It is important to conduct a sensitivity analysis for close decisions. In some cases, taking no corrective action may be the best of the alternatives.

Evaluation Criteria		Alternative 1 One 12 hr shift			Alternative 2 Two 8 hr shifts			Alternative 3 Three 8 hr shifts			Alternative 4 Two 12 hr shifts		
Musts (Go-No Go): • Certified Software Testers • Available within 3 weeks								X X					
				Score			Score			Score			Score
Wants	Weight (W)	Comments	Raw	R x W	Comments	Raw	R x W	Comments	Raw	R x W	Comments	Raw	R x W
Factors													
Maximizes productivity	10		5	50		7	70					10	100
Highly experienced in our software	8		10	80		8	64					8	64
Low average labor rate	8		7	56		10	80					5	40
Max Score (10xW) Total Score	260			186			214						204

FIGURE 7.71　Evaluating alternatives by weighted scoring.

also consider the consequences of doing nothing at all—always an alternative worth evaluating. In critical situations, it may be important to provide for a justification trail should conditions change or the decision need to be reversed.

Having conducted the decision process, two important steps remain:

1. Develop an implementation plan.

2. Get the appropriate commitments.

The project manager approves the decision and is responsible for the timely execution of the corrective action plan.

SUCCESSFULLY IMPLEMENTING CORRECTIVE ACTION

Major problems often require major actions.

The most prevalent management error in reacting to variances is that corrective action is usually applied too late and with insufficient vigor. You need to rush to ownership and be sure to do enough to solve the problem the first time:

- Problems prevented are least expensive.
- Problems solved quickly are cheaper!

The other common errors are:

- Corrective action is usually insufficiently imaginative to consider all viable options.
- The effect of labor burn rate is usually ignored.

Problems that occur during high burn rate periods are expensive (Figure 7.72). Extraordinary action may be justified to avoid runaway deviations. If too many critical path activities are in variance, or if the burn rate renders the variance irrecoverable, it may be necessary to redefine the baseline since the current plan may be unachievable. This situation may also indicate that the statusing system, itself, is inadequate.

> Paying high fees to expert consultants could be a real bargain . . . if they help avoid schedule slips during high "burn-rate" periods.

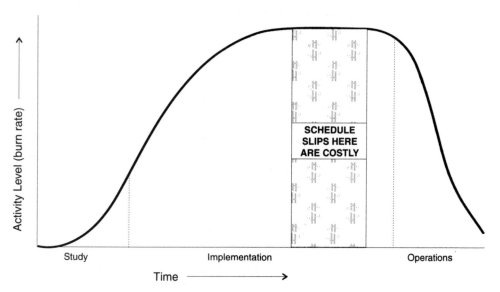

FIGURE 7.72   The high costs of schedule slips.

To ensure that all viable actions are considered:

- Identify the total problem.
- Establish and define several courses of action as strawman solutions.
- Brainstorm the problem and course of action.

Finally, to ensure that the plan is successfully implemented:

- Seek a consensus for the solution.
- Thoroughly develop the plan.
- Advertise the plan and authorize the action.
- Status and control the corrective action plan the same as the master plan.

10. PROJECT LEADERSHIP

The only way in which any one can lead us is to restore to us the belief in our own guidance.

Henry Miller,
The Wisdom of the Heart

THE ESSENCE OF LEADERSHIP

Distinct among the ten management elements, the proper exercise of leadership ensures that the other nine elements are accepted and utilized. In this section, we address the three primary aspects of project leadership:

- Situational leadership model—the relationship of leadership to management.
- Techniques for inspiring and motivating individual and group performance.
- Style—determining and communicating your leadership style.

In the context of project management, leadership represents the ability to inspire—to ensure that project members are motivated—on both the individual and the team level. Several leadership professionals, quoted below, have captured the essence of inspiration and self-motivation. Regarding self-motivation, Peter De Vries wryly commented, "I write when I'm inspired, and I see to it that I'm inspired at nine o'clock every morning."

As Peter Drucker defines it, "Leadership is not a magnetic personality—that can just as well be a glib tongue. It is not 'making friends and influencing people'—that is flattery. Leadership is lifting a person's vision to higher sights, raising a person's performance to a higher standard, building a personality beyond its normal limitations." He contrasts leadership, "doing the right things," with management, "doing things right."

Efficiency is associated with management, even in climbing the ladder of success. But as Warren Bennis observes, "leadership determines whether the ladder is leaning against the right wall."

Stephen Covey reminds us that management is clearly different from leadership. "Leadership is primarily a high-powered, right brain activity. It's more of an art; it's based on philosophy. Management is the breaking down, the analysis, the sequencing, the specific application, the time-bound left-brain aspect of self-government." His own maxim of personal effectiveness: "Manage from the left; lead from the right."

Motivational experts seek to explain why some projects succeed while others do not. Some studies have related project success to the source and number of initiatives made that are actually incorporated into the project. These studies result in leadership success models based on the project environment, the characteristics of the leaders being studied, and the leader's ability to influence others. Some have studied the basis for leadership power and influence, notably Hans Thamhain[17] and the Wilson Learning Corporation,[18] by having various influence factors ranked by managers, peers, and support personnel. To highlight the consistencies among their findings, we've focused on four influence categories. They're listed below in the order of their effectiveness as perceived by team members:

> "Leadership is primarily a high-powered, right brain activity."

> "Leadership is lifting a person's vision to higher sights."

> Managing is doing things right. Leadership is doing the right things, like leaning the ladder against the right wall.

- *Organizational position or formal authority.*
- *The manager's personal factors*—Expertise, interpersonal skills, information, connections and alliances, trust and respect.
- *The project work itself*—Work interest and challenge; future assignments.
- *Rewards and penalties*—Salary and promotion; coercion and penalties.

While the order varies somewhat among surveys and industries, most personnel rank the project manager's authority and expertise at the top along with the work itself. Surprisingly, salary and promotions are perceived only a little more positively than coercion and penalties, the later being seen as the least influential.

When we discussed forming the project team, we emphasized that the project manager should be given as much formal authority as possible. But we need to add one important caveat. The *existence* of the authority is considered to be a positive influence; however, its *undue exercise* can be perceived as coercion—diminishing the net influence. Selective use of formal authority in only the appropriate situations will produce the best overall results.

> In the absence of adequate formal authority, strong personal skills and leadership techniques are indispensable.

THE SITUATIONAL LEADERSHIP MODEL

Leadership techniques are nearly all situation-driven—they vary according to the task to which they are applied. To portray the situational nature of leadership, we use the orthogonal model we introduced at the end of Chapter 3. The cylinder shows the typical sequence of actions that occur in any well-managed task. After task work is assigned, a work plan is prepared. The plan may vary in detail from back-of-the-envelope ideas for a simple task, to a logic network detailing a complex project's sequence of resource-loaded work elements. Ideally the plan is created by the team intending to do the work. Someone on the team—the team leader, a project manager, or a team member—provides oversight during

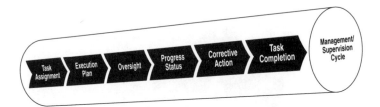

FIGURE 7.73   The sequential management/supervision cycle.

execution, and work actually done is compared against the plan to note status. When unacceptable deviations in cost, schedule, or technical compliance are detected, corrective actions are taken to return the project to the plan. This sequence is repeated throughout the project cycle, as represented by the axle in Figure 7.73.

The wheel (Figure 7.74) shows groups of leadership techniques and tools that may be needed during the task sequence. The tools include training, creating environment, maturity, interpersonal traits, reinforcement, setting examples, and rewarding achievement—all held together by the leader's vision. How the

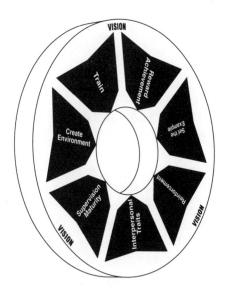

FIGURE 7.74   The situational leadership techniques.

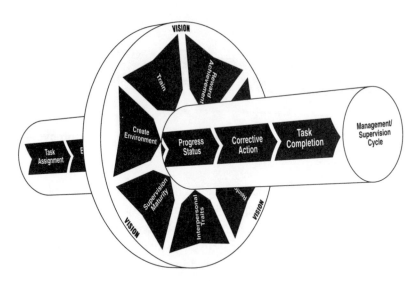

FIGURE 7.75   The orthogonal leadership model.

techniques and tools are applied can vary widely as a function of the skills and style of the leader and according to the situation.

Our model (Figure 7.75) positions the situational techniques of leadership orthogonal to the sequential management/supervision cycle. Leadership techniques must be applied situationally and responsively, relative to the active project phase and the specific team or individual circumstances at the time.

THE MOTIVATIONAL TECHNIQUES OF PROJECT LEADERSHIP

Nothing exercises leadership skills more than the complexities of motivation. Yet the payoff is very high. According to the results of studies by The Public Agenda Foundation, a private research organization in New York, 88 percent of workers responded positively when asked if they considered it important to do their best job. However, 44 percent of those surveyed admitted that they "exert no effort over the minimum." And only 23 percent believe they work to their full capacity. The leader's motivation challenge is to tap that available discretionary effort.

All the limitations of control and authority stated earlier demand that project managers be able to differentiate motivational causes and effects, and be able to relate them to the specific project team and member needs. Misplaced or ill-conceived motivation often turns into demotivation—much worse than no motivation at all. The following groups of techniques, when properly applied, have proved effective in the project environment.

Vision   Above all else, we demand that our leaders have a vision and be able to articulate and structure its attainment. Whether it's successful task completion or a company reorganization, the ability to visualize success and then affect its realization is the glue that holds all the other leadership techniques together. Leaders must accept the goals of the larger organization, of which their work is a part, or work to change those larger goals. They must understand the driving forces of the various stakeholders who will gain or lose by the vision's fulfillment. Finally, they must be able to communicate that vision to the team in relationship to their work. (Incidentally, visionaries who cannot lead to realization of their vision are called hallucinators.)

> Vision attainment is the glue that holds all the other leadership techniques together.

Creating the Environment   How we manage vision attainment is the heart of the rest of the technique set. Attainment begins by creating the environment in which work is to be accomplished. Initially, this means defining a set of management practices to be used on the project and determining your style (discussed in detail at the end of the chapter).

In Chapter 5, we addressed the decision-making process as a major environmental and teamwork factor. The work of Douglas McGregor[19] is also useful in characterizing the leadership environment. He defined two types of environments illustrated in Figure 7.76, Theory X (authoritative) and Theory Y (challenge). Theory X is the militaristic environment based on the assumption that people really don't like to work and must be coerced into

> The leader knows the plans and focuses on the process.

FIGURE 7.76   Theory X (authoritative) and Y (challenge) environments.

following orders, most of which originate with top management. But direct orders cannot always be depended upon, as the following story, originally appearing in the Naval Institute's *Proceedings*, illustrates.

This "beacon of information" provides several metaphors regarding position power, perceptions of authority, and the need to act on complete information.

> Two battleships assigned to the training squadron had been at sea on maneuvers in heavy weather for several days. I was serving on the lead battleship and was on watch on the bridge as night fell. The visibility was poor with patchy fog, so the captain remained on the bridge keeping an eye on all activities.
>
> Shortly after dark, the lookout on the wing of the bridge reported, "Light, bearing on the starboard bow."
>
> "Is it steady or moving astern?" the captain called out.
>
> Lookout replied, "Steady, captain," which meant we were on a dangerous collision course with that ship.
>
> The captain then called to the signal man, "Signal that ship: We are on a collision course, advise you change course 20 degrees."
>
> Back came a signal, "Advisable for you to change course 20 degrees."
>
> The captain said, "Send, I'm a captain, change course 20 degrees."

"I'm a seaman second class," came the reply. "You had better change course 20 degrees."

By that time the captain was furious. He spat out, "Send I'm a battleship. Change course 20 degrees."

Back came the flashing light, "I'm a lighthouse."

We changed course.

Theory X often results in an adversarial relationship between manager and subordinates—totally inappropriate for most project teams. Theory Y assumes that people want to work and can be self-directed with an appropriate reward system.

Subsequent to McGregor's original work, William Ouchi[20] introduced Theory Z to refer to the participative format that grew out of the Japanese "community circles" movement and broadened with Total Quality Management. It is typified by closely knit teams that develop common goals to which they are committed through shared values (Figure 7.77).

Z - Management Environment

FIGURE 7.77   Theory Z (participative) environment.

Variations in performance often stem from the leadership style used by the accountable person—the way the task work is assigned, planned, etc.

In their pure forms, each of these concepts has shortcomings for most projects. While Theory Z represents the project environment most closely—especially small, well-controlled projects—it has been found deficient in atmospheres of conflict. Larger projects involving multiple organizations, customers, subcontractors, etc., work best when the environmental elements of both Theory Y (individual) and Theory Z (team) are combined. For your project, you need to determine the appropriate environment and decide how to set that environment in place.

Regardless of the specific style, a leader creates a problem solving environment by:

- Building urgency and "admiring" the problem.
- Removing roadblocks so the team can do their things.
- Eliminating window dressing.
- Rising above bureaucracy and politics.

The same sequence of actions should be taken for a task managed by a self-directed team or by McGregor's worst nightmare X-style manager. After assessing the team and the stakeholder expectations, adopt or adapt a project cycle for the project and announce what tailoring the team is expected to do to that cycle. Identify the training needed, both on the team and individual levels, for the members to be able to work effectively together. You also need to define the balance of decision-making authority among the team, you as the project manager, and higher level management.

The leader knows the people on the team and recognizes their needs.

Due to the interdependent nature of project people and the teamwork culture, each team member wants to be involved and to feel responsible for proactive participation in management activities. These include planning, measuring, evaluating, anticipating, and alerting others to potential problems. To become committed to project goals, as Stephen Covey observes, ". . . they want involvement, significant involvement. And if they don't have involvement, they don't buy it. Then you have a significant motivational problem which cannot be solved at the same level of thinking that created it."

Project failures can frequently be traced to unrealistic technical, cost or schedule targets. Such targets may be entirely arbitrary or based on bad assumptions—setting team members up for failure. Furthermore, the specific goals that motivate you may not motivate another team member. This isn't to say that all tasks have to be inherently motivating—that's not sensible. But there have to be motivating elements, if by nothing more than participating in goal determination. This also helps ensure adequate risk analysis and acceptable risks.

> Involving team members in the goal-setting process has several important benefits.

We've found that it is better to aim high and to occasionally miss than to aim low. For example, one high-tech leader encourages employees to include goals in their MBOs for which there is at least a 50 percent chance of accomplishing. An overall MBO score of 75 percent is considered good—encouraging a stretch. Even overly aggressive goals, if set by the team member rather than the manager, can stimulate the extra effort needed to meet them. And they pay an extra dividend—On-the-Job-Training.

> Goal-setting by team members ultimately leads to greater self-confidence and more aggressive goals.

Meetings—lots of them—are an inherent part of the project management process. Nearly everyone complains about the time they waste in meetings. But meetings are the major vehicle for exercising leadership. In the section on Project Visibility, we provided conduct guidelines for the various types, from one-on-ones to formal reviews, beginning with justifying the need. Too many meetings, or poorly conceived or poorly executed ones, can be a major demotivator.

> Meeting formats and conduct is a significant aspect of creating the environment.

Effective meetings are no accident. They demand management skills for preparation and leadership skills for conduct. For example, people who are needed for decisions, but who arrive late or not at all, waste everyone's time. Attendees who are not needed at all, also feel that their time is wasted. On the other hand, one of the most needless and damaging demotivators is exclusion. Occasionally a team member will be "spared" from an important meeting or a difficult task with no explanation. With proper explanation, that person might have been relieved not to be involved, but now feels left out—perhaps even penalized.

> A pattern of ineffective meetings is a sure sign of weak leadership.

A problem-solving meeting is a contest. The leader's challenge is to convince others to: change their positions or realign

Major meeting demotivators include: lack of an agenda, indefinite start/stop times, and failure to stay on schedule.

priorities, overcome prejudices and accept another point of view, extend commitments and increase vulnerability. But the leader needs to recognize and control counterproductive power struggles.

More obvious in meetings than in other leadership situations, the leader is an orchestrator, keeping the meeting balanced and on track. As Figure 7.78 shows, this often requires drawing out needed participation by others and preventing domination by certain vocal members, the leader included.

Studies by industrial psychologist Frederick Herzberg[21] examine specific factors that motivate people in their work environment—and those that don't. Herzberg and his co-authors identify several maintenance or "hygiene" factors that are not motivational. Pay and working conditions (safety, security, and comfort) reduce motivation when absent. But maintenance factors were found to lead to discontent only when they are missing or perceived as deficient, otherwise they have very little attitudinal affect. They are never motivators.

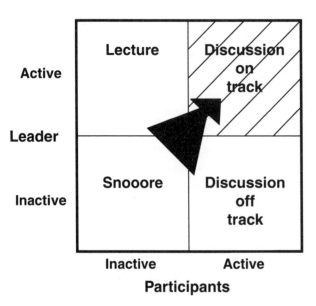

FIGURE 7.78 Keeping the discussion on track.

The presence of motivational factors, such as the work itself and recognition, can significantly improve job satisfaction, goal-orientation, and productivity. But they must not be manipulative. Alfie Kohn, in *Punished by Rewards*,[22] observed "Do this and you'll get that is not much different from do this or else."

The maintenance and motivation factors are listed in order of their relative importance revealed by Herzberg's research:

Motivational (positive)	*Maintenance (negative)*
Achievement	Policy and procedure
Recognition	Supervision
Work itself	Salary
Responsibility	Interpersonal relations
Advancement	Working conditions

Company-wide employee relations campaigns involve maintenance factors, whereas motivational factors are generally in the domain of the project manager and others in a direct leadership role.

Supervision Maturity   A good leader evaluates each team member's ability to supervise tasks and to accept delegation. Every opportunity should be taken to match the job assignments with interest and skills, keeping in mind that a perfect match is impractical. This means assessing every member's individual job knowledge and maturity, then planning their growth from the point where *detailed direction* can progress to *coaching* on important points; where *coaching* can transition to *supporting* as needed; and where *supporting* can mature to full *delegation*.

A leader's effectiveness depends on the ability to assess maturity levels and to adopt the appropriate delegation style.

- Delegating—Assigning the responsibility.
- Supporting—Answering questions when asked.
- Coaching—Reminding how it is to be done.
- Directing—Step-by-step instructions.

Hersey and Blanchard[23] have developed a comprehensive situational leadership theory and process that helps in assessing

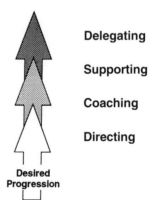

Delegating

Supporting

Coaching

Directing

Desired Progression

As the maturity level moves from low to high, leaders need to vary their style from Directing to Delegating.

maturity and determining the appropriate delegation style by considering the interaction between two major determinants (see Figure 7.79):

Task Behavior—the degree to which a leader *tells* people what, why and how. Generally, task-oriented leaders set the goals and define the detailed steps to reach them.

Relationship Behavior—the degree of *support* provided by the leader and the extent of feedback sought. Relationship-oriented behavior is characterized by good bilateral communication and active listening.

Follower Readiness—The degree to which the followers need direction from the leader, individually and as a team. In the project environment, readiness depends on the level of experience and knowledge available for the specific project and the interpersonal growth from working together as a team, all of which can be expected to grow as the project moves through its stages. The four basic situational leadership styles are summarized in Figure 7.79, followed by their appropriate application.

- Telling (S1): This style is most appropriate for followers who are unable or unwilling to take responsibility because they lack knowledge or experience.

- Selling (S2): This style can be practiced when selling concepts to top management and customers. It can be effective in obtaining team buy-in through selling the benefits of decisions. It is the natural training style.

- Participating (S3): This style is appropriate for a moderately mature team. The leader and followers share in the problem-solving, decision-making process, with the main role of the leader being facilitator.

- Delegating (S4): This style matches the needs of a team or individual which has reached a high maturity level. They have acquired both the motivation and ability to allocate project tasks and then to accomplish them with a minimum of supervision. The leader delegates and follows up.

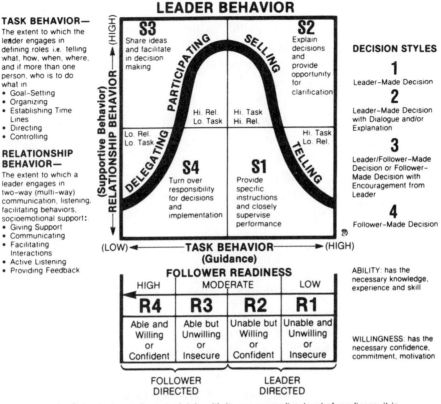

TASK BEHAVIOR—
The extent to which the leader engages in defining roles i.e. telling what, how, when, where, and if more than one person, who is to do what in
• Goal-Setting
• Organizing
• Establishing Time Lines
• Directing
• Controlling

RELATIONSHIP BEHAVIOR—
The extent to which a leader engages in two-way (multi-way) communication, listening, facilitating behaviors, socioemotional support:
• Giving Support
• Communicating
• Facilitating Interactions
• Active Listening
• Providing Feedback

DECISION STYLES

1
Leader-Made Decision

2
Leader-Made Decision with Dialogue and/or Explanation

3
Leader/Follower-Made Decision or Follower-Made Decision with Encouragement from Leader

4
Follower-Made Decision

ABILITY: has the necessary knowledge, experience and skill

WILLINGNESS: has the necessary confidence, commitment, motivation

When a Leader Behavior is used appropriately with its corresponding level of readiness, it is termed a High Probability Match. The following are descriptors that can be useful when using Situational Leadership for specific applications:

S1	S2	S3	S4
Telling	Selling	Participating	Delegating
Guiding	Explaining	Encouraging	Observing
Directing	Clarifying	Collaborating	Monitoring
Establishing	Persuading	Committing	Fulfilling

FIGURE 7.79   **The Hersey situational leadership model. Reprinted from Paul Hersey and Ken Blanchard, *Management of Organizational Behavior: Utilizing Human Resources,* Englewood Cliffs, NJ: Prentice Hall, 1993, Sixth Edition, All rights reserved.**

Appropriate delegation is an effective technique for avoiding over-management while, at the same time, improving job satisfaction. As a project or task manager, a particularly strong motivator is the confidence demonstrated by turning over one of your own plums to another team member.

Be sure to delegate whole tasks—as large a piece as possible—not bits and pieces.

People that can handle delegation, don't complain about it.

If they're not ready now, then consciously grow them to the point where they can accept delegation. Mismanaging this growth can mean either delegating too early and experiencing performance problems or giving overly detailed directions and micromanaging. Whether a project manager or a junior team member, a sign of maturity is knowing when to use the following three techniques with one's boss:

- It's my responsibility, and I am taking care of it.
- It's my responsibility, and I am taking care of it. But you need to be informed because you will probably be asked about it.
- It's my responsibility, but the best solution is beyond my authority and I need your help in implementing it.

Interpersonal Traits   Leading people is, in part, the skill of knowing how to draw on their strengths and minimize their weaknesses. It takes time to understand others—to understand why a single act of ours can have a positive effect on some and the exact opposite effect on others. It's not merely a one-time event of being type-cast by Wilson Learning[24] or Myers Briggs[25] or other good assessment tool, and then wearing a label. It requires conscious attention to the needs of each team member and hard work to understand their complexities so as to work with them and benefit from that complexity.

Much of traditional motivation theory is based on Abraham Maslow's five hierarchical levels (psychic, status, social, security, physical), each level becoming an intrinsic motivator after the lower-level need has been met. It has been our observation that any one of the levels may be dominant in a particular person. For example, some people are more responsive to psychic than to social incentives, regardless of how well their social needs have been met.

Needs can regress as the environment changes. Stephen Covey[26] dramatizes the point:

> If all the air were suddenly sucked out of the room you're in right now, what would happen to your interest in this book? You wouldn't care about the book; you wouldn't care about anything except getting air. Survival would be your only motivation.
>
> But now that you have air, it doesn't motivate you. This is one of the greatest insights in the field of motivation: Satisfied needs do not motivate. It's only the unsatisfied need that motivates.

Interpersonal clashes are inevitable, even in the most compatible teams. The techniques suggested here seek to channel the conflict in constructive ways so as to prevent a significant demotivator: prolonged or unresolved conflict.

The traditional conflict resolution methods are:

- Confrontation/Collaboration (Integration)
- Compromise (Negotiation)
- Smoothing (Suppression)
- Forcing (Power or Dominance)
- Withdrawal (Denial/Retreating)

In many situations, constructive confrontation, by providing a win-win strategy, is the best approach.

Confrontation is the most favored mode for resolving conflicts, especially in dealing with superiors. It has grown from a technique to a methodology complete with its own textbooks. But it is not a panacea.

Compromise is usually the best mode for dealing with functional support departments. At the other extreme, withdrawal is usually seen as capitulation, at best a temporary resolution. A skilled leader employs the full range of conflict resolution modes.

Group brainstorming can be very beneficial, but also very time consuming, so make sure it is time well spent.

Brainstorming techniques are often used to attack the most difficult problems while enhancing interpersonal skills. The leader needs to ensure an open and noncritical atmosphere. For example, unusual or impractical ideas should be encouraged—they often lead to new combinations and improvements. You may want to use a tape recorder to keep the session from backtracking just to clarify something for a note taker. Remember—the more ideas, the better.

The one-on-one meeting is one of the best vehicles for exercising leadership on an interpersonal level. It provides the opportunity to demonstrate four important leadership qualities:

- Sensitivity to personnel issues.
- Accessibility and friendliness.
- Trust—respect for confidentiality.
- Training and coaching.

> A leader's spoken and body language, and job performance especially, will provide reinforcement.

Reinforcement   Reinforcement refers to techniques used to remind team members of the vision and the continuing requirements of working as a team. Because the project process includes difficult aspects which may not yet be intuitive, team members may resist or circumvent them. At every opportunity, the leader should emphasize the benefits of the project management essentials. Posters and slogans around a team room reminding people of important things are good if there is follow through to make them credible. The project leader's spoken words and body language, and job performance especially, can be expected to reinforce those points.

> Every action, every day sends a powerful message to each team member.

Setting the Example   "Walk the walk, don't just talk the talk," if you expect others to follow. It is less what you say that counts and more what you do that influences behavior. Your attitude and body language set the tone for the entire team. You need to establish an atmosphere of openness by your willingness to seek advice, as well as bad news.

> Never ask your team to do what you would be unwilling to do yourself.

It's damaging to continually harp on the need to bring in a project on schedule, and yet begin every meeting late. Act as you want your team to act:

upbeat, punctual, decisive, untiring, enthusiastic, fair, dependable

Group activities such as planning and problem solving offer ample opportunity for setting examples. Make sure that you begin meetings on time and operate by the same standards that the team has committed to.

Rewarding Achievement   It may be time to put away the carrot and stick for good. Recent studies are calling into question the maxim of "You get what you reward." These studies show that, while some rewards can bring about short term compliance, others often backfire in the longer term. Rather than getting sidetracked trying to resolve reward controversies, managers can benefit most by simply being aware of the issues. Much of the conflict simply confirms that different people respond to widely varying rewards. Some do not respond to external motivations at all. In the next chapter, we discuss the long term implications of rewards such as salary increases and promotions. Our purpose is to characterize these forces so that they can be made part of everyone's awareness—managers and team members alike.

> Interesting assignments are often their own reward. People willingly work harder, as well as smarter, at motivating tasks.

Some rewards can be perceived as denials of self-control and freedom of choice, especially if they don't address a need. Even though there are many techniques for finding out what people want, managers hesitate to pursue them. You may not be prepared to deal with the answer. But you'll discover that asking about motivations, whether by a formal survey or a simple one-on-one question, is motivating in itself. You need to follow-up to prevent a backfire.

> Most people simply want to have interesting work and to be recognized for their accomplishments.

A Hilton Hotels Time Values survey revealed that 70 percent of people earning over $30,000 would trade a day's pay each week for an extra day of free time. This phenomenon exists even in the lower pay brackets. Almost half of those surveyed earning less than $20,000 would also make the trade.

You should take advantage of every opportunity to recognize good performance, but it's most effective when done in a group environment such as at meetings or reviews—even off-site pizza

> Most time-off incentives tied to productivity or schedule improvements get results.

> It's important to recognize significant accomplishments frequently—but not routinely.

breaks. Just be sure you're aware of the supporting details and that you don't leave somebody out. A further note of caution: intrinsic motivation, so fragile in the team environment, can be destroyed by anything that is perceived as being manipulative or controlling—even praise. Those who receive excessive praise can become so self-conscious that they have trouble concentrating. They may even duck challenges to avoid potential failure.

Rewarding individual performance doesn't necessarily result in a lack of teamwork. But cooperation does need to be one of the major performance rating factors. Accomplished leaders recognize and reward cooperation with teammates as an essential element of individual merit. One motivator for team performance is to do away with individual reviews. Some managers consider an entire task group's effort as one performance.

Regardless of your reward philosophy or the details of your rewards, they need to be systematically aligned with the goals and values of your project, environment, and company.

Training   Trying to do a job you haven't been trained for is no fun. This applies double to the project manager who needs to be trained to select appropriate project personnel, depending on the project type and size, and then to contribute to their career development.

We are frequently retained by clients to train their in-house teams and executive management. We find that any technique is valuable which brings groups together and encourages them to practice common goal setting, problem solving, and acknowledge their interdependencies. We've used managed delegation exercises, joint buyer-seller project planning sessions, project simulations, and a host of other techniques. As professional trainers, we've learned that some specific subjects work best when we train the in-house trainers—a group motivated to train others and to be involved in on-going follow-ups. But this doesn't work with most project management elements unless the trainers have extensive—and successful—project management experience and can credibly address detailed issues from that perspective. As one

> Rewarding team performance can work as it does in sports—motivating stronger players to help weaker ones improve.

> Training does not work as a one-shot seminar, regardless of how long or how intensive it may be.

of our clients asserted: "Someone with that kind of capability is usually very busy managing a hot project."

Not all people are emotionally or technically equipped to take on the teaching role. A teaching attempt at the wrong time, or by the wrong person, can be seen as a form of judgment or rejection. On the other hand, being taught by one's own management, if done well, can be extremely motivating. The higher the management doing the training, the more stimulating and effective it is in establishing a consistent culture (assuming that manager has progressed through the project trenches).

DETERMINING AND DECLARING YOUR LEADERSHIP STYLE

The practice of project management is increasingly influenced by human relations. Developing human relations skills, in turn, depends on awareness of one's own operating style and behavior patterns as well as a willingness to adapt those qualities to the specific project environment.

Firefighting provides a good metaphor for looking at how extreme a rigid personal style could be:

- Reactive—run for water.
- Inactive—watch the blaze.
- Counteractive—apply gasoline.
- Distractive—send the fire trucks to the parade.
- Retroactive—"I could have told you to install sprinklers if you'd asked."

The proactive manager would have already installed a sprinkler system.

The project manager's ability to get the job done usually depends more on operating style than on any other factor—even more than power or authority. A true leader knows what is going on at all times and anticipates situations, consciously operating in the appropriate style. While most leadership *techniques* are directed towards motivation, leadership *styles* characterize the methods for applying the techniques.

There are numerous texts and self-study guides for analyzing one's own style tendencies and preferences. We introduce two models that have proved to be particularly effective. However, the details of any specific self-typing or group analysis scheme are less important than the process itself—exploring your own preferences and stretching your range of styles. To benefit from that process you first have to be self-aware.

Before analyzing further, you may find it useful to jot down your own behavior patterns, both formal and informal. As Frankl says, we "detect" rather than "invent" our missions in life. Think about the way in which you respond to different situations. Think about the situations in which you're comfortable—and others where you're uncomfortable. In which kind of relationship problems do you invest time and energy on a regular basis—which ones need more of your time? Identify your motivation source (personal need served) in each.

Wilson Learning Corporation's Interpersonal Relations Model[24] has been widely used in the business environment for characterizing one's style. It is usually associated with a formal training seminar which includes a preliminary survey of selected peers. Your interpersonal style is determined by a blending of your peers' perceptions. This is done through formal questionnaires similar in format to psychology and aptitude profiles. The process begins with the interpretation of your individual results relative to a four-quadrant model (Figure 7.80).

Combining your primary style—Analytical, Driver, Amiable, or Expressive—with your secondary or backup style (one of the same four quadrants in the basic model), places you in one of the 16 style categories, for example, an Expressive/Driver (Figure 7.81).

The utility of the Wilson Learning model becomes clear when you consider the interactions among the various categories.

As the leader, you need to be motivated to adapt your own behavior rather than to "shape up" someone else.

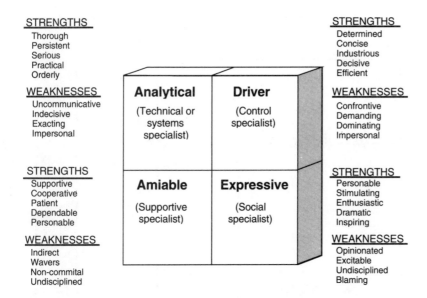

STRENGTHS
Thorough
Persistent
Serious
Practical
Orderly

WEAKNESSES
Uncommunicative
Indecisive
Exacting
Impersonal

STRENGTHS
Supportive
Cooperative
Patient
Dependable
Personable

WEAKNESSES
Indirect
Wavers
Non-commital
Undisciplined

STRENGTHS
Determined
Concise
Industrious
Decisive
Efficient

WEAKNESSES
Confrontive
Demanding
Dominating
Impersonal

STRENGTHS
Personable
Stimulating
Enthusiastic
Dramatic
Inspiring

WEAKNESSES
Opinionated
Excitable
Undisciplined
Blaming

Analytical
(Technical or systems specialist)

Driver
(Control specialist)

Amiable
(Supportive specialist)

Expressive
(Social specialist)

FIGURE 7.80   The basic Wilson Learning model.

The result is a much-improved insight and awareness, not only of your own styles, but of others' patterns as well. Perhaps most important is this newly acquired means to recognize behavior patterns and then anticipate interactions so as to extend your own personal behavior boundaries.

The Myers-Briggs model is broadly supported in psychology and self-help. It uses a questionnaire to help you determine your dominant trait in each of four pairs of traits:

E/I   Extrovert or Introvert
N/S   Intuitive or Sensing
T/F   Thinking or Feeling
J/P   Judging or Perceiving.

The model is based on the theory of psychological types described by C. G. Jung (1875–1961). Jung's model places you in one of 16 categories based on combining that one dominant trait

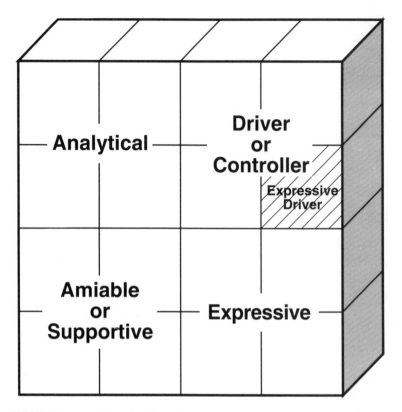

FIGURE 7.81   The sixteen Wilson Learning style combinations.

from each pair. The characterizations in Figure 7.82 are adopted from Keirsey and Bates,[27] one of several guides for interpreting the results.

Rather than consolidating peer- and self-review into one composite result, you are encouraged to characterize yourself and to independently have others respond to the same questions about you. Additional insight can thus be gained by comparing your results for each trait with the perception of others. As with the Wilson model, most authors provide detailed advice and insight regarding the dynamics of one style interacting with another (e.g., an ENTN interacting with an ISFP), whether it be as team members, manager/subordinate, or spouses.

INFJ	INFP	ISTJ	ISFJ
Author	Questor	Trustee	Conservator
ENFJ	**ENFP**	**ESTJ**	**ESFJ**
Pedagogue	Journalist	Administrator	Seller
INTJ	**INTP**	**ISTP**	**ISFP**
Scientist	Architect	Artisan	Artist
ENTJ Field Marshall	**ENTP** Inventor	**ESTP** Promoter	**ESFP** Entertainer

FIGURE 7.82   Myers-Brigg's sixteen types, characterized by Keirsey and Bates.

Regardless of your preferred style, your actual style at any time should be affected by such factors as the maturity level of team members and the gravity or priority of the situation. Variety and shifts in style are not only healthy—they're necessary. Leadership requires flexibility and adaptability in dealing with the task at hand, the personalities involved, events, and the situation.

The newspaper article in Figure 7.83 describes how Lt. General William G. Pagonis' leadership style literally moved mountains in the Gulf War. Note the use of "daily 'stand-up' meetings and the 'articulation' of each leader's management style, so that subordinates need spend zero time and energy guessing how the manager manages."

Anticipate necessary changes in your own style and declare what will trigger a change. A good time to announce these to the team is at the kick-off meeting. Here's an example: "I'll implement news flash meetings, budget violation meetings, daily

You need to develop the ability to vary your style.

Once you determine your preferred styles, declare yourself and make it good.

Gulf War Leader
Offers Lessons On Leadership

"In Moving Mountains: Lessons in Leadership and Logistics from the Gulf War" (Harvard Business School Press, $24.95), Lt. General Willian G. Pagonis tells how he served 122 million meals, moved 31,880 tons of mail, pumped 1.3 billion gallons of fuel, processed 730,000 personnel, set up 2,746 miles of main supply routes, and logistically supported an integrated military force equal to the population of Alaska.

The leadership style and techniques Pagonis used are equally fascinating. First he publicly gained the confidence of his boss.... (He) responded to the challenge... by signing his John Hancock on his logistical charts in front of Schwarzkopf and the rest of the command, as the latter stood by in disbelief and incredulity....

An expert on strategic mobility, it comes naturally to Pagonis to say, "if you have good people, and if you have the capability to expand and delegate, and you have a centralized plan, imagination and ingenuity will always win. I believe in centralized control and decentralized execution."

"Moving Mountains" explains... the outlines of Pagonis' demonstrated effective leadership style. **That style includes a constant, informational flow of communications on 3-by-5 cards, daily "stand-up" meetings and bulletins, and the necessary "articulation" of each leader's management style, so that subordinates need spend zero time and energy guessing how the manager manages.**

"If you can articulate your leadership style, you can cause a transition to go 20 times faster," he says. "Then everybody knows what you want. I am convinced too many chief executive officers want to keep their subordinates guessing, keep them at a distance and a little bit of an edge, and I think that's wrong."

—*San Jose Mercury News, 16 November 1992*

FIGURE 7.83   Leadership lessons in the Gulf War.

stand-up meetings, and as needed, red teams and tiger teams. I'm an expressive/driver. I will operate in the Y-mode most of the time. I will be proactive and reactive—seldom inactive. I want to delegate as much as possible, but if I'm the one to recognize a slip in a delegated task, I'll switch to driver/directing mode."

8

THE IMPLICATIONS FOR A SUCCESSFUL FUTURE

People ask for the secret to success. There is no secret, but there is a process.

Nido Quebin

That process, starting with our visual model, has been unfolding for several chapters. We've demonstrated the strong connection leading from a systematic process—our process—to successful projects, and by implication, to successful careers. The purposes of this chapter are to:

- Make evident the trends and forces that are shaping future management careers.
- Identify the barriers that need to be broken.
- Remove the need to take that leap of faith.

Project management is indeed the wave of the future. But that kind of broad claim has been made for other concepts that became popular, only to fade away. Why will the future of project management be different from, say, Total Quality Management?

THE FUTURE WAVES AND UNDERCURRENTS

In most industries, quality is still considered the top competitive success factor.

In many ways, project management is evolving much like quality assurance did—from an obscure servant of line management; to broad consciousness; to formal disciplines, processes, and organizations with professional status; and finally, to the world's foremost competitive factor.

The bottom-line expectations for TQM have not been fulfilled—at least not in the short term. Japan's TQM culture shift took some 30 years.

Total Quality Management and Continuous Quality Improvement developed great expectations on the part of project stakeholders, company shareholders, and all levels of users. But for many, the TQM bubble burst when The Wallace Company filed Chapter 11 bankruptcy shortly after receiving national acclaim for its TQM program (the Houston-based oil-supply company had just won the Malcolm Baldridge National Quality Award). Recent surveys on TQM results and attitudes have concluded that U.S. firms may not fully embrace TQM until it demonstrates more dramatic results at the bottom line. For example, the American Electronics Association found that 40 percent of the 455 companies it surveyed has realized less than a 10 percent defect reduction over 3 years (attributable to in-house TQM programs). That same survey found that Quality is by far the top competitive success factor, ranking far ahead of Service (#2) and Technology (#3).

The perceived value of high quality is increasing even while TQM programs are being abandoned! This apparent dichotomy can be explained by our cultural priorities which demand that bottom line improvement initiatives bear significant fruit in the near term. The TQM concept will ultimately be successful, but only when embodied in disciplines such as system engineering, as part of an integrated project management process.

Project management is not a single idea or campaign. It's a confluence of several concepts (quality management being an important one) that offer both short-term and long-term bottom-line performance improvements. Waves which roll into project management include:

- Right-sizing the organization.
- Re-engineering the business process.

- Reducing middle line management.
- Shifting toward project teams and product teams.
- Using comprehensive, integrative processes.

Project management is moving from a specialty to the mainstream—from a management or organizational option, like a task force, to the way the enterprise is run. We're just beginning to feel the potential impact. The wave, building from many synergistic currents, is between the stages of broad consciousness and professional formalization.

Many associations and conferences are devoted to furthering project management development and recognition. The growth of project management's professional status and its reservoir of practitioners is reflected by international associations such as the Project Management Institute, the Performance Management Association, and the International Project Management Association. For example, the Project Management Institute membership is now growing at some 36 percent annually (Figure 8.1).

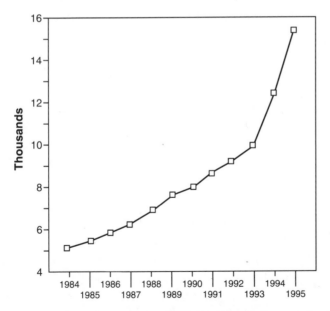

FIGURE 8.1 The accelerating Project Management Institute growth.

Thousands of
independently certified
Project Management
Professionals are now
advancing the field.

A solid career path depends on the ready availability of education and training. To that end, project management is being widely recognized as a fundamental management process with specific professional competency and knowledge criteria, including graduate programs at several universities. The Project Management Institute certifies those who have passed a rigorous eight-hour exam, as a Project Management Professional. Almost half of the members have applied, with just over half of those being certified. In addition, many corporations offer competency-based certification of project managers.

The U.S. government strongly supports project management training and education, usually at the agency level. As Undersecretary of Defense, David Packard, co-founder of Hewlett Packard, initiated the formation of the Defense System Management College at Fort Belvoir. While the 14-week curriculum emphasizes negotiation techniques and contract management for DoD and industry managers, the principles of project management are covered as well.

It remains for system
engineering to be
recognized as a process
integrator rather than as a
technical specialty.

Another encouraging sign of professional growth, at the process and discipline level, is the formalization of system engineering practices through organizations such as INCOSE, the International Council on Systems Engineering. From a modest beginning just six years ago as NCOSE, a national organization with 30 members, INCOSE membership now exceeds 2,000 and is growing at over 50 percent annually. Although its formation was encouraged by the American Management Association, it is only loosely connected with the project management profession.

When challenged to call on
personal power to marshall
the troops, some project
leaders may feel like
responding as did
Shakespeare's Hotspur:
"So can I, and so can any
man; but will they come?"

Even though that beleaguered middle level of line management appears convinced that the future lies in project management, just what that implies is not clear to those more comfortable with conventional power structures. That problem is not new, as evidenced by this heated exchange related by David McCullough.[1] In 1904, after the Panama Canal project team had protested an international mandate for a sea-level canal, Lord Kirchener reacted to President Roosevelt's support for team authority by saying: "I never regard difficulties, or pay heed to protests like that; all I would do in such a case would be to say, 'I order that a sea-level canal be dug, and I wish to hear nothing more about it.'" Roosevelt's retort strikes a familiar chord for any present-day project manager: "If you say so, I have no doubt you would have given such an order; but I wonder if you remember the conversation between Glendower and Hotspur, when Glendower says, 'I can call spirits from the vasty deep,' and Hotspur answers, 'So can I, and so can any man; but will they come?'"

That anecdote sums up the major leadership challenge facing the new breed of project managers: obtaining a full and continuing commitment by the team. An undercurrent of dissatisfaction, based largely on past exposure to flawed processes and inconsistent implementations, continues today. We call this undercurrent the hidden enemy of project management (Figure 8.2).

With all this knowledge and intensity, why aren't major projects more consistently successful?

EXPOSING THE UNDERTOW—THE HIDDEN ENEMIES OF PROJECT MANAGEMENT

A negative attitude and lack of confidence in project management often turns out to be a self-fulfilling prophesy:

At a software engineering course for aspiring managers, the participants were asked: "If your team of programmers developed airplane control software, and one day when you were flying, you

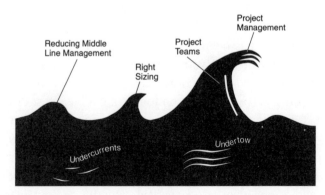

FIGURE 8.2 A teacherous undercurrent: The hidden enemy of project management.

found out before take-off that this plane was one of those equipped with *your* software, how many of you would get out?"

All except one person raised their hands. The course instructor asked the only one left whose hand was not raised, "What would you do?" She said, "Stay in my seat—if my team wrote the software for this plane, it wouldn't move, let alone take off."

Project success depends on the team members' attitude as much as on the leader.

While this story is told with tongue in cheek, it comes close to characterizing the attitudes of many frustrated team members in this era of vaporware and getting to market at any cost. In an attempt to understand why some teams succeed and others do not, experts have studied the magic of the natural born leaders who have been successful at leading project teams. These studies produced project manager attribute models similar to those we referenced in the last chapter. Although relevant and important, this leadership approach alone, based on the characteristics of the leaders in the studies, cannot yield teams that are consistently successful. This approach fails to consider the importance of the process and tools, and the team members' attitudes toward essential project management techniques.

Professional organizations have recently taken a more scientific approach to understanding project success and failure. They evaluate work practices, and then develop and apply maturity models. For example, the Carnegie Mellon Software Engineering Institute has developed the SEI Capability Maturity Model (CMM) to assess the work practice maturity of software development teams (Figure 8.3).

This model has been in use since 1987 and is becoming the de facto standard for software development maturity. Five levels of maturity are used to rate organizations as to their ability to reliably produce software based on four evaluation areas: Processes, People, Technology, and Measurement. The model is based on the theory that the more effective the people, processes, tools, and measurement, the higher the probability for project success.

The capability approach to success needs to account for the team's attitude.

We reported above on the expanding use of competency-based and knowledge-based certifications for project managers. Currently, The International Council on System Engineering

Implications of Advancing Through CMM Levels.					
	Level 1	**Level 2**	**Level 3**	**Level 4**	**Level 5**
Processes	Few stable processes exist or are used.	Documented and stable estimating, planning, and commitment processes are at the project level.	Integrated management and engineering processes are used across the organization.	Processes are quantitatively understood and stabilized.	Processes are continuously and systematically improved.
	"Just do it"	Problems are recognized and corrected as they occur.	Problems are anticipated and prevented, or their impacts are minimalized.	Sources of individual problems are understood and eliminated.	Common sources of problems are understood and eliminated.
People	Success depends on individual heroics.	Success depends on individuals; management system supports.	Project groups work together, perhaps as an integrated product team.	Strong sense of teamwork exists within each project.	Strong sense of teamwork exists across the organization
	"Firefighting" is a way of life.	Commitments are understood and managed.	Training is planned and provided according to roles.		Everyone is involved in process improvement.
	Relationships between disciplines are uncoordinated, perhaps even adversarial.	People are trained.			
Technology	Introduction of new technology is risky.	Technology supports established, stable activities.	New technologies are evaluated on a qualitative basis.	New technologies are evaluated on a quantitative basis.	New technologies are proactively pursued and deployed.
Measurement	Data collection and analysis is ad hoc.	Planning and management data used by individual projects.	Data are collected and used in all defined processes.	Data definition and collection are standardized across the organization.	Data are used to evaluate and select process improvements.
			Data are systematically shared across projects.	Data are used to understand the process quantitatively and stabilize it.	

FIGURE 8.3   The implications of advancing through the capability maturity model.

(INCOSE) is crafting a maturity model for system engineering to be used to assess organizational capability in that domain. Unfortunately, while these capability models assess the presence of practices within an organization, they fail to examine the team's underlying support or resistance to these practices.

We support the leadership approach to success and the need for a comprehensive project management maturity model, but we caution against their use without assessing and accounting for the team's underlying resistance to the fundamental practices of project management. Even though effective leadership can provide the direction and a capable team can provide the vehicle, these hidden enemies can still cause the trip to be bumpy, if not downright hazardous.

> Team empowerment depends on winning over the hidden enemies of project management.

In the early 1980s, we became aware that most project failures were not caused by the problems of advanced technology, but rather by the failure to implement fundamental and basic project management techniques. Teams within companies, known for their expertise in project management, would violate basic practices and as a result would experience failures of the worst kind. For example:

Failure	*Poor Practice*
NASA Challenger disaster	Inadequate qualification
Hubble defect	Ignored test results
Intelsat VI failure to achieve orbit	Inadequate change controls
Denver International Airport debacle	Failure to rebaseline with added requirements
FAA air traffic control system failure	Inadequate risk management
AT&T telephone system shutdown	Failure to test after change

In each of these cases, a fundamental project management practice was overlooked, ignored, or circumvented. In every case, the properly applied project management technique would have prevented the project failure.

We set out to discover what caused project teams to ignore proven practices. Fortunately, our business causes us to routinely interface with substantial numbers of leading project personnel from government agencies and contractors, commercial hardware, and software companies, and with graduate students, at several universities, pursuing project management careers.

We designed a survey to be administered to participants entering our training room. The survey collects the participant's candid attitudes about "how they value" a selected group of important project management techniques prior to receiving training. The summary of responses (Figure 8.4) from some 20,000 participants represent the percentage of "Positive" responses for some of the most important techniques. Our premise with this questionnaire is that personnel who are negative, neutral, or have no opinion toward a technique cannot be expected to pursue and support the technique in the project environment. The "Somewhat Positive" person may support the technique if implemented by others, but will usually not be the initiator. The only person that is a possible candidate for championing the technique and cultivating its effectiveness in the project environment is the person that checks "Positive." And even if positive, the person might not have the leadership skills to instill a technique in a resistant climate.

The survey results are sobering on two accounts, the wide range of group results and the low averages. The negative biases carried into the room when the survey was taken are a major cause for concern. The 45 percent averages for Project Business Management, Change Control, and Requirements Traceability means that less than half of the 20,000 participants felt positive towards these techniques. Inadequate attention to one or more of these specific techniques caused the failure of the Intelsat commercial satellite, the Challenger disaster, and the Denver airport delay and cost overrun. Thus the results of this survey are particularly alarming when you consider that clients send only their best project personnel to a week or two of project management training.

Further analysis reveals that one of the main factors contributing to the nearly 85 percent range is the variation in management levels and corresponding knowledge/experience. The perceived value of project management techniques diminishes significantly with descent into the organization (Figure 8.5).

No competent project manager would think of managing a project without these important techniques, effectively practiced.

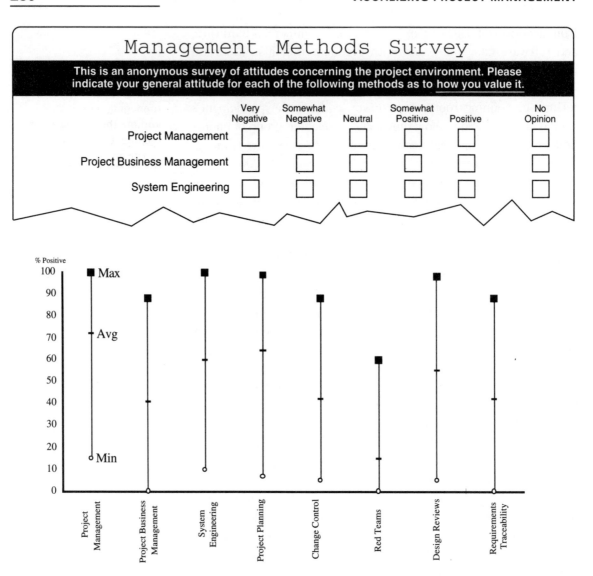

FIGURE 8.4 Management methods survey form and summary results.

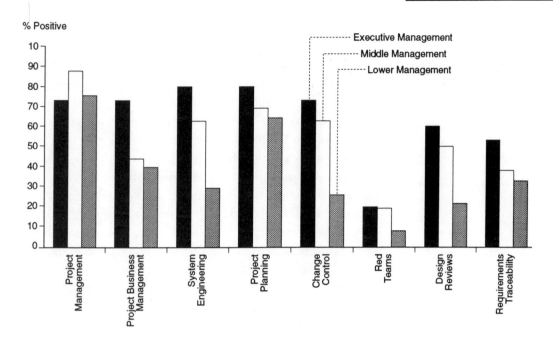

FIGURE 8.5 How three management levels value important techniques.

Fortunately, this trend can be reversed with proper training and positive experience. In early applications, we administered the survey both before and after training without discussing the reasons for the survey. The results showed a positive attitude shift of up to 60 percent to 70 percent for most techniques as a result of understanding the rationale, the proper implementation, and the appropriate application of the technique. This attitude reversal demonstrates the power of the visual model. The success of projects which follow the model instills confidence in the process. Being able to visualize the overall project management process removes the need to follow the individual steps on faith, or by edict.

SO MUCH TO LEARN—SO LITTLE TIME

Our surveys and personal experiences reveal a strong tendency for people to abandon discipline in favor of ad hoc practices if given the opportunity. Thus, it is incumbent on all organizations to establish a culture based on fundamentals and to maintain it through training and consistent practice. While campaigns and promotions can help get everyone's attention, they are a reinforcement, not a substitute, for ongoing, long-term fundamentals.

> To some organizations, assimilating the new processes is like learning that the earth is round.

The broadest concepts may not work well without systemic changes from the top down. Effective and lasting process renovation requires a far greater commitment than banners, hype, and a 5-day seminar. A growing consensus believes the system changes have to begin at the public education level and include "remedial" training at all levels and by all levels of the organization.

The recently declassified Corona reconnaissance satellite program, considered by many to have given birth to the integrated product team concept, illustrates the sweeping changes that may be required for successful project management. Since all subsequent U.S. space reconnaissance evolved from the CIA's Corona program, which spanned 13 years and 145 launches, its importance to U.S. security is inestimable. However, it very nearly didn't succeed, with only two successes in the first two years of operation. Eventual success is credited to the establishment of a project management process based on integrated project teams and many of the fundamental techniques we've included in our process. The results were completely turned around with only two failures during the last 8 years of the program.

But very few organizations could survive a two-year hiatus in order to effect the acculturation process. We need to attain the intuition and level of commitment that comes from several years of successful projects, but without expending those years. As the saying goes, "We have the technology." We can systematically learn from the successes and failures of others. And we can develop our intuition through conditioning and mental gymnastics.

There needs to be a mechanism for the lessons learned to get into the hands (and minds) of those who would benefit most. If project teams are prematurely dispersed to other projects, just at the time they should be documenting those learning experiences, it goes undone.

Many government and industry standards and regulations have been inspired by lessons learned and are maintained and updated as a means of promulgating those experiences. Training and cross-project technical meetings are major techniques for communicating lessons learned.

Files and manuals, if developed by the project team after a project is complete, can be invaluable to other project managers, present and future. An example is the DoD's Best Practices Manual.[2] The project requirements should include the relevant lessons from prior projects. A file or manual of lessons learned should be available for every project, in readily accessible documents or files (Figure 8.6). They should be formally required, regardless of the size and complexity of the project.

Albert Einstein has been quoted as saying, "Everything should be as simple as possible—but no simpler." One corollary might be, at any level of complexity, make sure you have a management process up to the task, and that you follow it to the letter. Management formality increases with the project size, risk, or complexity as illustrated in Figure 8.7. In general, more complex or higher risk projects require tighter controls, such as more frequent statusing and smaller percentage thresholds for the performance measurement systems. Furthermore, as size and risk increase, so do the needs for planning and documentation (Figure 8.8).

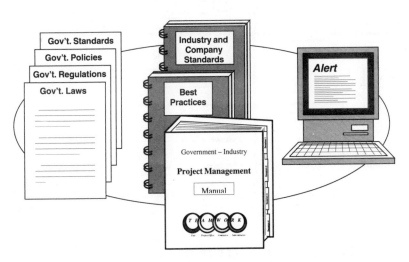

FIGURE 8.6 Lessons learned can take many forms.

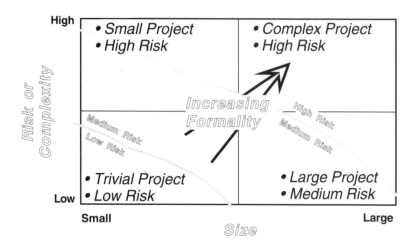

FIGURE 8.7   Management formality increases with size, risk, or complexity.

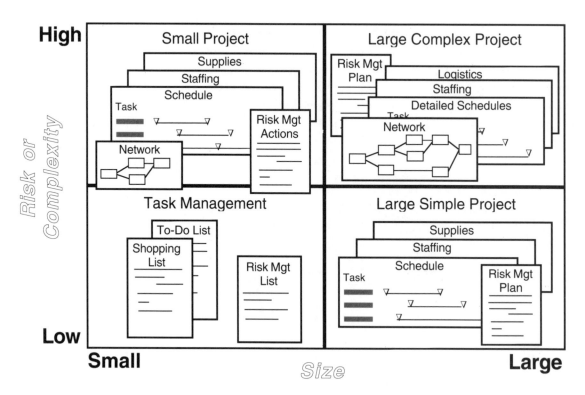

FIGURE 8.8   Planning increases with project size, risk, or complexity.

"Overwhelming complexity" is often cited as the reason project management processes defy our intuition. But complexity alone does not preclude intuition. Intuition develops from observing and understanding key principles. For example, the behavior of a gyroscope is not intuitive to most of us. But to an inertial guidance specialist, gyroscopes are second nature.

Managing a project without some intuition is like looking at a road map through a soda straw. Generating that intuition is perhaps the most important contribution of our visual model. Effective empowerment is confirmed by the positive attitudes on the part of team members who embrace the model and the process. The obvious correctness of the model instills confidence in the process. A team that understands the value of a credible process, and follows it because they believe in it, will be far less likely to omit an important step or to perform a practice incorrectly.

In project management, familiarity breeds intuition that dissolves contempt.

Being able to confidently internalize the overall project management process, removes the need to follow the individual steps on faith, or by edict.

THE PAYOFF

- Successful projects.
- Improved bottom lines.
- Successful careers.
- A healthy stand of highly-qualified executive timber.

We'd all be hard-pressed to come up with a better training ground for general management.

BIBLIOGRAPHY

INTRODUCTION

1. Stewart, Thomas A. "The Corporate Jungle Spawns a New Species: The Project Manager." *Fortune* 10 July 1995: 17.

CHAPTER 2

1. Fayol, Henri. *General and Industrial Management.* New York: IEEE Press, Rev. ed. 1984.

2. Royce, Winston W. "Managing the Development of Large Software Systems." *Proceedings, IEEE WESCON* August 1970: 1–9.

3. Boehm, B. W. "A Spiral Model of Software Development." *Tutorial: Software Engineering Project Management.* Ed. R. H. Thayer and M. Dorfman. Washington, DC: IEEE Computer Society Press, 1988. 128–142.

CHAPTER 3

1. Forsberg, K., and Mooz, H. *The Relationship of System Engineering to the Project Cycle.* Proceedings of the National Council for System Engineering Symposium. Chattanooga, TN: October 1991. 57–65.

CHAPTER 4

1. Beckley, John L. *The Power of Little Words.* Fairfield, NJ: The Economics Press, 1984.

CHAPTER 5

1. Covey, Stephen R. *The Seven Habits of Highly Effective People.* New York: Simon & Schuster, 1989.

2. Drucker, Peter F. *People and Performance: The Best of Peter Drucker on Management.* New York: Harper & Row, 1977.

3. Kezsbom, Deborah S., Schilling, Donald, and Edward, Katherine A. *Dynamic Project Management.* New York: Wiley, 1988.

CHAPTER 6

1. Forsberg, K., and Mooz, H. *Application of the "Vee" to Incremental and Evolutionary Development.* Proceedings of the National Council for System Engineering Symposium. July 1995. St. Louis, MO: National Council for System Engineering Symposium, July 1995.

CHAPTER 7

1. Covey, Stephen R. *The Seven Habits of Highly Effective People.* New York: Simon & Schuster, 1989.

2. Drucker, Peter F. *People and Performance: The Best of Peter Drucker on Management.* New York: Harper & Row, 1977.

3. Kezsbom, Deborah S., Schilling, Donald, and Edward, Katherine A. *Dynamic Project Management.* New York: Wiley, 1988.

4. Peters, Tom I., and Waterman, R. H., Jr. *In Search of Excellence.* New York: Harper & Row, 1974.

5. Kerzner, Harold. *Project Management.* New York: Von Nostrand Reinhold, 1984.

6. Ibid.

7. Ibid.

8. Covey, Stephen R. *The Seven Habits of Highly Effective People.* New York: Simon & Schuster, 1989.

9. Kezsbom, Deborah S., Schilling, Donald, and Edward, Katherine A. *Dynamic Project Management.* New York: Wiley, 1988.

10. Kerzner, Harold. *Project Management*. New York: Von Nostrand Reinhold, 1984.

11. Rosenau, Milton D., Jr. *Successful Project Management*. Belmont, GA: Lifetime Learning Publications, 1981.

12. Sawyer, K. "Space Station Officials Queried on Overruns." *Washington Post* 3 March 1993: A10.

13. March, J., and Shapira, Z. "Managerial Perspectives on Risk and Risk Taking." *Management Science*, 33:11 1987.

14. Forsberg, K., and Mooz, H. *Risk and Opportunity Management and the Project Cycle*. Proceedings of the National Council for System Engineering Symposium, July 1995. St. Louis, MO: National Council for System Engineering Symposium, July 1995.

15. Kazmier, Leonard J. *Principles of Management*. New York: McGraw-Hill, 1969. 309

16. Drucker, Peter F. *People and Performance: The Best of Peter Drucker on Management*. New York: Harper & Row, 1977. 498.

17. Gemmill, G., Thamhaim, H., and Wileman, D. L. "The Power Spectrum in Project Management." *Sloan Management Review*, 12 (1970): 15–25.

18. The Wilson Learning Corporation, Eden Prairie, MN.

19. McGregor, Douglas. *The Human Side of Enterprise*. New York: McGraw-Hill, 1960.

20. Ouchi, William G. *Theory Z: How American Business Can Meet the Japanese Challenge*. Reading, MA: Addison-Wesley, 1981.

21. Herzberg, Frederick, Mausner, Bernard, and Snyderman, Barbara. *The Motivation to Work*. New York: Wiley, 1959.

22. Kohn, Alfie. *Punished by Rewards*. New York: Houghton Mifflin, 1993.

23. Hersey, P., and Blanchard, K. H. *Management of Organizational Behavior: Utilizing Group Resources*. Englewood Cliffs, NJ: Prentice Hall, 1993.

24. The Wilson Learning Corporation, Eden Prairie, MN.

25. Consulting Psychologists Press, Inc., Palo Alto, CA.

26. Covey, Stephen R. *The Seven Habits of Highly Effective People.* New York: Simon & Schuster, 1989.

27. Keirsey, David, and Bates, Marilyn. *Please Understand Me, Character and Temperament Types.* Del Mar, CA: Prometheus Nemesis Book Company, 1984.

CHAPTER 8

1. McCullough, David. *The Path Between the Seas, the Creation of the Panama Canal 1870–1914.* New York: Simon & Schuster, 1977. 488.

LIST OF ACRONYMS

The acronyms that are included are those that are undefined in the text, or that appear more than once, with or without a definition. (We have not duplicated those that appear with their definition in one section only.) For those acronyms appearing here without a definition, one may be found in the index.

Acronym   **Name and Definition**

AR   **Acceptance Review.** A control gate at which the Buyer determines that the item presented for acceptance complies with its specification. Acceptance Reviews occur at all levels in the system hierarchy. The verification results are presented as evidence of specification compliance.

COW   **Cards on the Wall Planning.**

CCB   **Change Control Board.** A board established to review all proposed changes to an approved baseline. The scope includes all technical and program changes to the project. The project manager is chairperson of the Change Control Board.

CEO   **Chief Executive Officer.** A company's most senior manager, responsible and accountable for all activities and business units in the company.

CSC   **Computer Software Component.** A distinct part of a Computer Software Configuration Item (CSCI).

CSCI   **Computer Software Configuration Item.** A major software component of a system that is designated by the Buyer for configuration management to ensure the integrity of the delivered product. It, therefore, may exist at any level in the hierarchy, where interchangeability is required. Each CSCI is to have (as appropriate) individual design reviews, individual qualification certification, individual acceptance reviews, and separate user manuals.

CI   **Configuration Item.** A hardware, software, or composite item at any level in the system hierarchy designated for disciplined configuration management. CIs vary in size, type, and complexity but each has four common characteristics: (1) a defined functionality; (2) is replaceable as an entity; (3) a

Acronym	Name and Definition
	unique performance specification; (4) a disciplined control of its form, fit, and functionality.
CDR	**Critical Design Review.** A series of control gates at which the Buyer reviews and approves the Seller's Build-to baseline as evidenced by detailed Build-to documentation and approves proceeding with fabrication and coding. All hardware, software, handling equipment, test equipment, and tooling should be reviewed in the ascending order of assembly to system.
CPM	**Critical Path Method.**
DoD	**Department of Defense.** A department of the executive branch of the U.S. federal government. DoD is responsible for the armed forces and provides for the common defense.
ECR	**Engineering Change Request.** A request to consider a technical change to the technical baseline submitted to a Change Control Board.
EAC	**Estimate At Completion.** Actual cost of work completed to date plus the predicted costs and schedule for finishing the remaining work.
ECD	**Estimated Completion Date.** The predicted date at which all requirements for a defined task will be completed.
FAA	**Federal Aviation Authority.** The agency of the executive branch of the U.S. federal government that manages the national airways.
FQR	**Formal Qualification Review.** A joint control gate at which the Buyer, based on analysis and test data, determines that the Seller's design will survive the qualification environment as defined in the System Specifications.
FCA	**Functional Configuration Audit.** An engineering audit of a Configuration Item (CI) or system conducted by the Buyer to verify that the performance test results of the "As-built" item are in accordance with the performance specification of the item. The FCA, with the results of the Physical Configuration Audit (PCA), is the decision point to confirm that the design is ready for either integration or replication.
HWCI	**Hardware Configuration Item.** A hardware component of a system, which is designated for configuration management to ensure the integrity of the delivered product. It may exist at any level in the system hierarchy, since configuration management must be imposed down to the lowest level where item interchangeability is required. Each HWCI is to have (as appropriate) individual design reviews, individual qualification certification, individual Acceptance Reviews, and separate operator and maintenance manuals.
HMO	**Health Maintenance Organization.** A commercial business which combines a health insurance program with health care delivery.
IEEE	**Institute of Electrical and Electronic Engineers.** A professional association of electrical engineers.

Acronym	Name and Definition

MBO   **Management By Objectives.** A management theory that calls for managing people based on documented work statements mutually agreed to by manager and subordinate. Progress on these work statements is periodically reviewed, and in a proper implementation, compensation is tied to MBO performance.

MBWA   **Management By Walking Around.** Part of the Hewlett-Packard legacy and popularized by management theorist Tom Peters, MBWA works on the assumption that a manager must circulate to fully understand the team's performance and problems. The best managers, according to Peters, spend 10 percent of their time in their offices, and 150 percent of their time talking and working with their people, their customers, and their suppliers.

NASA   **National Aeronautics and Space Administration.** The agency of the U.S. federal government responsible for the Nation's space program.

PCA   **Physical Configuration Audit.** An engineering audit of a Configuration Item (CI) or System conducted by the Buyer to verify that the item "As-built" conforms to the "Build-to" documentation. The PCA is a method of verification. Results of the PCA are part of the Acceptance Review.

PDR   **Preliminary Design Review.** A series of control gates at which the Buyer reviews and approves the Provider's proposed Design-to baseline as evidenced by lower level performance specifications and associated test plans and authorizes the Provider to proceed with detail design. All hardware, software, handling equipment, test equipment, and tooling should be sequentially reviewed in the descending order of system to assembly.

PERT   **Project Evaluation Review Technique.**

PIR   **Project Initiation Review.** A control gate at which the Provider executive management reviews, approves, and commits the company to the Provider's Project Plan and approves the project start. The PIR is the forum for executive management to constructively challenge the readiness of the Provider Project Manager and project team to initiate the project effort and successfully meet the project requirements.

PPL   **Project Products List.**

PWAA   **Project Work Authorizing Agreement.**

QA   **Quality Assurance.** The design and implementation of design features and procedures to ensure that performance specifications can be verified. This includes performance specification analysis, quality engineering for inspectability and testability, manufacturing process control, and the use of techniques and training to implement the measurement and testing process.

RFP   **Request For Proposal.** A document prepared by the Customer to solicit proposals from potential Providers. The

Acronym	Name and Definition
	Request For Proposal consists of a Solicitation Letter, Instructions to Bidders, Evaluation Criteria, Statement of Work, and a System Specification. The Provider issues an RFP to potential subcontractors.
SWCI	**Software Configuration Item.**
SQA	**Software Quality Assurance.** The design and implementation of design features and procedures to ensure that software requirements and specifications can be verified.
SSR	**Software Specification Review.** A control gate at which the Provider reviews the functional performance specifications of the software and firmware configuration items. The SSR is the decision point to proceed with preliminary design.
SOW	**Statement of Work.** The part of the Request For Proposal and resulting contract which describes the actual work to be done under the contract. It includes a description of the tasks the Provider shall perform and the identification and schedule of the deliverable contract end items.
SCR	**System Concept Review.** A Buyer control gate which reviews and approves the recommended system concept configured to satisfy the System Requirements Document. The SCR is the decision point to proceed with the development of the system specification.
SDR	**System Design Review.** A Seller control gate which reviews and approves the top-level system design solution and rationale. The SDR is the decision point to proceed with system specification flowdown to hardware and software configuration items.
SRR	**System Requirements Review.** The Buyer control gate which reviews and approves the System Requirements Document to determine which needs of the total User Requirements Statement will be satisfied by the proposed project. The SRR is the decision point to allow the project to proceed with the in-depth analyses and tradeoffs necessary to select a preferred system concept with associated budget and schedule estimates.
TRR	**Test Readiness Review.** A series of joint Buyer/Seller control gates at which the Buyer concurs that the Seller is ready to conduct official "sell-off" tests during which official verification data will be produced. Each TRR is the decision point for approval to proceed with planned qualification tests or acceptance tests to verify that performance specifications have been satisfied in accordance with the Verification Plan.
TBD	**To Be Determined.** Plan content such as dates, specifications, or criteria that have yet to be defined.
TBR	**To Be Resolved.** Plan content such as dates, specifications, or criteria that are not final, and are to be resolved by the Provider or by the Customer as part of the development effort.
TQM	**Total Quality Management.**
WBS	**Work Breakdown Structure.**

INDEX